dear sister

dear sister

*a memoir of secrets, survival, and
unbreakable bonds*

michelle horton

GRAND
CENTRAL

New York   Boston

Grand Central Publishing
Hachette Book Group
1290 Avenue of the Americas, New York, NY 10104

grandcentralpublishing.com
twitter.com/grandcentralpub

First Edition: January 2024

Grand Central Publishing is a division of Hachette Book Group, Inc. The Grand Central Publishing name and logo is a trademark of Hachette Book Group, Inc.

The publisher is not responsible for websites (or their content) that are not owned by the publisher.

The Hachette Speakers Bureau provides a wide range of authors for speaking events. To find out more, go to hachettespeakersbureau.com or email HachetteSpeakers@hbgusa.com.

Grand Central Publishing books may be purchased in bulk for business, educational, or promotional use. For information, please contact your local bookseller or the Hachette Book Group Special Markets Department at special.markets@hbgusa.com.

Print book interior design by Taylor Navis

Library of Congress Cataloging-in-Publication Data

Names: Horton, Michelle, author.

Title: Dear sister : a memoir of secrets, survival, and unbreakable bonds / by Michelle Horton.

Description: First edition. | New York : GCP, 2024.

Identifiers: LCCN 2023036406 | ISBN 9781538757154 (hardcover) | ISBN 9781538757178 (ebook)

Subjects: LCSH: Addimando, Nikki. | Abused women--United States--Biography | Women prisoners--United States--Biography | Justifiable homicide--Law and legislation--United States.

Classification: LCC HV6626.2 .H685 2024 | DDC 362.82/92 [B]--dc23/eng/20230811

LC record available at https://lccn.loc.gov/2023036406

ISBNs: 978-1-5387-5715-4 (hardcover), 978-1-5387-5717-8 (ebook)

Printed in the United States of America

LSC-C

Printing 1, 2023

Wild, Purple Flowers

there's something wild growing inside me—
thriving still despite it all.
for years it hid in the shadow of Fear.
a vine, climbing the dark corners of my home.
its prickly stalk grew around my lungs.
strangled the words out of my throat.
well, they cut it down when they tried to
break me, but they didn't realize
how deep my roots go.
they spread my seeds when they forced me open,
and now we are growing wild, purple flowers.

—NIKKI ADDIMANDO, WRITTEN IN DUTCHESS COUNTY
JAIL AFTER HER 2019 TRIAL AND CONVICTION

* * *

This book is for Nikki, whose roots are deeply entwined with mine.

For Noah, Ben, and Faye, as one step in healing our collective trauma.

For the wild purple flowers—all those who Stand With Nikki—who are out in the world spreading seeds of change.

In honor of that *something wild* that grows inside us all—that indestructible, unaffected *something* that endures and thrives, stubbornly rising toward the light, continuously and miraculously finding hope, grace, and connection in even the bleakest situations. Despite trauma and loss. Despite violence and imprisonment. Despite it all.

May my *something wild* be expressed through this writing. And may my words shed light on the issues in ourselves, our families, and our societal systems that need healing.

contents

author's note

You may have heard the name *Nicole Addimando* before picking up this book—perhaps from a news show, or a podcast, or a film. She's known as "Nicole" in legal documents, headline news, and the New York State inmate directory, but she's "Nikki" to everyone who really knows her. Maybe you, along with hundreds of thousands of others, signed petitions and shared #FreeNikki posts, becoming emotionally invested in seeing my sister gain freedom. Her case began as the stuff of True Crime intrigue and small-town gossip; and over time, it morphed into the focus of national news, grassroots advocacy, and eventually, precedent-setting case law.

Or maybe the case flew under your radar, one of many injustices in the #MeToo #BelieveWomen #BlackLivesMatter era. Hers was yet another story of a woman criminalized for surviving her abuser, happening at the same time as several other high-profile cases, such as Brittany Smith's in Alabama, Cyntoia Brown's in Tennessee, and Chrystul Kizer's in Wisconsin.

There are many Nikkis out there, living the same cruel fate—born into a body that is abused and traumatized, trapped by unthinkable violence behind closed doors, and then, after fighting back, ushered into a prison system that replicates the tactics of an abuser. Overwhelmingly, these bodies belong to Black women, Native women, trans women, immigrants, and gender-nonconforming people.[1] Because Nikki is a young white mom from a middle-class suburb with an unusual amount of organized advocacy around her case, she attracted media attention and support, but she is just one of a staggering number of women who survive domestic violence only to face State violence. She became a part of what journalist Justine van der Leun once described to me as "the abuse to prison pipeline." Very little data exists on the phenomenon, hiding its full scope, but even limited research shows a clear, persistent pattern: In 2005, 67 percent of the women in New York State prisons who killed someone close to them were abused by the victim of their crime.[2] According to the ACLU, as many as 94 percent of the nation-wide women's prison populations have a history of physical or sexual abuse before incarceration.[3] We don't hear their stories because they usually come from communities that are invisible, marginalized, or discriminated against. We don't hear their stories because these survivors are State property, having disappeared behind rows of barbed wire, identified by inmate numbers, deemed unworthy of basic hygiene and nutritional care. Many of them are enduring the most unbearable punishment imaginable: being separated from their children.

Nikki's children, Ben and Faye, were toddlers when she was imprisoned. There are many more Bens and Fayes out there—kids traumatized on multiple levels by events beyond their control, and treated like collateral damage by a system that should have protected them. Children serve their parent's prison sentence, too. So do family members who are left behind to raise the kids, pay for phone calls and commissary needs, and manage the ripple effects of imprisonment.

The circles of impact are vast, spreading far beyond an incarcerated person—out to the community that donates their time and money, and taxpayers who foot the incarceration bill. According to Vera Institute, in 2015 New York State had the highest cost per inmate in the United States at $69,355 a year,[4] a cost that's only rising. When Nikki was arrested, I was standing at the epicenter. We don't often tell the stories of people like me, who are left behind to pick up the pieces of a shattered family and a broken system.

And just as there are more Nikkis, Bens, and Fayes out there, I know that there are many more Michelles—good, loving people who, for a variety of reasons, don't see the red flags of domestic violence waving in front of our faces. Not until it's too late. I know it's hard to believe that's true. You'll probably think that, in my shoes, you would have done things differently.

Trust me, I've spent the last few years trying to understand my blindness. Why didn't I see? Was some part of my subconscious unwilling to take in information that would challenge my belief in a safe and just world? Was my desire to keep the peace stronger than my curiosity to find out the truth? The more digging I've done into my own family patterns, the more universal this blindness seems. We don't like to imagine that something this terrible could happen to the people we love—or to ourselves—and so we collectively blame victims and find excuses for why it couldn't happen to us. We don't want to accept that the societal systems around us often fail at keeping victims safe, and so we defer to the authority of police and district attorneys. The more I examine my past, the more clearly I see a complex system of concealment and denial—because of fear, shame, and above all, because of our defenses. Nikki hiding the most disturbing parts of her life, and my brain's ability to unsee the evidence in front of me, grew from the same root: self-preservation. She was preserving a sense of "normal," keeping her life as intact as possible. I, on the other hand, was preserving my belief system—which, I've come to realize, fights to live just as vigorously as our bodies do. This system of hiding and denying works well—until, quite suddenly, it doesn't.

What happened to my family is not unique. As a society, we have a tendency to look away. To avoid. To deny. My hope is that, in telling my story, we can bring more of the silent violence in our homes and social structures out into the light—which is the only place that healing and change can happen.

Nothing about writing this book has been easy. The secondary trauma I experienced from someone else's domestic violence and incarceration—plus the experience of having our family's stories weaponized against us—complicated my ability to relive some of the most painful moments in my life. Writing was often accompanied by the disembodying effect of shock or the numbing quality of adrenaline that carried me through the moments as they happened. I have done my very best to write about the people and events I encountered as I experienced them, and I relied heavily on documentation, transcripts, therapy notes, jail calls, and my personal recordings. All people in this book are either in the public record or consented to be included.

I recognize that parts of this book may be difficult to read, especially if you have a history of intimate partner abuse and/or sexual violence. Please take good care of yourself, pause if overwhelmed, and reach out to a professional if you need help processing.

Yet as I sift through memories and try to find their meaning, it's clear that even in the darkest situation, even amid perpetual uncertainty and compounded grief, there's also levity, resilience, and deep hope. Beauty can coexist with exquisite pain. The solidarity of community can accompany the most crushing injustice. Sisterhood is a powerful force. And the bond between a mother separated from her children is unbreakable.

PART I

truth

"That is my prayer to God every day: 'Remove the veils so I might see what is really happening here and not be intoxicated by my stories and my fears.'"

—Elizabeth Lesser

before

I felt *good*.

It was a Wednesday in late August, days after I turned thirty-one years old. A fresh decade lay before me, and for the first time in a long time, I felt an expansive feeling of freedom and possibilities ahead.

That day, I came home from work to find my apartment bustling with activity—my sister, Nikki, had come over with my achingly adorable niece and nephew. As a newly single mom, I needed all the help I could get during the workweek—and Nikki was my solution. She stayed with my third-grader after school, got him snacks, and most days, cooked him dinner, too. She made my life easier, only wanting to help.

We were all outside playing under the day's last gasps of sunlight—Ben, my four-year-old nephew, was freshly showered and wearing pajamas, kicking a soccer ball to my eight-year-old son, Noah. Faye, who was two, was also in pajamas, cheering with apricot-size fists in the air. Nikki and I sat on the grass, pulling at the blades like we used to do as kids.

I was on the other side of the hardest experience of my life. I walked through my days feeling lighter and happier than I'd felt...maybe ever.

It had taken me years to cut myself free from the man I loved deeply, but the truth was, my marriage had hurt. In the way my bones ached after another near-death scare, another call from the cops, *come to the hospital quick the accident is bad.* In the way my wrists tensed from gripping the steering wheel, feeling my arms go numb, preparing to see my husband's mangled body, feeling the pulsation of ambulance lights down to my nerve endings. It was the throat-tightening rage at logging into my separate, protected bank account and seeing six or seven consecutive withdrawals in a row from a random ATM in Poughkeepsie, all slightly under the notification threshold for bank alerts. It was the red-hot sting of embarrassment when checking out at a grocery store, staring at the credit card reader and willing it to say "Approved."

Now it had been almost one full year since I'd separated from my husband, Justin, who'd struggled through various stages of addiction, mostly to opiates, over our ten-year relationship, and who had become disruptive, chaotic, and even dangerous after I asked him to leave. It had been a year of learning, healing, and letting go. Life was finally settling down.

"I'm really proud of you," Nikki said suddenly, as if reading my mind. Could she, too, feel the relief radiating off me?

"You're really different than you used to be."

She wasn't wrong. I saw my decision to leave my marriage as the most courageous thing I'd ever done—the first real, radical, self-honoring choice I'd made. Before that, I'd been caught in a cycle of enabling, denying, being consumed by my need to save and change the men in my life. I was drowning, and I needed to live.

After I had asked for a separation, Justin then spiraled down a destructive path beyond anything I could have foreseen: He had two head-on car accidents in the span of a month. A mysterious new stab wound appeared on his abdomen, probably from a drug-related scuffle. He took out a credit card in my name and continuously siphoned money from my account (no matter how many times I changed PINs, passwords, and entire banks). He tracked my phone, stalking my movements. Finally a strange woman messaged me photos of my ex in her bed, along with money-related threats. It was Nikki who convinced me to get a restraining order.

"Listen," she'd said, sitting across my dining room table, scrolling through the messages on my phone. "I've been holding my tongue for a while." The house echoed with children's voices shrieking and yelling and singing, but my sister's eyes stayed locked on me. She lowered her voice. "If anything ever happened to Noah, God forbid, and they find out that you knew that Justin was using and acting dangerously—you could get in trouble for not protecting him. You could lose custody."

The next day, I filed for a restraining order and sole custody.

It was a hell of a year, but now, finally, the rest of 2017 into 2018 was going to be *my* year. I had a job I liked, a little boy I adored, and no one stealing my money. I had family who loved and supported me, friends who'd rallied around me with love, and a sister—the greatest gift my mom ever gave me.

I hadn't always seen Nikki that way. Because she was born only twenty-seven months after me, I can't remember a time before she was in my life.

I'd have described our sibling relationship as "normal," growing up in the suburbs of New York's Hudson Valley in the 1990s and early aughts— at least the way sisters were depicted on sitcoms and through other friends we knew. We were playmates as little kids—playing rousing games of Spit and slapping piles of cards on our hardwood floor, trading lanyards that we made at summer camp, and predicting our futures by playing MASH (Mansion, Apartment, Shack, House) on loose-leaf paper in the back of our parents' station wagon. But I spent a lot of time in my head, constructing the world around me like a storybook, while Nikki was more grounded into the earth—quite literally. She was constantly digging through the dirt for bugs and tiny creatures, always on the hunt for something slippery and slimy, something to crawl over and around her curious fingers.

We also bickered and blamed, slammed doors, and pranked. In a lot of ways, we grew up side by side, but worlds apart.

Sisterhood can be complicated, and it certainly was for us.

I'd always wondered if we'd become as important to each other as my mother had promised we would. When Nikki and I teased each other or raged at one another, she'd reprimand us, "You better be nice. One day you're going to need each other." My mom had two older sisters herself. They'd all shared one bedroom in the small apartment they grew up in. Even after they'd gone their separate ways and started their own families, they always stayed within arm's reach of one another. As Nikki and I squabbled, our mom would spend hours with our cordless phone tucked between her ear and shoulder as she washed dishes—talking to one sister, then the other, on what felt like an endless loop. Watching them, I learned that sisters show up for each other, no matter what. My dad would say that the Moriarty sisters knew every detail of each other's lives, down to the snacks they'd eat. "One would eat, one would chew, and the other would swallow," he'd joke.

Now I could see that my mom had been right. We needed each other.

Nikki and I were enacting the core code of sisterhood in my family: we showed up. Whenever I needed someone to watch Noah, to bring us food when we were sick, to vent and cry to when I was grieving my marriage—she was there. Faithfully.

Throughout our twenties, we had actually started to *enjoy* each other. Nikki was funny in a way I'd never fully appreciated as a kid, and her daily texts—videos of the kids, throwback memories from childhood, or witty one-liners—made me laugh out loud. We shared recipes, we planned birthday parties and outings together, and we each warned the other when she was likely to get her period, because we were on the same cycle. It was the kind of sisterhood we'd both always wanted but, for whatever reason, hadn't seemed available before.

Maybe because our grown-up version of sisterhood was interwoven with motherhood—and there was nothing more impressive to me than Nikki as a mom. She was so attuned to the kids, pouring all of herself into nurturing their talents and interests—like Ben's astounding musicality, and Faye's free-spirited, animal-loving personality. Motherhood was her source of creativity, generosity, and selflessness—and I, along with so many others who followed her on social media, learned from her example. She was her very best self as a mother—and even though we commiserated about the hard parts of raising young kids, as any mom needs to do, I was a better mother and person because of what she taught me.

With each subsequent kid, it was like a string between us tugged us closer together, like two boats that had drifted out in opposite directions, forgetting that we were anchored together underneath it all. We were finding our way back to each other. We were finally friends. And at this point I didn't know how I'd have functioned without her.

"There's leftover pasta in the fridge," said Nikki as we stood up, brushing grass off our hands. "And I tried to do the dishes but I didn't get to all of them," she added, adjusting her oversized sunglasses.

"You didn't have to do that, Nik, but thank you."

"Oh, and I have a load of the kids' clothes in the dryer," she told me. Nikki and her partner, Chris, didn't have a washer-dryer unit in her apartment, and I always made mine available for her. "I'll come get it tomorrow."

"No worries," I said, and I meant it.

"Come on, kiddos, it's time to go!" Nikki called out. "Bedtime! Say goodbye to Aunt Mimi!"

They ran over on little legs, wide smiles on their tiny faces.

"Don't leave me," I joked, pulling them into big bear hugs, smooching their faces.

Then I sat on the grass a little longer, breathing in the fresh air, watching them climb into their car.

I had no idea how quickly that season would pass, how soon we would be ripped apart, how my sense of freedom would vanish like the falling leaves.

CHAPTER 1

homicide

Day 1, September 28, 2017

A loud knock punctured the routine of an ordinary Thursday morning. It was around 8 a.m., nearing the time I would head out to work and my mom would put Noah on the school bus. I hurried down my apartment's steps, opened the door. A uniformed Town of Poughkeepsie police officer stood outside. His face looked tense.

I held my breath, as I had learned to do when a cop was in my doorway. What had happened this time? Another car crash? An arrest?

Justin hadn't lived with me for a year, but we were still legally married—so if a police officer was looking for someone to identify a body, they might just knock on his wife's door.

In the split second before the officer spoke, I braced for impact. A part of me whispered, *This is it. He's dead.* I'd imagined this scene hundreds of times, I knew what would come next.

Except—

"Are you Nicole Addimando's sister?"

My brain went blank. It didn't know what to formulate to replace the "Daddy died" talk I'd been preparing. Why was Nikki's name coming out of this man's mouth?

The cop assured me that she was fine, but said someone had to come pick up her kids at the police station. That's all he could say.

"You'll need to bring clothes for them," he added.

My mom had just joined me in the doorway. For the past few months, my parents had been staying in my apartment, helping me adjust to my new single-mom lifestyle. Her mouth began spinning as fast as my mind: *Was Nikki hurt? What had happened to the kids' clothes?*

The officer brushed off each question with a curt, "I can't answer that, ma'am, you just need to go pick up the children."

My mom started to say we'd have to stop at Nikki's apartment to get their clothes. "No, you can't go there," the officer said quickly. He offered us no clarifying information. He needed us to obey, not understand.

So we did the only thing we could do: follow the officer's directions and hope it would all make sense soon. I had a suspicion that I might know where this was coming from. The day before, Nikki had messaged me on Facebook while I was at work.

She was in a panic, sending short, choppy, one-line messages, saying that Child Protective Services had opened an investigation. "I can't believe this is happening," she wrote. The gist was that an anonymous reporter suspected Nikki was being abused by Chris, her long-term boyfriend, father of the kids, and that it was emotionally affecting their preschool-aged son. CPS had shown up at her house, investigating the claims, and they might be calling me soon, she warned.

My gut instinct was that she was panicking for no reason. This had to be a misunderstanding that would soon be cleared up. Nikki had two young, rambunctious kids, and she *did* often have bruising on her lately.

"You can help by saying that I've always had random bruises but nothing suspicious and that you are close with us and trust us and our kids are totally loved and safe," she wrote.

Of course I'd say that. Everything *was* okay, right? Nikki would have told me otherwise. She would have talked to me about it, just like I talked to her about my own toxic marriage during countless heart-to-hearts over the past year.

It was true she almost always had a dark bruise on her left cheekbone nowadays—some days it was deep purple, others a more faded green-blue, but it was in the same spot. I didn't know about bruises anywhere else, but I assumed she didn't want me to tell them that her shoulder had recently popped out of its socket and she had to wear an arm sling. It wasn't the first time that she'd dislocated her shoulder. She blamed a lifetime of gymnastics and, this last time, even wondered out loud if she had a connective tissue disorder. "I was just picking up Faye, and *pop*," she'd motioned, indicating that her shoulder just fell out of its own socket. *Weird*, I'd thought, not questioning too deeply. "You should get that checked out," I told her.

If I didn't know Nikki and Chris as well as I did, I might have wondered if Nikki was being hurt, too. A CPS call didn't seem *unreasonable*, given her bruises, but it did seem hasty and extreme.

This must be why the police were at my door. They were investigating the claims—claims that they, like CPS, were obligated to look into but would ultimately be for nothing. But I couldn't tell my mom that. I knew Nikki hadn't told her about CPS, and she wouldn't want me to, either. That's what our family did—we hid unpleasant news, sparing one another unnecessary worry or stress, especially when our mom's Crohn's disease was flaring up as it had been recently. All our lives, we'd heard "Don't upset Mom, she's sick today" or "You're giving me a stomachache" enough times to internalize the rules.

I watched my mom scurry out the door after the police officer, but I was more concerned about being late to work than anything else. It was all a misunderstanding. I arranged plans for a neighbor to take Noah to school, and then went to work.

I had an easy twenty-minute commute to my job at the Omega Institute, a nonprofit retreat center tucked in the deep woods of Rhinebeck—a town best known for shaded village sidewalks that spill into restaurant patios and boutiques, and for hosting the county fair each summer. Though I had grown up in the area—a historic stretch of land on the Hudson River, positioned halfway between New York City and Albany—I'd only recently learned that Omega existed. It was like a hidden gem, accessible only through dirt and gravel backroads winding away from commuter highways and cell phone service.

Omega is an oasis-like campus with blooming gardens, meandering trails, a meditation sanctuary, and a small private beach on a peaceful lake. But for me it was also a job, where I helped craft the organization's social media messaging and run Facebook ads for hundreds of workshops and events. That day I had a standard Thursday to-do list, which my body performed on autopilot. My mind kept circling back to the morning's strange beginning. *What the hell is happening?* I couldn't make sense of it. Why were the police keeping Nikki? Why did the kids need new clothes, and why couldn't we go to their apartment? Where did CPS fit into this?

In a hushed voice, I filled in two of my closest colleagues. *Is this a family emergency?* I asked, as if maybe they'd know. *Do I need to leave?*

I went to the dining hall for lunch and poked around at my falafel and green goddess salad, silently replaying the morning in my head, searching for any clues I may have missed.

When I got back to my desk, I saw a text from my mom. Chris's mom had called her. He hadn't shown up at work. No one knew where he was. I had assumed he was at the police station with Nikki, but now—wait. *Where was Chris?*

I did not think, *Maybe she was being abused by him and Chris was arrested and Nikki was at the station dealing with paperwork.* It didn't even occur to me as an option to disregard. Instead my imagination searched for an explanation, coming up with nothing.

Around 5 p.m., just after most of the office hallway had emptied for the day, I got a text from my mom. It was just one word: "Homicide."

I looked at my phone for one, two beats, not understanding what I was seeing. I wheeled my office chair over to the door, shut it, and called her.

My mother picked up on the first ring. She was screaming.

Chris was dead.

Nikki had killed him.

CHAPTER 2

groundless

Numbness spread from my head, down my neck, through my arms as I absorbed the shock. I felt my lungs expand and contract, out and in. My breath was the only thing I could be sure was real.

No.

No no no.

My sister—the least rebellious, least violent person I knew—who never so much as had school detention, who wouldn't even squash a bug—was in jail for murder? The girl I'd known my entire life, who'd never met a stray animal she didn't take in, the girl whose bleeding-heart compassion was so intense that she wouldn't even eat meat—she took someone's life? My sister—a stay-at-home mom whose life orbited around the needs of her children—killed their father? What the hell?

"How?" I said.

"A gun," my mom cried.

"Where did she get a gun?" I yelled into the phone. "How does she know how to shoot a gun?"

Mom didn't have answers. I told her I'd be home soon and hung up the phone.

I felt groundless, but stood up anyway, looked to the doorway, and let adrenaline carry me outside. The warm September sky was jarringly blue. Omega guests volleyed a ball back and forth on the tennis court, colleagues waved as I passed—unaware that my body was a walking shell. To them, I must have appeared totally normal.

I got into my car, left the Omega parking lot, and turned down the familiar single-lane road flanked with towering trees. I'd driven home through those winding country roads hundreds of times. I could anticipate each turn with my eyes closed—and I knew that this time I was driving to an unrecognizable place.

What was happening? All I could do was keep driving. Keep driving home—toward Ben and Faye who, *holy shit*, had no idea they'd seen their dad for the last time. Had no idea their mom wasn't coming back tonight. *My God. Who's going to tell them?* I wondered.

Except I already knew the answer. It was going to be me.

The twenty-minute drive wasn't long enough. I took a deep breath, and walked through my front door. The scene was disconcertingly familiar. Except for the grief-stricken look on my mother's face, you'd have had no idea we were in the middle of a family crisis.

Noah, eight years old, had a couple of neighborhood friends over, and they were chasing each other and scream-laughing from room to room. Ben was delighted at being included in the "big kid" play. He ran past me giggling in Noah's outgrown clothes, the same clothes I had handed to my mom before she went to the police station. Faye was on the living room carpet with my mom, lying on her lap and playing a game on mom's iPhone. She was wearing a pink polka-dot shirt that Nikki had left in my laundry, and a Cookie Monster diaper.

I watched the kids, willing time to stop—to somehow keep us cocooned in this moment before we'd have to tell them that their parents weren't coming back that night. They had never spent a night away from Nikki. Faye had spent most of her two years nursing before falling asleep—and even though she was now (thankfully) weaned, I knew she'd need her mom's touch in a matter of hours, as would Ben.

My mom walked over, looking like a scared little girl. She pulled me in for a long hug, and I could feel her shoulders tremble. Then she composed herself, wiped her face, and handed me a piece of paper with a name and phone number scrawled in pen. "Elizabeth."

I had never met Elizabeth, but I recognized the name. She taught Ben's Music Together classes—a real bright spot in his life. Ben had musical gifts beyond other toddlers I've known, and Nikki and Ben often talked about "Miss Elizabeth" during his impromptu living room concerts.

"She wants you to call her," my mom said. "She said she has information."

I stepped out the front door and paced along the sidewalk in front of our duplex. I lived in a quiet gated community of apartments and town houses, and my home was bordered by a white picket fence. I looked out toward the wooded wetlands beyond the yard, hearing chirps and croaks that, under other circumstances, would have been soothing. The sun dipped toward the tree line as I dialed.

"Hi, Elizabeth? It's Michelle." I held my breath.

"Hi, Michelle," she said, her voice soft and sweet. "I'm sorry to be meeting you this way."

"Me too," I said.

"He was a really bad man, Michelle," she started. "Really bad."

I sat down at my small outdoor table set and exhaled. "Tell me everything."

CHAPTER 3

clarity

H e was hurting her," she said.

I took the sentence in. It was as if her words flipped on a light switch in my mind, and the totality of my memories slowly began lighting up under flickering fluorescent bulbs, illuminating a life that was always here. A life I hadn't seen.

Memories popped into my mind, asking to be put into this new context. Her clothes, for one. All summer Nikki had worn ankle-length black leggings, long-sleeve open-front cardigans over a baggy black T-shirt, a lightweight scarf, and sunglasses, even on the hottest of days. I'd thought it was her style.

"I only have, like, two shirts," Nikki would say, shrugging, as if she just didn't care that much about what she wore; as if she couldn't put their limited money toward frivolous fashion decisions. Now I realized—

Oh my God, she was hiding injuries.

At the beginning of Nikki's relationship with Chris, nine years earlier, they'd coached gymnastics together. Every now and then she'd say she got kicked in the face while spotting a kid, which was reasonable enough. But it wasn't until the past year or so that her face was regularly black and blue.

I'd seen the bruising on her face, and I'd accepted all of her explanations. Three-year-old Ben had hit her in the face with his toy guitar, she'd tripped again—and again and again. A few times I had seen Ben throw a toy or book across the room at Nikki, or accidentally head-butt her. Yet the next day Nikki would have an injury that often looked worse than anything I'd expect would come from what I saw happen. "I bruise easily," she'd say with a shrug.

She didn't have excessive bruising growing up, and certainly not as regularly before Faye was born, but bodies change. And Nikki—like most of the women in our family, myself included—tended to take care of everyone else before getting to her own needs. Doctor appointments weren't on her agenda; it was probably nothing. But in the sharp clarity of hindsight, the bruising *had* been excessive over the past year or two, becoming so frequent that I stopped asking; eventually it became normal, expected. If I did mention a fresh injury, I'd do it with a laugh, like "*Geez*, what happened to you now?"

I assumed she was accident-prone because she was exhausted. She was in the new mom stage of life and both kids were terrible sleepers. I assumed she needed to take better care of herself, and suggested she join a gym, take some spin classes with me. She would have confided in me if she needed something. Motherhood had forged a bond between us. If I had a problem or needed to vent, she was at the top of my text list. I'd assumed she felt the same.

I assumed.

It was suddenly frighteningly obvious. But I had never questioned whether Chris was hurting her—not even behind her back, not even in the safety of my own mind. *Why?*

"The bruising…" I trailed off. Was he punching her? Did he have a rage I didn't see beneath his soft, quiet exterior?

"The bruises were from him," Elizabeth said. "He'd hold her down, or slam her face into a counter."

She said *he would*, not *he did*; it wasn't a one-time incident.

A deep, hot shame washed through my body. There I'd been, calling in help from the family to extricate myself from my own version of abuse, while Nikki was being physically hurt. My own relationship issues had pulled eyes toward me, while she had no one. Except, it seemed, Elizabeth.

Had I been too focused on my own life, that I didn't see the full picture? What else wasn't I seeing?

I stood up and walked in a small circle next to the table. My body needed to process what I was hearing; I needed to move.

I didn't think Nikki was *happy* in her relationship—I didn't see romance, public affection, or shared interests—but I also didn't see big blow-out fights or dramatic breakups that I associated with abusive households. I didn't see danger. It looked like quiet resignation. Eye rolls. Deep sighs. It looked like two young parents tolerating one another, surviving on little sleep and zero intimate connection. The few times I *did* talk to Nikki about her relationship, I told her she deserved to find someone she was attracted to, someone she enjoyed. I was feeling the winds of freedom in my own life, and wanted that for her, too. She always responded with shrugs and head shakes. She said she'd never take the kids away from Chris, even if she were unhappy. She'd never break up the family.

I understood her stick-with-it instinct and the goal of keeping a family intact at all costs. The only reasons I had stayed with my husband for as long as I did was to avoid separating a boy from his dad, and the hope that things would get better over time.

"But how did she get a gun?" I asked Elizabeth. I was nearly yelling into the phone. This was a crucial component to my confusion. Nikki hated guns. Nikki was the one who regularly reminded me to ask parents if there was a firearm in the house before letting Noah go on playdates. She certainly wouldn't keep a gun around kids.

"It was his gun. I think it was legally registered to him," Elizabeth said.

I'm sorry, what? Chris had a gun? They never, not once, told me there was a gun in the house. Noah had played there countless times without me, even sleeping there a few times. How could she keep something like that from me?

It was a short call, but a lot to digest. After promising to keep in touch with Elizabeth, I hung up the phone. I stopped pacing along the sidewalk and took a seat at my outdoor table. I needed a few minutes.

I couldn't stop myself from thinking back to the day before, when Nikki was panicking about the CPS visit. At the time, I both believed that she was overreacting and also understood how scary it must be to have a government agency knocking on her door with a bombshell accusation. Something she wrote to me, amid her CPS freak-out, came screaming back into my mind: "If Chris were abusive and a CPS case opened? We would be in the most danger ever. An abusive man would flip out and could just kill the whole family."

It was when I'd read those words that I'd called her. When she answered, her voice was unusually high, and she talked fast. She sounded markedly different, disproportionate to what I understood was happening, and she seemed to be in a full-blown panic. And so I went into calm-down mode. I tried to reassure her they were probably just covering their asses.

"Nikki, you do have bruising on you a lot. And your arm was just in a sling. It's not crazy for someone who doesn't know you to think you're being hurt." For good measure, I offered: "Listen, if something *is* going on . . ."

"Oh my God, you too, Michelle?" she'd interrupted, angry and abrupt.

"Let them do the investigation, Nik. If you're safe, you're safe. They can't take kids away from a safe home."

That was the last phone call we'd have that wasn't on a recorded line.

collect call

After I made my way back inside, I'd barely exhaled before there was a knock. Pulling the door open, I saw two young women with laminated badges hanging from their necks. CPS. Their investigation was still open, of course; and now a gun had been fired within hours of their visit.

They introduced themselves and apologized for interrupting during such a sensitive time. But they had some questions.

I led them inside and introduced them to my mom, who was pacing from room to room. Faye was now asleep, and Ben was watching TV in bed with my dad, a fun treat. Noah had gone to play at a neighbor's house, but would be home any minute.

One case worker, a woman named Jenna who couldn't have been much older than thirty, did all the talking. The other woman, who looked even younger, stood like a shadow in the background. Jenna asked to speak with my mom somewhere private, and said she'd need to talk with me next. My mom led them back outside to the small bistro table and chairs near my front door.

While they talked out of earshot, I stood over the trash can and mechanically scraped the kids' leftover raviolis off their plates, waiting for someone to tell me what to do next. I don't know how long the interview took: Two minutes? Twenty? Time was not moving in a way I could track. It was fully dark by the time my mom came back in the house, motioning for me to take her place outside.

I stepped back out into the unseasonably warm night when my phone rang. It was a Poughkeepsie number I didn't recognize, but decided to answer, just in case it was Nikki.

"This is a free collect call from Dutchess County Jail…"

My throat tightened. This was it. My sister.

I politely excused myself and ran back upstairs, three steps at a time, and into the bathroom for privacy.

The connection was staticky, but it was her voice, saying words that fit into this new reality like a puzzle. "He pulled a gun, he threatened to kill me…" She whimpered out the end of her sentence, trailing off. I repeated *I know* as she cried, the way a mother might console a child. I didn't *know*, clearly, I was only now learning just how much I didn't know, but I did know she'd been faced with an impossible situation.

Nikki's voice was high and barely audible. "I didn't want it to end like this, I begged him, I said, 'Just let us leave and I won't tell anyone.' I will continue to tell everyone that everything is fine, I've been doing it for years, I said please let us leave, and he wouldn't let us go." She spoke in long continuous sentences, gulping for air as she went.

She started talking about Chris's family. I, too, had been thinking about them all night—imagining the agony they were all feeling, the utter devastation currently ripping through their own phone lines.

"I mean, I love them, and I don't know how they're ever going to face me because this is their son, and I have a son." Her voice cracked and cried out the last four words. *I have a son.* "Ben." His name came out like a sob.

"I know," I repeated.

"I begged him to let us leave," she said again. "And he wouldn't. And he just looked at me and said, 'You won't do it.' And when he said, 'I'm going to kill you and myself and your kids will have no one,' I just…I don't know what else I could have done…"

Before that moment, I simply could not imagine Nikki knowingly pulling a trigger and killing *anything*. Even if he were a "bad man" as Elizabeth had said. Even if he slammed her face into counters and dislocated her joints. But when she said that she squeezed the trigger because Chris had said, *The kids would have no one*, it clicked. She wasn't killing, she was saving.

"Nikki, you did the right thing," I said instantly. And I meant it. If I were in that situation, I'd hope to have the strength and luck to live. I'd wish that for anyone. I was glad she was alive.

"No, this is not the right thing," she said quickly, firmly, breaking into tears.

"It was the only thing you could do," I said, talking over her moaning. I felt an urge to claw my way through the airwaves, through whatever bars were keeping her away, to make my way to the phone she was crying into and be there next to her. She sobbed until, seconds later, our time ran out.

I hung up the phone and my body folded in half, my head practically in my lap. And for the very first time since the knock on our door, I cried. The tears came violently, like a purge, and part of me wanted to stay on that floor and cry until I stopped breathing altogether. But a different part of me, flooded with adrenaline, knew this was a red-hot emergency, and maybe if I said the right things to the right people, we could manage. We could get her home.

I steadied myself before walking out of the bathroom, into the hallway where Ben and Faye slept in rooms at either end. They had assumed this was an unexpected and exciting sleepover (Their very first one! Yay!), but I knew it wouldn't be long until they'd demand answers that we weren't ready to give. My parents and I hadn't even begun to imagine how we'd break the news to them. For right now, the only thing to do was resume my seat in front of two impassive case workers: one sitting in the same seat that I left her, pen and notebook ready; the other standing to her side like a witness overseeing a document signing.

I apologized for making them wait, and proceeded to parrot everything I'd heard from Elizabeth and Nikki. I spewed facts, but I also needed them to know who Nikki was—a kind friend, a good mother, an educator who had taught preschool before quitting to raise her kids, and now sewed baby slippers to make money. Not a killer. They wrote down notes as I spoke.

Jenna asked me to tell her more about the bruising. I opened my mouth to speak but all that came out were sobs.

"It's okay to be emotional," she said flatly. "It's normal to be this upset." Nothing about this was normal.

No matter what I said, or how I sobbed, her face remained neutral. Every now and then I saw her eyes dart to the right, where her colleague was standing, as if to telepathically communicate something I couldn't decipher. Did they believe that Nikki was abused, or did they think Nikki was a murderer? Did they need to cover up wrongdoing on their part for how they had handled the investigation? It was impossible to ignore that CPS opened a case, and within twenty-four hours of leaving the apartment, someone was dead. Much of what I told Jenna were minutes-old revelations—was I making sense?

I'd later read how Jenna documented it:

"Michelle reports that Nicole did not confide in her often..."

"Michelle reports that recently Nicole had a dislocated shoulder that she sought treatment for but always had an excuse when someone asked her what happened..."

"Michelle reports that Nicole also has a history of sexual trauma from age 5 and that nothing was ever done about it."

CHAPTER 5

unkle butch

I had heard Elizabeth's words, *bad man*, and they called up a memory, clear and vivid in my mind: Butch.

I hadn't thought of him in years, just as I hadn't thought of the other neighbors, teachers, and friends' parents who had once made up the constellation of my childhood. Yet while sitting with the case workers, I knew with certainty *Butch* was at the root of this story.

I told them that, years ago, when Nikki and I were teenagers, I saw his name scrawled in crayon, in a child's handwriting, on a page in Nikki's diary. *Unkle Butch is a bad man,* it said.

It was an older diary, one of many, from a pile of Nikki's private journals that I was absolutely not supposed to be reading. I wasn't even supposed to be in her room. We were in high school at the time, and so reading through her hidden journals—hidden from me, specifically—was a serious offense.

It's not that Nikki and I hated each other as teenagers. We had family game nights of Pictionary and Yahtzee. We watched our *Parent Trap* VHS again and again, reciting Lindsay Lohan dialogue back and forth. We pitched in on chores and painted each other's nails. But there was also name-calling and finger-pointing, and some low blows to each other's fragile teenage egos, after which we were expected to forgive and be forgiven. We were sisters, after all. That's what sisters did.

After fifth grade, Nikki and I moved to a small white house in the village of Hyde Park, in Upstate New York, in what felt like quintessential suburbia. We had a drive-in movie theater, a roller rink, and a classic fifties diner with an aluminum roof and a black-and-white-checkered floor.

Our neighborhood, known as Crumwold Acres, was nestled between two historic estates—the Roosevelts' to the south, and the Vanderbilts' to the north—and had hundreds of nearly identical houses on quarter-acre plots, in rows, loops, and cul-de-sacs. They were "Cape Cod–style" houses, as my mom liked to say, known for cozy single-story frames and steep slanted roofs. Ours had a circular driveway, an in-ground pool, and a tire swing out front. And at the top of the house, behind the two gabled dormers, were our attic-shaped bedrooms. Mine was on the left, Nikki's was on the right. Between us was a bathroom just barely large enough for a stand-up shower, and a short hallway that often reverberated with slammed doors, thrown shoes, and on occasion, the tiptoes of a sister snooping through another sister's things.

I don't even know what I was looking for in Nikki's diaries. An embarrassing secret to hold over her head? I certainly wasn't looking to better understand her, or to connect with her.

Something about reading those six words made my stomach drop.

I brought the diary to my mom. I knew I was risking Nikki finding out that I'd invaded her privacy. But something about that page made me know I needed a grown-up's help.

During my high school years, my mom was like a girlfriend. I thought of her as an extension of myself, a part of me whose purpose was to help clarify what I thought and felt and wanted. If I didn't understand something, no matter how weird or embarrassing, I went to my mom. My friends came to her, too. She was empathetic. She was easy to talk to. She was cool.

So now, with six words written in crayon and an icky feeling in my stomach, I went to her, book in hand.

Unkle Butch is a bad man.

Butch had lived across the street from our old rental house, the place we'd lived during most of elementary school. It was where I'd made some of my warmest memories, wrapped in innocence. My bedroom had been across from Nikki's. Our doors stayed open. She had a bunk bed in her room in case a guest, usually an aunt, would take my room for the night. The bottom bunk was mine whenever I wanted it. I remember whispering and laughing in the dark, and how on every Christmas Eve, after we'd sung in our church choir for the evening candlelight service, I'd lie in that bunk bed and swear I could hear sleigh bells over our heads. The backyard smelled like lilac and fresh-cut grass, like muddy magic potions of soil and herbs, thick chlorine, and wet dog.

As often as not, when Nikki was in the backyard, her friend Caitlin was by her side. Caitlin was the same age as Nikki, and they were each other's first best friends. They both had a free-spirited wildness to their personalities, as if they were made to dig their toes into grass and howl at the moon. Both of them had hair that refused to be tamed—Nikki's thick and dark, Caitlin's blond with wispy curls. One of my earliest memories of Caitlin was watching her dance in the rain, and then kneel and scoop mud into her hair before washing herself in a street puddle. I thought she was weird. Nikki, on the other hand, saw the magic in her. And oftentimes when they'd play together, it was under the watchful eye of Butch.

If I hadn't known better, I would have assumed he was Caitlin's grandpa. He was a grandpa-aged man with coke-bottle glasses and graying hair, and Caitlin and her mom had lived in his house for as long as we'd lived across the street. Butch was the father of Caitlin's mom's boyfriend, a twenty-something guy with a cool red Jeep. I knew Butch and his wife as well as any kid knows their aging neighbors who politely wave as you drive by.

Unkle Butch is a bad man.

My memories are fuzzy—I don't know where we were in the house, or where Nikki was. But I know that when I handed my mom Nikki's diary, I didn't expect her reaction. She barely emoted. I think she even nodded, as if it were a confirmation. And then she shook her head *no* as she handed it back. I absorbed her body language, confused as to why she wasn't assuring me that it was nothing.

"Yeah, I think something may have happened between them," she whispered.

"Like what?" I asked, thinking that maybe he reprimanded or embarrassed her. No part of my teenage brain thought the *something* was sexual; he was an old man, and she just a baby.

Mom let out a sharp exhale. "Remember that sleepover at Caitlin's?"

Of course I remembered. It was Nikki's one and only sleepover. She was five years old, I was seven. And early the next morning, our mom got a call that Nikki wanted to come home. She said her "foot hurt"—a lame excuse I mercilessly teased her about. *Aww, yittle Nikki's too much of a baby for sleepovers.* From that point on, the only sleepovers she'd have were at our house.

"Well, some weird things happened after that sleepover," my mom confessed. "Nikki's personality changed a lot—she was scared to go to school, and she could only make it through the day if she wore a locket with my picture, remember that?" I nodded. It was as if she were thinking out loud, at times even looking to me for answers. "Maybe it wasn't just separation anxiety?"

I wasn't fully following, but I was paying attention.

"And I did find blood in her underwear," she added, as if just remembering in that moment. "And she started wetting the bed—but when I brought her to the doctor, he said nothing was wrong," she said quickly.

I remembered being at our yearly pediatrician physical, my sister's turn on the paper-covered table, and hearing our (male) childhood doctor say that Nikki probably tore her hymen doing gymnastics, happens all the time, no big deal. (A hymen isn't just a "cherry to pop"; they can tear through other activities. So the doctor wasn't lying.) I'd clung to that information through middle school, jokingly questioning whether she was even a virgin.

"Maybe something *did* happen," my mom said, looking down at the diary in my hands.

Mom didn't define what that *something* was, but over time, it became the context to explain Nikki's "personality quirks." Her modesty, refusing to change in front of anyone; the ways she starved her body to stay small and hidden; why no one could touch the back of her neck without her flinching or jumping away; why, right after the sleepover, Nikki suddenly couldn't stand the texture of meat in her mouth, and would spit it out on her dinner plate across the table from me. And as we got older, why Nikki was visibly disgusted by the topic of sex.

Something happened with Butch that made Nikki cringe and shrink and avoid sex. We didn't talk about it—in fact, I never brought up the diary to Nikki, ever. It felt intrusive, as if I'd be poking around at a core wound, causing her unnecessary pain. My parents didn't get Nikki counseling; I don't even know if my parents talked about it privately. Maybe we were all waiting for Nikki to tell us herself.

I didn't explain all of this to the CPS workers, only the stripped-down truth: Something happened at a sleepover when she was five years old, something that felt foundational. For the first time, the name *Butch* wasn't accompanied by a question mark in my mind; it was a definitive statement. Why did it take so long for me see that?

CHAPTER 6

red flags

I watched the CPS workers slowly and silently walk to their car. I sat for a while, after their car pulled away, one hand leaning on my forehead, the other steadying my chest. I didn't have the energy to hold on to thoughts or feelings like guilt or fear for too long. There would be a time and a place for ruminating and blaming, for stewing and raging, and now was not it. Now I needed to calm my jacked-up nervous system, having just purged more tears and words than I thought I had in me.

But I couldn't. Another memory nagged at me, keeping me rooted to the chair. It was buried under a jumble of recollections begging to be reexamined, one I'd glossed over with the CPS workers because there was still so much I didn't understand.

It was around six or seven years earlier—back when I was in the early stages of young motherhood. I lived with Noah and Justin in a duplex in Poughkeepsie, right down the road from my mom. Nikki was still finishing up her bachelor's degree in early childhood education, and she lived in my mom's apartment while commuting to class. And because we lived less than five minutes apart, Noah and I spent a lot of time visiting Grandma and Aunt Nikki. Mom nearly always kept her door unlocked, so many days Noah and I would walk in and have the place to ourselves.

One day I walked in and saw my mom standing in the living room with a man in jeans and a T-shirt. They both smiled, an air of friendship between them. I didn't have a clue who he was, but their conversation seemed to stop mid-sentence when I walked through the door. We all made some awkward pleasantries, and he quickly said goodbye.

I nodded toward the door with a look that said, *What was that about?*

Mom's face responded with a *wait until you hear this one* expression.

She explained that the man's name was Dave—a name that was vaguely familiar, and mom clarified that Nikki coached and sometimes babysat his daughter.

"He's a police officer, and he thinks someone hurt Nikki," she said, launching into what sounded like a wild story. "He said that she came to him for help, and he saw blood in the shower," she said, adding, "Her hands were zip-tied together?" Mom's face was contorted into a question mark, as if this was all too dramatic, too fantastical, to be true. "Why would Nikki say that?"

Ordinarily, if I heard that a mother was visited by a police officer, and was told that her daughter was being hurt, I'd expect that mother to run toward her with help—not question if her daughter was making it up. But given the dynamic between Nikki and my mom—one where my mom seemed to second-guess what Nikki said—her reaction tracked.

I don't know where it started or why, but there was a consistent undertone, from the time we were little, that Nikki was "looking for attention." Which doesn't make sense, because she wasn't one to chronically lie or get caught up in risky, dangerous behavior. She was a quiet girl, a good girl. In fact, if you watched our childhood home movies back then, I was the one belting off-tune notes into a makeshift microphone and vying for the spotlight, while Nikki blended into the background. I danced on a stage, I wrote short stories about my life. If anyone appeared to be "looking for attention," it was me, not Nikki.

But she was dodgy and distrustful of other people, particularly my mom. Over the years, Nikki had watched me spill my guts to my mom about everything and anything, and then heard Mom go and tell her sisters what I had said. Nikki paid attention like an animal being preyed on, always listening, always taking the temperature of a room. Did that contribute to my mom thinking that Nikki couldn't be trusted? Was her quietness misinterpreted as sneakiness?

Or maybe it was the way that Nikki would drop hints that something was wrong with her, instead of coming right out and saying it. She'd say it through bouts of starving her body, while simultaneously mentioning that she hadn't eaten all day. She'd say things like, "I don't cry in front of any of you," and "I have so much going on in my life that you know nothing about." Now, looking back, I wondered if someone looking for help looks an awful lot like someone looking for attention.

It was the zip-tie detail that got me—"Mom, you can't zip-tie your own hands together." But I don't remember talking to her about it again.

This incident didn't seem like something Nikki could make up. So much that I did something we rarely did in our family: confront the issue head-on. I asked Nikki about it directly. I'm sure I did it tentatively, mentioning the police officer. I don't remember our exact conversation, but I remember her icy response—like talking to a frozen wall. She didn't look me in the eye; she wouldn't engage. She insinuated that it was a one-time assault by a stranger, but wouldn't even go so far as to put language to it. It was clear that she didn't want to talk about it; she didn't want the police involved; she just wanted it to go away. I said okay. We never talked about it again, mostly because I didn't want to upset or embarrass her. If she needed me, she'd come to me.

Still—I couldn't let it go entirely, and I pulled her brand-new boyfriend, Chris, into the conversation.

No part of me thought that Chris could be the one hurting her, and I didn't ask him to come to my apartment to accuse him. Maybe because he seemed too *nice* and timid to violently attack someone. But I wanted to know what he knew and see how we could help.

He sat at my dining room table wearing a newsboy-style hat over his prematurely balding head. He was about as tall as me, barely five feet five, and a year younger than me. I knew very little about him, only that he lived with his parents, was in community college for cinematography, and was quiet. An awkwardness hung in the air between us; I wrapped my arms around my body as I talked, and he kept his hands in his lap and looked down at the table for most of the conversation. Through the nine years I would know him, we'd never get comfortable around each other.

I asked him about the police, the assault, and said Nikki wouldn't talk about it. What did he think?

"I think she's making it up." He shrugged his shoulders. "I don't think anything happened."

It should have been a red flag—why didn't he have her back? Why would he assume that his girlfriend was lying? And why would he stay with someone who would create such a disturbing fabrication? But he was new in our lives, and I didn't know how long he'd stick around. My most immediate reaction was that he must not know all the details. Plus his denial was a familiar response; it aligned with the unsaid assumptions in my mom's reaction. My family may not have said it as bluntly as Chris did, but the idea that nothing actually happened was an *easier* belief to choose. I didn't yet recognize that the "she's crazy" eye roll can also be a tactic.

We all dropped the conversation entirely.

This individual and collective denial or avoidance, I'd come to learn, wasn't unusual—especially in a family that carried their own generational trauma, and had a tendency to take on each other's problems. It made sense that, on some level, we'd avoid knowing an overwhelming, anxiety-producing truth. Denial is a well-traveled path of self-preservation.

I *had* thought about it through the years, particularly the zip-tie part. It bothered me not to have a solution to the mystery—but not enough to ask her again. That came with a risk—a risk that she'd shut me down, a risk that I'd have to feel her palpable discomfort or anger, a risk that she'd say something I didn't want to hear.

A few times over the years, I almost brought it up again with Nikki. And then I'd chicken out, assuming that one day she'd be ready to tell me what happened; I thought we had more time.

Time was up.

My brain scanned for more intrusive memories, and jumped from that unexplained assault years ago, to several moments within the last few months—to a series of waving red flags that I saw but didn't *see*.

Earlier this past spring, I had seen a circular burn on Nikki's chest peeking out from behind a scarf, while she touched up her makeup in the bathroom. It looked raised and oozy. She quickly dismissed it by saying she had dropped a hair straightener on herself while multitasking, *what else is new, no big deal*. I didn't question it.

Not long after, in the early weeks of summer, she pulled me into the same bathroom, shut the door, and whispered, "I think something's wrong with my vagina. It looks like my insides are coming out." My exact response was, "Ew. You need to go see a doctor." I didn't ask to see. I didn't ask how it happened. I've always been squeamish around body stuff. If you'd have asked me at the time, I think I'd assumed that she was having some kind of prolapse from two back-to-back pregnancies.

Long red marks on her upper arm—the image flashed in my mind. I remembered even having the thought, *Wow, those look like finger marks,* but never saying it out loud. *Why?* My brain couldn't place when I saw it: Was it last month? Last year?

I was only now stringing the memories into a pattern, instead of brushing them off as isolated moments. I had a hard time coming up with a word for what this felt like. It wasn't exactly *denial*, because I wasn't presented with cold hard information that I had disregarded or rejected as untrue. It was more like *misinterpretation*. I had come up with more palatable explanations. I'd accepted excuses without further questioning. I'd filled in the blanks with my own version of reality.

I wish I could have asked all the questions I had dismissed. Maybe I could have helped her. Saved her.

Maybe Chris wouldn't have had to die, either.

CHAPTER 7

booth visit

It was fully dark now, as I sat at the small table outside my door with bright pinholes of light scattered above my head. My body was surging with some kind of adrenaline concoction that narrowed my vision like a hawk's, making my thoughts and actions crystal clear and super simple. At that moment, I knew exactly what to do next. *Go to her.*

I picked up my phone and looked up the number for the jail. A man answered and I awkwardly fumbled out a sentence about my sister being there and wanting to see her. He said I'd need to come down to the jail and sign up for a booth visit, and suggested I come soon; it was first-come, first-served. Two visitors max. I sent Elizabeth a text, asking her if she'd meet me. *Of course.*

The only other person who might have needed to go see Nikki as fiercely as me was my mom. But now that all three kids were asleep, she was practically pulsating with anxiety, eyebrows stuck high on her forehead, her hand on her heart. *Nikki called? Can I talk to her? What did she say? Oh, Michelle, what's happening?*

Even if my parents wanted to go, they couldn't. While I walked out the door, Mom was deflated on the couch, while my dad sat next to her, completely silent, leaning on his knees with his head in his hands.

I, however, felt wide awake.

I googled the address, 150 North Hamilton Street—an area of Poughkeepsie tucked between the sheriff's office and low-income houses, down the road from multiple organizations that help families navigate poverty, violence, and unemployment. I'd spent years driving those city streets. I'd waitressed only a mile and a half from North Hamilton through high school and college, but I'd never had a reason to drive down that road.

Starting route to Dutchess County Jail, 6.4 miles, a 12-minute drive.

Jail. Everything felt surreal as I hovered my way down familiar roads in a dreamlike state, feeling like a déjà vu in reverse. I felt implanted in a life that looked eerily similar to the one I knew, but wasn't.

I'd assumed that the closest I'd ever get to a public tragedy would be reading about it in the paper. I'd seen such reports in local news stories, and heard the inevitable refrain: *This kind of thing doesn't happen in a place like this.*

And yet, they do.

When I was in middle school, a man who lived across the street from my pediatrician's office killed nine women, nearly all sex workers, and hid their corpses in his house. For months the bodies piled up until the odor grew so bad, it was undeniable. On national news, I watched a team of people in hazmat suits carry body bags down the steps of the familiar white house. I wondered how many times I'd driven past these women's bodies, disposed of like trash.

More recently, a neighbor in our gated community killed his wife and two sons before killing himself. They were a quiet family. The father was a pharmacist; the kids, both in our local elementary school, rode bikes past us and shared neighborhood friends with Noah. The day it happened, helicopters circled above and cops knocked on doors asking if we'd heard gunshots or screams (we hadn't). I soon found out that the father had killed his wife in their car on a nearby road, in broad daylight. Later, he shot both kids before killing himself. I knew the stomach-turning details because my mom was the property manager for their rental. She organized a vigil in front of the apartments as a handful of people held candles and each other through the shock and grief. The newspaper barely reported it, and no one talked about it again.

*   *   *

I didn't have any expectations about what the jail might look like, or even the faintest idea what the process might be to see her. Before I had time to formulate a plan, I pulled into a large parking lot in front of a long, squat three-story concrete building. It looked cold and unfriendly.

Yanking open the heavy steel doors, I stepped into a room lined with small bluish-green lockers and white cinder block walls littered with flyers and laminated signs. There was a desk in the front of the room under an American flag, but no officers. Two women sat in the waiting area—one was petite with tight brown curls; the other had fair, shoulder-length hair and a friendly look in her eyes. They both watched me as I walked in.

"Are you Nikki's sister?" the brunette asked. Something about her demeanor and Italian-looking features felt familiar, as if we could have been related.

"Yes," I said hesitantly.

"I'm Sarah," she said, putting her hand on her chest. "This is Lori." She gestured to the woman sitting next to her, whose face spread into a cautious closemouthed smile.

I sat down, leaving a blue plastic chair between us.

"I was Nikki's therapist," Sarah added. My face must have given away my surprise, because she then began explaining. "I started working with Nikki when Ben was a baby and through her pregnancy with Faye, over at Family Services," she said. "When I left to open my private practice, we stopped working together but stayed in touch."

I had no idea Nikki was in therapy.

Then Lori introduced herself as Nikki and Chris's former landlord. She had sublet her one-bedroom condo to Chris and Nikki until around a year ago, when their growing family needed more space. I knew the apartment well. It was where I'd stop over with Dunkin' Donuts and watch two-year-old Ben perform Laurie Berkner Band songs. It was where Noah had his first sleepover, playing video games with his cool Uncle Chris. Faye was born in the bedroom, in a birthing tub, in the middle of a snowstorm.

"We just saw Nikki, and before that, we were at the police station," Sarah said. She went on to describe how they'd spent hours talking with the cops who'd arrested Nikki, trying to make them see that Nikki was a victim—that she'd killed her abuser.

I was both confused and impressed that they were so on top of this, quicker than me.

"I only just learned about this," I said. "Elizabeth told me—do you know Elizabeth?"

"Yes," Sarah said quickly. "She'd been trying to help Nikki safely leave. She was one of the only people Nikki confided in—besides me, in therapy sessions."

I felt the sting of embarrassment. Here I was, her only sister, yet I wasn't on her short list of confidantes. I blinked, took a deep breath, and let that thought go. There was no room in my body to carry that shame. Not yet.

Lori took a turn speaking. "Nikki didn't tell me directly, but I saw the signs of abuse and I'd been concerned for years." She went on: She had worked as a social worker with the local children's home, mainly with abused and sex-trafficked girls, and she knew Sarah because they both sat on the board of a local coalition against sexual and domestic violence in our county.

"We were shocked, but also relieved that she lived," Lori said. "I always thought she'd be the one dead."

The next few minutes went by in a blur, as Sarah and Lori told me what they knew and how long they'd known it. I could hear the words they were saying, but it was as if I were hearing them through protective glass, distant enough that I didn't have to feel the full weight of their impact.

Lori described dropping by Nikki's apartment for a lease renewal two years before, and she said things like "signs of strangulation," having observed what looked like a thin rope mark around Nikki's neck and redness in her eyes. Nikki was visibly pregnant with Faye at the time.

I nodded, as if that was a completely reasonable thing to hear, as if I was ready for her to go on and keep talking. But the part of me trapped behind glass was screaming, *What???*

"Whatever legal team represents Nikki *has* to have an understanding of sex trafficking and its psychological effects," Sarah said. Lori nodded. Sarah offered some names and resources, and said she'd be happy to put us in touch.

"I'm sorry, go back. *Trafficking?*" This was too much. "Are you saying he was *selling her*? Were other men involved?" I was suddenly talking faster, louder.

Sarah took a sharp inhale and sighed, as if she really didn't want me to learn about it this way.

"Yes and no," she said. "Other men weren't raping her, but they were watching her be raped on the Internet." She said Chris would film her and he was "good at it," and he would tell Nikki that the videos were "in high demand."

Nausea broke through the glass. If I'd had to rank every single person I'd met in my entire existence based on their likelihood to appear in pornography, Nikki would have been dead last.

Without question.

Sarah went on, "A police officer was tracking the videos on Pornhub,[1] which were getting more and more violent and disturbing, and wanted to arrest him. But Nikki was scared to press charges. She was embarrassed and scared of the repercussions. We think he eventually moved to a more underground website, Extra Lunch Money, where he was taking requests for what to do to her and likely making a profit."

There was no way Nikki would have willingly participated in any videos. By the time we were teenagers and throughout our twenties, Nikki was completely uninterested in, and often disgusted by, sex. She'd cringe at the mention of blow jobs or anal sex, even if they came up as a joke. Mom liked to say she had "hang-ups" and teased her for being a "prude." Her motherly advice was to "learn to like it," because "boys have needs."

Whenever she gave advice like this—which she did, to both of us, in varying degrees—it was always with an air of, *Sorry, kid, this is the curse of being a woman, just accept it and your life will be easier.* As if this was a hard-earned lesson passed down from a long line of women trained into submission.

Even though the idea of Nikki having sex on camera was wildly incompatible with who I knew her to be, I also knew that Chris *was* good at filming videos—he was a trained videographer. I'd seen several of his amateur projects, like a beautiful montage of Nikki's first pregnancy and a quirky comedic reel for Noah's new YouTube channel. I knew that he'd been to community college for cinematography and owned video-editing programs. But filming and uploading rape videos?

"And he made money doing this?" I asked, my head spinning.

Sarah nodded. "We think so."

I stared at the gray linoleum floor. The thought of someone filming and uploading rape videos was disturbing all on its own, but to know it was being done to *Nikki*? If someone close to Nikki wanted to hurt her—to make her freeze and submit; to expose and exploit her deepest wounds—they would do exactly what Chris had done: Broadcast her naked body out to the world, and then hold that humiliation over her head. If I'd had access to the full range of my emotions—which, in that moment, I did not—I would have been brimming with fury. It was abjectly cruel.

I sat for a minute, scrambling to make sense of these shattered pieces of reality.

"How could I not have known?" I asked, mostly of myself. "*I pay attention.*"

Sarah looked at me blankly, both of us probably thinking the same thing: *Obviously not.*

CHAPTER 8

fever dream

The dark night pressed against the wall-size window behind us, reflecting one metal detector, two horseshoe clusters of plastic chairs, and three exhausted women.

Then two more women walked in. Despite never having seen Elizabeth, the music teacher, before, I knew it was her: She appeared to be in her forties, with shoulder-length red hair, and despite an obvious exhaustion behind her eyes, a kind smile. She looked warm and approachable, the kind of mom who bakes brownies for the PTA sale. The kind of person who you'd stop and ask directions, or trust to watch your bag while you went to the bathroom.

Trailing behind Elizabeth was another woman, around the same age, but taller. Elizabeth had told me she was bringing a friend named Wendy, who had spent all day at Elizabeth's dining room table making phone calls to lawyers and domestic violence organizations—but as they got closer, I also realized that I knew her. She had a daughter who had been in Noah's preschool class, the same preschool where Nikki taught. I recognized Wendy from drop-offs and pickups, and the occasional easy conversation at a birthday party. I hadn't run into her in years.

Wendy reintroduced herself. She said she knew Nikki as a gentle and caring teacher, and she remembered Noah fondly.

"Wendy's been helping me navigate this for, what, a little over a year?" Elizabeth said, looking at her friend, who nodded back.

A year of Elizabeth and Wendy knowing and helping. Lori had been concerned about Nikki for the past two years. Sarah had been working with Nikki, on and off, for nearly four years. For me, this was day one.

A correctional officer showed up behind the desk. I excused myself from the group.

"Um, hi, I signed up for a booth visit? I'm here to see Nicole Addimando?" Everything out of my mouth was a question. I didn't have the capacity for definitive sentences. And the officer, it appeared, didn't have the capacity for much beyond grunts and heavy exhalations.

I don't remember Sarah and Lori leaving. I don't remember giving my bag and coat to Wendy for safekeeping, although I must have. But I do remember following a blank-faced man in a black uniform toward a cold metal door that slowly slid open. He led Elizabeth and me across a narrow hallway and into a room the size of a closet, with two chairs and a black corded phone on the wall. We sat down and looked at the window ahead of us. On the other side was another room, a mirror image of the one we were sitting in, where inmates were brought to talk to visitors on the phone.

And then the door opened, and Nikki, *my* Nikki, was led into the room. She was dressed head-to-toe in orange, her black hair loose and wild. Her face looked depleted, as if the life force had been drained from her body. She took small steps into the room, wearing slip-on shoes, the exact ones on the cover of the *Orange Is the New Black* memoir sitting on my bookshelf at home.

She looked small—the short-sleeve jumpsuit hung loose on her body. She looked young—far younger than her twenty-eight years, entirely too young to be in jail.

In the time it took for her to sit down, my eyes pulled to the correctional officer in the corner of the room—a young uniformed Black woman, very pregnant, smiling right at me. *Wait a minute, is that...Ronda? My friend in sixth grade?* I hadn't seen or thought about her in years, not since the days of goofing around at recess, playing pretend.

None of this felt real.

The scene was too much for my brain to compute. It had all the trappings of a nightmare concocted by my subconscious—random people from my nearly forgotten past, names I'd heard in passing, and an outrageous stranger-than-fiction plot. This was the kind of thing I'd wake up from and immediately text Nikki. *I just had the weirdest dream—first of all you were in jail for killing Chris…* And then we'd laugh and joke because nothing as crazy as that could ever happen to us.

And yet there I was, picking up a phone in a jail visiting booth, looking like a scene from a TV show I'd seen a thousand times.

The left side of Nikki's mouth lifted into a reluctant acknowledgment as she locked eyes with me and sat down.

"Hi," I heard her small, tired voice through the phone. Her shoulders rounded forward and down toward her waist, as if her spine couldn't hold her up.

"I'm sorry," I blurted out. "I'm so, *so* sorry." I suddenly felt twice as heavy, as if those words released the full weight of my guilt. I pressed the receiver to the left side of my face.

She looked down. "No, *I'm* sorry, I—" She left the sentence hanging, as if she'd run out of energy for talking. Instead she looked up and shook her head *no*. Then her eyes quickly shifted to Elizabeth. I sensed a comfort, an ease, between their shared *hellos*.

I passed the phone to Elizabeth, who then passed it back to me. We did that for the next twenty minutes, going into fix-it mode—exchanging what we knew about the kids (*someone needs to file for emergency custody ASAP*), legal help (*Wendy already called the National Clearinghouse for the Defense of Battered Women…*), and the jail protocol. Facts were still foggy, but from what Nikki had absorbed, she now had to stay under "constant watch" to make sure she didn't kill herself—standard protocol for someone facing a possible murder charge—and so she had to eat, sleep, and pee in front of a guard. Once she was "classified," which would determine where she would be placed in the jail, then she could have two hour-long visits a week in a different visiting room. She'd be strip-searched after every visit, forced to take off her clothes in front of strangers.

But Nikki wasn't thinking about future visits in the jail—she just wanted to get out of there.

"How can Ben and Faye be away from me for an entire night? You have to get me out of here, please."

Elizabeth and I met her with a steady *we'll get this straightened out, we'll help you* attitude, but we couldn't change the fact that this separation was a gigantic unmovable reality, and none of us knew how long getting her out would take. The theoretical *who do I want to take my kids in case anything happens to me* thought experiment was suddenly happening, and Nikki was alive enough to make a decision in real time.

Nikki looked right at me. "Will you keep them, Michelle? Please keep my babies safe until I can get to them?" She asked with a shaky voice. *"Please,"* she whispered, barely audible.

I nodded. Of course. It wasn't a question.

"The last thing I said to the kids was, 'I'll be right back.'" Nikki started to cry deep, heaving sobs. "I never would have said that if I didn't think I'd be right back." She wiped her face with the back of her free hand, and I realized it was the first time I could remember seeing Nikki cry.

I left the jail holding a piece of paper with handwritten directions on how to pay for phone calls and put money in Nikki's commissary account. A white-haired correctional officer took the time to advise us to find a private attorney instead of relying on the overworked public defenders for "this kind of thing"—meaning a murder charge.

"This will take a while," he said. I assumed he meant it would take days, maybe weeks. I wasn't ready to know how long *a while* could be.

Back home, my parents were still awake. They were sitting on the floor of the living room like children waiting for direction. *Did you see her? Is she okay? What's next?*

I filled them in on most of what I'd learned in a hushed whisper, all three of us huddled around the coffee table. My mom mumbled *oh God* in a loop, shaking her head. I couldn't get the words *sex trafficking* and *porn* out of my mouth, but I relayed most of what I had learned about Chris and the police investigations. I also let them know that Nikki had a support system in place that none of us were aware of.

Then we sat, mostly without talking, audibly sighing. My dad rubbed his temples, as if that might turn back time. My mom cried into a tissue.

"How did the kids do falling asleep?" I asked.

"I rocked Faye to sleep," my mom said. "She cried for Nikki but settled down pretty quickly. I promised her that Nikki would be back soon."

I let out a long exhale, replaying what the correctional officer had told me: *This will take a while.*

"Ben asked for Nikki a lot, and he was starting to get pretty upset, but we got through it," my dad said.

His face suggested that he himself had just *barely* got through. His olive skin was pale, his eyes glazed. My mom was almost green—she looked as though she could vomit any minute.

Noah was old enough to put himself to bed with a mind full of questions I'd soon have to answer. He could tolerate Ben and Faye in small doses, but I knew he'd like them to leave soon, *thank you very much.* He enjoyed his quiet only-child lifestyle, and Ben—the boy who never met a surface that wasn't a drum, or a wall that couldn't be scaled—existed just beyond his tolerance zone.

I quietly jogged up the stairs to Noah's bedroom and peeked in at his sweet sleeping face. The past year had been so hard and confusing for him. His dad had moved out—something he long feared would happen and was devastated to see come to fruition. A couple of months after that, he learned that his dad was living a whole separate life with a new girlfriend, without us, and he'd soon have a little brother. And now this.

His Aunt Nikki (or "Aunt Didi," as he called her), was the closest mother figure he had besides me. Back when he was an infant, I had worked full-time, with a two-hour commute each way. Nikki, who was in college, stepped up as his consistent caregiver, and the two of them forged an unusually tight aunt-nephew relationship. She hand-made toys—like soft felt blocks when he was a baby, and an elaborate train table when he was a toddler—and planned special days to take Noah out, just the two of them. She'd show up with genuine enthusiasm, waving wildly to Noah as he looked out the window with anticipation, celebratory hands in the air, yelling, "Aunt Day!" She started taking photographs of him to capture his beauty and innocence, which then turned into a small local photography business. She was like a second mother to him, without the rules and *no*'s—the perfect aunt.

And as for Chris—they were buddies. They'd play video games and chat about Marvel characters, and Chris had started to teach Noah how to use video-editing programs.

I'd spent so many years wanting to put a force field around Noah, to protect his sensitive heart from the disappointments and dangers that come from living with an addicted parent. I wanted to do the same now—to shield him from the terrible truths that I was only just beginning to uncover. I wanted him to retain whatever glimpses of innocence he had left—but how? How would I explain that one person he loved had killed another person he loved? And that Chris had actually been hurting Nikki, and none of us knew? How could I articulate that people can be both good and bad, when the "bad" was this violent and extreme? Would he ever trust anyone again?

The only thing I knew for absolute certain was that holding back the truth under the guise of "protection" was a kind of magical thinking I no longer wanted any part of.

CHAPTER 9

everyone knew

September 29, 2017: Day 2

I woke up on my couch the morning after Nikki was taken into custody. In the time it took my eyes to focus, it hit me: *It all really happened. Nikki is in a cage. Chris is dead.* The facts landed in my stomach like a sucker punch.

Then I heard a small familiar voice. "Aunt Mimi?"

Ben. I'd been *Mimi* for the past four years, ever since he'd tried to say the word *Michelle* and those two syllables were all that came out. The name stuck. He was standing at my side wearing only a pair of dry disposable Pull-Ups.

Normally, at his own house, he'd wake up, grab a ukulele or guitar, and compose a melody for the day. Nikki would post the videos on Instagram, or send me morning texts about her little musician. As a baby, he sang before he could speak. But there was no music in his voice today.

"Come on up, bud." I grabbed my glasses, propped myself up, and made some room under my blanket.

We were the only two awake in the house. He had slept next to my dad in one room, Faye had slept next to my mom in another, and Noah was still asleep in the loft above the living room. He'd soon be up for another Friday in third grade, probably expecting to find me sitting on my yoga mat in the corner of the living room with a lit candle, a journal next to me. I liked modeling that routine, and for the past six months, we'd had a quiet morning ritual. He'd come down and join me on the floor until I blew out the candle ("Make a wish for your day," I'd say), and together we'd sit on the carpet and look out the window, watching a sky that slowly and then quickly brightened into a new day.

But the sun wouldn't be up for another hour. I did some quick math and realized I'd slept less than four hours, yet didn't feel tired at all. *Adrenaline*, I thought, amazed at our body's ability to operate in survival mode.

"I'm hungry," Ben sighed.

"Well, let's get you some food," I said cheerfully. I gave him a squeeze around his narrow shoulders and a kiss on his head before getting up to rummage through the kitchen. His skin felt a little warm, and I worried he might be getting sick. I narrated different breakfast options in a singsong voice.

While I went through the breakfast-making motions, words like *custody* and *attorneys* swirled in my mind, forming a jumbled to-do list. I imagined what Nikki must have been doing right now, sitting alone in a jail cell. Stress drummed in my ears, propelling me forward. Luckily, that was my comfort zone. I liked a task. I liked having a list of items to cross off. I preferred to stay busy, especially when the alternative was to feel bad feelings. I could sense my body start to chase my mind, armoring up to Fix and Do and Go, Go, Go.

Then something came over me like a deep, soothing hush: the words *Stay here.* Maybe it was the effect of my morning ritual, from training my brain to be contemplative at this early hour. It felt like a reminder from my body not to run away into my mind. It was an invitation to drop down right where I was—not on a mat, but in the kitchen, hands on the counter, bare feet pressing against the cold tile floor. The Fixing and the Doing could wait; Ben needed my whole undivided self. In that moment, some wiser part of me rose to the surface—a part I'd met before, always in times of crisis, one I'd found through the healing work around my marriage. I was glad to hear her.

For today, I was giving myself only one big task: Drive into the City of Poughkeepsie and file for emergency custody. I'd take a personal day from work.

Ding. The toaster oven told me that Ben's waffles were done. I pulled out a blue plastic Spider-Man plate that Noah hadn't used in years, and arranged the waffles and some cut-up fruit into a smiley face, just like my mom used to do for me.

"Mom, what's the lunch today?" Noah soon called from upstairs. I looked over to the orange paper menu on the fridge to see what the school would be serving. "Chicken drumsticks." He approved. He walked downstairs fully dressed, book bag packed for the day. He didn't ask if he could stay home with everyone, and I didn't suggest it. *Update Noah's teachers on home life*, my brain scribbled on its mental checklist.

After Noah was off to school, I tried to keep my phone out of reach, giving myself a few hours without a barrage of new information. Whatever terrible truths were lurking would still be there later. But I was only human. Once the morning routine had settled and Ben and Faye were contentedly eating a second breakfast, dry cereal, and watching *Mickey Mouse Clubhouse*, I sat at the dining room table and unlocked my phone. Thirty-two unread texts.

Messages came in shock or panic or deep concern for my well-being. "Michelle, what's going on? Are you okay? Is this really happening?"

There was also a message from my boss: "Take the time you need." She said a coworker saw a Facebook post about Nikki in a private group, recognized that Nikki was my sister, and relayed the severity of the situation.

"Thank you," I wrote back, relieved not to have to explain. And also thinking, *It's on Facebook already?*

I opened the app and saw the post immediately. It was made in a private group for local moms with more than a thousand members, linked to a small business in Poughkeepsie that sold baby products and held classes for new and expecting parents. I scanned the post.

> Good morning mommies. As some of you already know,
> one of our members is in the papers for murder. Nikki
> Addimando has been a member for years. She has been
> accused of murdering her boyfriend. I know this board

includes members of both sides of this story. Those of us
that know Nikki know that she was in an abusive situation
and are devastated for her and her children, Ben and Faye.

Something about seeing Nikki's situation in writing made it more real.

Elizabeth had told me that others in town had been concerned, but I hadn't understood the extent. As I scanned through nearly one hundred comments, I realized *those who knew Nikki* really meant *those of us who've known Nikki for the past year or two.* Those with fresh eyes on Nikki saw the bruising with a clearer perspective. Comment after comment expressed either suspicions or knowledge of abuse, or disbelief that Nikki could be a cold-blooded murderer. Not one person commented negatively about her.

I googled the *Poughkeepsie Journal* and my maiden name. There it was: POLICE CHARGE GIRLFRIEND IN POUGHKEEPSIE MAN'S DEATH.

They'd posted her mugshot, and when I saw it, my heart hurt. *Oh, Nikki,* I whispered out loud. The top half of her face looked frozen in despair— eyebrows slightly raised, worry lines in the center of her forehead, and dark circles under her glazed eyes. Her mouth was straight, her jaw visibly clenched. Her hair was air-dried and poofy—not the shiny straightened version others were used to seeing.

Some might say she was unrecognizable, but I saw the sad, scared little girl I used to know, before she found hair straighteners and eyeliner. I saw a teenage Nikki who'd just learned our ten-year-old dog, Evan, needed to be put to sleep. I saw a six-year-old Nikki sitting in a hospital room, looking at our mom, who was sick again from her Crohn's disease. I saw the little girl hurting with secrets she didn't share, and it broke me.

Another message came in from the woman who'd posted in the private Facebook group. "We have bags of clothes for the kids at the store, come stop in anytime." Nikki's car and the entirety of their apartment were off limits for evidence collecting, so we had nothing for the kids beyond the car seats that the police gave my mom, and two teddy bears that the kids got at the station.

And so, on my way to the one big task of the day, I stopped at the small store. It was nearly empty, but I felt eyes on me as I stood in front of tables displaying muslin blankets and teething toys. Jenn, the owner of the store, waved me over and pointed out the two big garbage bags of toddler-size clothes. "Everyone knew," she said from behind the checkout counter.

"Everyone. Knew," she said again, shaking her head and looking right into my eyes this time. She said it as if she were talking to someone who *also* knew, someone who'd share in the outrage that *so many people* knew she was being hurt and yet *she's* the one arrested.

I don't know what my face looked like from the outside, but I know how it felt from the inside: hot. How could I explain that I—Nikki's only sister, a person who saw her more often than nearly anyone—was not part of the "everyone" who knew?

I didn't respond.

"Michelle, do you know how many parents walked out of music class and came to me with concerns about Nikki?" Jenn said, gesturing to the two empty rooms off the back wall where she held classes and support groups. "She came in here with black eyes, everyone saw," she went on. "There were text threads about it."

She explained there was a specific group of people—people I knew and considered friends—who had been discussing Nikki's injuries for the past year. They debated whether to confront Nikki or call Child Protective Services, especially once the injuries became impossible to hide.

Those in the group who understood the realities of domestic violence and how our local system worked, like Sarah, advised caution—they didn't want to ignite a flame and unwittingly cause an explosion. They were witnessing what looked like an escalation in violence, and they were scared Chris would kill her. Others were pushing for an intervention because they knew they'd never forgive themselves if something happened to Nikki and they hadn't said or done anything to stop it.

All these silent observers and group texters also happened to be *moms*, conditioned to scan a room for boo-boos and find the people who need help. But I was a mom, too. I was a part of this community. I *knew* these women who were concerned about my sister. I wasn't active in the Facebook group anymore—far past the potty training, sleep regression, *is this poop color normal* stage of parenting—but I was a member.

I was one message away.

Everyone knew, but no one thought to include me?

I couldn't even identify the mix of feelings muted under lingering shock. Was I angry that no one told me? Was I embarrassed? Was I looking for someone to blame? It was as if I didn't have an ounce of excess energy to process feelings.

I thanked Jenn and genuinely meant it. She said she'd be in touch. From there, I continued down the arterial toward the courthouse, processing the new layer of information I had just received.

It's not exactly true that *everyone* knew. Most of us were seeing a curated, filtered, public-facing version of Nikki. I started going back to her Instagram page for clues that morning—looking for telling comments left on posts, or cries for help disguised as captions. But I didn't see anything, just emoji hearts and #supermom comments, and a smattering of heartfelt musings on motherhood.

One post from August 6, less than two months earlier, showed her lying next to a sleeping Ben, holding his small hand. Underneath she wrote:

> B: "Mommy, I didn't like not being with you today. I missed you too much . . . what would I do in my life without you?"
>
> Me: "I missed you so much, too. You don't have to worry about life without me. I'm with you always."
>
> B: "Because our hearts have an invisible string that connects us no matter what, right mom?"
>
> Yes. That. #theinvisiblestring

I had seen and "liked" it, along with sixty-nine other people. "Too sweet," one commenter wrote. And it was! That's the kind of post we'd come to expect from her—something that made us *feel* the powerful connection she had with her kids, and reminded us of that connection in our own lives.

The post references *The Invisible String* by Patrice Karst. It's a book that is often recommended when a child is grappling with losing someone they love—either through death or more routine separation anxiety. It had a simple message: "Don't worry, love connects us all through an invisible string, heart to heart, no matter how far."

I couldn't stop thinking how far that string now had to stretch.

Out of the *everyone* who knew Nikki, those of us who knew Nikki the longest, especially those of us who experienced the full trajectory of Nikki and Chris's relationship up close, were completely blindsided. Like two of Nikki's oldest childhood friends who called me while I was driving back with custody paperwork and two garbage bags of kids' clothes.

"Michelle, hi, it's Rachel and Laura, we're together." I heard Rachel's familiar voice. Laura, Rachel, and Nikki were a long-standing trio, going back to the days of elementary school sleepovers (at our house) and first-kiss milestones. I'd hear them across the hall playing Jewel in Nikki's five-disc CD player and giggling in a little-girl octave. Now Laura and Rachel were grown-ups who had just learned that their best friend, the nicest person they'd ever known, was in jail for murdering Chris, a guy they'd known for years.

"What the hell is happening?"

Yes. Finally. Someone else reeling from this complete breach in reality.

"Rachel," I said, relieved to hear her shock. "What, the, fuck," I started, unloading it all—all the messy, ugly, infuriating information I'd been holding, feeling my heart rate pick up speed as I said words like *rape* and *filming* and *trafficking*. I ranted into the speakerphone, driving up Route 44 from Family Court.

I felt like I was telling Rachel a story that belonged to someone else's life.

"Um, do you think we should be talking about these details?" Rachel interrupted. My stomach dropped.

Paranoia shot through my body. "Do you think someone's listening to my calls?" Absolutely nothing was outside the realm of possibility at that point.

Instead, she reminded me that communication can be subpoenaed and witnesses might need to testify. Before calling me, she'd talked to a family friend who was also a retired attorney, and he warned her about keeping witness testimony clean. You don't want your memories to be muddled with other people's information, and we'd have to be careful with what we say or write.

I hadn't even considered this.

Despite the risks, those of us blindsided needed to reach out to each other to make sense of our own memories and experiences. We needed each other, for our own steadiness, our own ability to function.

As it turned out, not everyone was telling the same story.

now they have no one

Later that day, after I filed my custody petition and school let out, sorrow broke through the cocoon of shock. Tears streamed, a steady overflow, through the mundane household tasks of dishes and laundry. My parents needed a break from around-the-clock parenting while emotionally crumbling inside. I needed to step away from the "I know a person who knows a person who knows a lawyer" messages, and "Just checking in on you, how can I help?" texts. It was a warm autumn day, and the kids needed my love and presence, so I sat outside under the low sun and watched them run barefoot up and down the small grassy hill in my backyard. They pulled out our basket of "outdoor toys," and suddenly Faye was wielding a blue Nerf gun that was almost as big as she was, shrieking and laughing as she chased Ben and Noah.

Ben looked off to the left and brightened. "Hey! Grandma Grover's here!"

Yep. There they were. I didn't know they were coming, and yet I wasn't surprised to see them; I doubted anything could have surprised me at that point. The kids smiled and waved, holding colorful plastic guns in their hands. I cringed, wishing they'd put them away.

The Grovers were a tight-knit family who lived in rural Red Hook, a forty-minute drive through Dutchess County's uppermost country roads. They raised all sorts of animals on a small backyard farm (*for the grandkids*, they said), which was where Chris had lived until Nikki became pregnant with Ben. His grandparents, parents, brother, aunt, and cousins all lived on the property, too, and many of them were now walking toward me with solemn faces, like a giant moving storm cloud.

I mostly knew them as one big group—as birthday party guests and Facebook friends. Nikki, Chris, and the kids visited Chris's parents every Sunday, and Noah had been going up to the Grovers' for years with his Aunt Nikki. I had last seen them a few months before, for a Fourth of July get-together, my second visit in the nine years we'd known each other. Nikki made us matching tie-dye shirts to wear. I gave the kids mini-American flags to wave for pictures. The Grovers had a barbecue, a fire pit for roasting marshmallows, and new baby goats—"*my* goats," two-year-old Faye corrected anyone who mentioned them, toddling in bare feet from the bunnies to the chickens. Ben rode over to us in his mini–John Deere play tractor, while Chris held up the goats for me to take pictures. Kids jumped on a trampoline, dogs barked and chased the cars coming and going from the driveway, and I felt truly happy.

And yet, here we were.

My dad walked toward the Grovers, aided by a cane for his bad back. He was starting to shrink with age, and now, in his early sixties, he was barely taller than me. His transition lenses darkened as he stepped into the sunlight and reached his free hand out to Chris's dad. "I'm sorry." They both nodded and shook hands.

I stood up and wiped tears from my cheeks. I wrapped my arms around myself as I, too, walked toward them. My mom went inside.

The kids started playing again, oblivious.

"We just don't understand," his mom said stoically, out of the kids' earshot. "They said Christopher was sleeping." Her voice carried an undertone of anger. She didn't cry.

This was new information to me. All I knew is what Nikki had said—*he pulled a gun, he threatened to kill me*—actions during which he would have had to be very much awake. Nothing in the newspaper reports said he was asleep.

Who are "*they*"? I wondered. How could "*they*" have made that determination before an autopsy? I didn't ask any of that—I barely said anything beyond "I don't know." I decided to respect their grief and let them believe whatever they needed to. We were all too fragile to start an argument. There was so much that we still didn't know.

"And now people are saying that he abused her?" His mother kept going. I guessed they had seen the Facebook comments.

I said nothing.

"He would never," his aunt cried out. "He always walked away from confrontation."

"I don't know," I said back, shaking my head, thinking that *surely* there would be professionals who would clear all of this up. It couldn't possibly be my job to break that news.

We all stood in silence, looking out at the children blissfully playing. I couldn't stop leaking tears. All I wanted was to shield their innocence, just a little while longer.

"Yesterday they had two parents who loved them. Now they have no one," Chris's mother said, her voice cracking. "The way I see it, both of their parents are gone forever." She said this firmly, with finality.

Oh God, I thought to myself, *not only would this woman have to grieve the loss of her son, but she'll have to grieve the imaginary image she had of who he was.* Right now she was operating with false information, and someone with more authority and irrefutable proof was going to break her heart all over again.

Almost as soon as the Grovers came, they left. They didn't threaten to take the kids. They weren't aggressive toward us. They just wanted to see Ben and Faye's faces, the last living parts of their son, and make sure they could still visit with them on Sundays. They knew that the kids didn't know details yet, and we all agreed to stay on the same page as far as what and when to tell them.

Their family was as blindsided as we were. Their loss and grief were intertwined with ours. And no matter what stories we were telling ourselves, and what fears threatened to consume us, I believed the truth would soon be revealed. And it would be undeniable, to all of us, together.

where is she?

It was late. The warm atmosphere of our second day had faded, and Nikki was still not back to rock Ben to sleep. He was pissed. He repeated *Where is she?* over and over, backing himself into the corner of the bedroom like a wounded animal. He got louder, his voice more frantic, with each subsequent ask. None of us gave Ben a straight answer.

Faye's questioning had been quieter throughout the day, as though she'd lost something important that she couldn't find. "Mama," she muttered to herself, toddling around the house, while the grown-ups around her held up shiny distractions. *"Mama's not here . . . but look at this!"*

Was this the time to tell them? And if it was, what should we say? We had no idea what was going on ourselves, completely at the mercy of a system that was moving at a glacial pace.

I was desperate for someone to tell our family exactly what to do. A ten-point action plan, or at the very least, a clear list of *dos* and *don'ts*. Sarah, being a therapist, was the first person I asked. She connected me to a local psychologist who, earlier that day, gave a suggested script, knowing only the bare-bones details of what happened: *Mommy and Daddy had a fight, and in the fight, Daddy died.*

But I wasn't sure. Would telling the kids that they'd had a *fight* be a vague enough explanation or put violent imagery in their heads? And was that even true? Was it a *fight*? I still didn't know exactly what had happened, and I had no way of knowing what the kids had already seen and heard. I didn't want to further distort their reality with an explanation that didn't fit their experience.

There were no easy answers. For tonight, as Ben's panic reached a fever pitch, I knew we'd have to wing it.

"Mommy is helping the police right now, taking care of some things," I told Ben, stroking his hair. "Mommy is safe and she loves you." It was a mantra I'd repeated to Noah before bed since he was a toddler—"You're safe and you're loved"—and so I offered it to Ben. When really, I'd never felt less safe in this unpredictable world. I was stalling for time.

"But *when* will she be home?" Ben demanded, grasping for the certainty I didn't have to give.

"Soon," my mom interrupted. I flashed her a side-eye glare: *Is that true?*

"We don't know when, Ben," I said. What else could I say?

I didn't think his screams would ever stop, but eventually he cried himself to sleep, curling up on the carpet. I picked up his small body and carried him to the bed, grateful to be getting one more night under our belts. We'd wake up tomorrow and do it all over again.

I knew Nikki didn't want us telling Ben and Faye the details. She wasn't ready. And truthfully, I wasn't ready for it, either. There's no age-appropriate way to tell kids that their mom shot their dad, not without implications of massive childhood trauma. This felt outside of my jurisdiction as an aunt.

But Noah? Noah was mine. And I knew he'd been watching, absorbing, more than the younger kids. I knew he was sitting in an uncomfortable place where his internal knowledge that something bad was happening didn't match the high-pitched "It's fine!" responses the adults had been doling out. I'd stalled long enough; I needed to break the news.

"Mom, can you come up here?" Noah called from his bedroom. A few weeks before, I'd had a spacious three-bedroom apartment for the two of us—a room for myself, with a bed I no longer had to share; an extra room for guests (where I imagined I'd create a zen space for my yoga and meditation practice); and a loft above the living room that Noah wanted for himself. We had talked about getting a dog, a sort of emotional bribe on my part to make up for how guilty I felt for asking his dad to leave.

But now, here we were, six of us sharing a suddenly cramped space. My parents took the main bedroom, as my mom's sickness required a private bathroom, and Ben and Faye were in the spare room. I slept on the couch.

The two littlest children were asleep as I dragged my body up the stairs to the third.

"Hi, honey, you ready for bed?" I arranged my face into a smile, but was sure he could feel my angst. Our typical nighttime routine of book reading and chats had fallen to the wayside. He was watching TV, pajamas on. His school clothes were crumpled on the floor. I sat down at his computer chair, in front of a large quote decal: "Happiness can be found in even the darkest of times, if only one remembers to turn on the light.—Albus Dumbledore."

It had been nearly three days since the police had knocked on our door, flipping reality on its head. Since then, it was as if I'd been swept out with a tide, away from him. I was briefly back, and he needed me.

"What's going on?" he asked plainly. "Is Aunt Nikki okay?" He asked with a tone that said, *Don't lie to me.* "Just tell me this," he continued. "Is everyone still alive? That's all I need to know." He said it like a joke—as in, *As long as everyone is alive, we're going to be okay.*

"Aunt Nikki is okay," I said, relieved to be able to start with the bright side. I lowered my voice. "But no, not everyone is alive. Chris died."

Chris died. I hadn't said the words out loud yet. I hadn't given myself a moment to fully think about it, even when his family was outside visiting. The magnitude of the shock was so all-consuming, it was as if my brain had swiftly assigned an avatar for him—an Other, separate from the man who had been in my life for the past nine years. I didn't feel sad that he was gone, I didn't feel loss—just a steady nothingness.

I felt the sentence suspend in the air between us, hanging in silence, unable to be sucked back in. I braced for his reaction.

Chris had been Noah's friend. He was goofy, with childlike interests— the same kinds of things Noah liked. Comic books. Video games. He'd come to Noah's fourth birthday party dressed like Spider-Man, articulating his body in a way most grown-ups couldn't, literally climbing and flipping off the walls. He'd come to every holiday event with a smile. He was always *there* in Noah's life, and now...he wasn't.

"Okay," Noah said blankly, nodding his head slowly. He was always so mature, so understanding. I wondered how much of him was processing what I had just said, and how much was compartmentalizing.

"I'm so sorry, Noah. I know how much you love him." I watched his expressionless face. He didn't ask me how Chris had died. Thank God.

"Well," he said, attempting to lighten the mood again. "I guess I'm not having a video game sleepover next weekend."

"Oh, honey, I'm so sorry." Tears welled in my eyes.

He shifted the conversation to Nikki. Noah was even closer to Nikki than he had been to Chris.

In an effort to get ahead of his next question, I continued, "Aunt Nikki was hurt, too, and she's someplace now where she's safe and getting help."

It wasn't *completely* untrue, I rationalized to myself. I minimized the severity, and how long the kids could potentially be living with us. And I did that—I thought—to protect him.

"Do Ben and Faye know Chris died?" he asked.

"No."

"How are you going to tell them?"

"I have no idea. I'm talking to a lot of smart psychologists who are helping me figure out the right time and place to tell them. Until then, please don't mention it."

He nodded. He seemed to understand the gravity of that news.

"Do you want me to sleep in here tonight?" I asked gently.

"Yes. Can we watch some TV to fall asleep?"

Book reading would have to wait. I welcomed the opportunity to turn off my brain and disappear into a show.

"Absolutely."

He scooted over on his twin-size bed, making room. I stroked his hair, feeling our nervous systems settle into a synchronized rhythm. Our world was upside down and on fire, but there, in that room, in that bed, with that boy, was exactly where I needed to be. I wished I could stay curled up in that moment forever.

CHAPTER 12

elizabeth

September 30, 2017: Day 3

Saturday was a pause. No school. No jail visits. Law offices were closed. I lay on the couch, which was now my bed, and exhaled for what felt like the first time in two days. Except I was breathing under water. And up above the surface of this alternate reality, there were people living an ordinary September weekend. On a typical Saturday, Noah would be getting ready for his 9 a.m. soccer game, the third of the season.

We'd been doing this routine every fall for four years, rain or shine: Noah in his oversized town soccer jersey, the name of a local business and a big number on his back, tucked into a pair of black shorts that inevitably went missing each week. It was a gathering place for our family—my parents brought egg sandwiches, my aunts often drove in to visit, Nikki and the kids met us with fold-up chairs and snack baggies. Seven days ago, we were all sitting on the sidelines of a game, Nikki, Ben, and Faye all in a row, wearing sunglasses and big smiles, waving out to Noah, who happily ran past his cheering section. Seven days. In one week, even the most immovable routines cemented into our lives can disintegrate and wash away with a riptide you never see coming.

I lay on the couch a little longer, dissolving in the current.

I knew what I had to do: Go out and talk to the people who knew my sister better than I did. Information would be my life raft, and no one, other than Nikki, had more information than Sarah and Elizabeth. We had plans to get together that morning.

I pulled my unwashed hair into a low bun and slipped on some day-old jeans, as my parents took care of the breakfast making. I couldn't believe how awake and alert I felt.

But before I could leave, my phone rang. It was her.

My mom and I stiffened as we saw the contact name: *Nikki DCJ*. The two of us disappeared into the bathroom, closing the door behind us, while the kids watched *The Sound of Music* in the living room. My mom took the phone and accepted the call, I could see her hand shaking. She put it on speakerphone.

Nikki's voice was trembling as she said hello. She explained that she could only call when the one phone in the unit was free—"If it cuts us off, I'll try to call you back," she said, crying through the words. "Can I talk to Ben?"

Mom and I looked at each other. Could she? Would the anguish in her voice disturb the kids? Was it better for them to hear that she was alive than to imagine that she was gone forever? The questions ticked one after the other in my brain. I took a seat on the edge of the tub, and Mom paced with the phone in her hand. I nodded, *yes*, they should probably talk.

"Yeah, yes, but I need you to calm down a little first," Mom said, sounding even more distraught than Nikki. "Listen, you should know that last night Ben kept asking where you were. He said, 'But why is it taking so long for her to talk to people?' He thinks that you're still at the police station," which was where he'd last left her. "I didn't know what to say—I said that you had to sew slippers..."

I rolled my eyes. As much as I tried to fight it, I had a rising irritation, a biting anger, deep in the pit of my stomach toward my parents.

My mom was still talking: "I mean, you could say that you're in another state sewing slippers? I don't know..."

The truth didn't occur to her as an option.

Nikki and I were not raised to believe that we could face the truth, or that the adults could, either. The grown-ups around us used lies and omissions as a protective shield. Their parents did the same. It was a family trait, stretching back generations. My dad's mother, my Nana, grew up thinking that her mother was dead; until, at age fourteen, her very-much-alive mom waltzed back into her life after having run off for a decade. My mom's mother, a woman who died before I was born, hid her husband's PTSD-caused mental illness from their three kids—despite the fact that he sometimes retreated to his bedroom for days at a time and openly wept at the dinner table, thought to be a side effect of his time in war. In his moments of mania, he'd pack the family into the car and show up at a relative's house unannounced, usually around dinnertime, staying for as long as he pleased. My mom told those stories with embarrassment. She hated the way her father's untreated illness controlled the ebb and flow of family life, and the way her mother would silently smile and go along with it.

Even when that secret was out and my mom was grown, our family didn't talk about his condition above a whisper, and *never* to my grandfather. There were things that were spoken about, and things that weren't. There were ways we acted in public and ways that we didn't. The house had to be clean before we could have anyone over. My mom had a "phone voice" and a regular voice. We were encouraged to make up white lies to get out of uncomfortable social situations, and always present our best selves to teachers, friends, and especially boys, only allowing the uglier parts of our personalities to come out in private.

I was ready to break that pattern. No more lies. No more pretending.

"*No, Mom,*" I whispered firmly. Mom looked back at me, confused, tears running down her cheeks. It was hard to stay mad at her when she was in such clear anguish. I was torn between wanting to hold her accountable for what I thought were epic fuckups—it should have been *her* job to keep Nikki safe, I reasoned, desperate to find someone to blame—and knowing that I couldn't reduce Mom to the sum of her mistakes. She was still the mom who showed up at our bedside when we were sick, saved her money to take us on trips, and was always available to talk—whether it was after a nightmare as a kid, or on the phone from my dorm room at 1 a.m. She showed up for me, every time. That version of her was real, too. She enthusiastically loved me through a young pregnancy right out of college, and helped me raise Noah with more hindsight wisdom than she once had—less criticism and stress. We had talked more about the deep stuff over the past two years—our fears, our *I'm sorry*'s. We had gotten to know each other as adults. We were friends. The anger was still coursing through me, but my broken heart softened me into a place of compassion. I put my arms around Mom and pulled her in for a hug. I felt her shoulders shake as she silently cried into my hair.

Nikki's voice broke in: "Can you please just put Ben on the phone?" There was a desperation, a pained longing, behind the words.

Mom cleared her throat and brightened her voice, "Ben? Ben honey!"

"Oh God," Nikki whispered quietly to herself.

"Ben, it's Mama!" she called as he came barreling into the bathroom. "It's on speaker."

"Hi," he said, sounding slightly annoyed. His hands were on his hips, and he stood across the room from the phone, not wanting to get too close.

"Ben!" Nikki cried out his name—if she had tried to compose herself, she failed. She audibly sobbed into the phone.

"Why is it taking so long?" Ben asked, his arms dropped to his sides.

"Ben, I love you so much."

She hadn't answered his question.

"Why is it taking so long for you to come?" he asked again, more forcefully. I heard Faye's distant voice getting closer, saying "Mama, Mama, Mama."

"It's gonna take a little while. You're gonna stay with Grandma and Grandpa for a little while until I can get there, okay?" It was the first sentence that she was able to speak clearly, without shaking into a cry. "But I'll be there."

"MA! MAAAA!" Faye shrieked excitedly, entering with my dad. Her face looked like the opposite of Ben's: She was smiling, eyes bright, happy.

"Faye! My Faye!" Nikki's voice collapsed again. "Hi, honey! Faye. I miss you, sweetheart."

"I. Miss. You!" Faye responded, hopping with each word, seemingly oblivious to the crying on the phone and around the room. Even my dad, who rarely cried, was misty eyed, listening to the speakerphone conversation. We were all crammed into the small bathroom, except Noah.

"FaceTime?" Faye looked up at my mom, pressing the button that, even at two years old, she knew brought people up onto the screen. "I want to see Mommy."

"I can't FaceTime right now, honey," Nikki answered.

Nikki repeated the same explanation that she had said to Ben, who was now gone—back to the television, away from the pain. "You're going to stay with Grandma and Grandpa for a while, and then I'll come, okay? I miss you so much. I miss you so, so much."

"I miss you, too," Faye said sweetly.

"Can you look at pictures of us with Grandma?"

"Oh yeah! 'K love you bye!" Faye said, ready to go find pictures.

"I love you, baby," Nikki called after her. "Can you get Ben?"

"I'll get him," my mom said, running out of the room with the phone.

"I know he runs away when he's upset, but can you just tell him that I can't call a lot." I heard Nikki's voice carried from room to room. I followed the sound.

"You're here with him," Mom said, holding the phone over the couch, where Ben laid with his face in the pillow.

"Ben?"

"What," he said angrily.

"I love you—more than all the blue whales lined up in the ocean." It was the line she'd been telling her whale-loving boy for years. "And I'm gonna be with you soon." She said it in a way that sounded like she'd maybe never be with him again. She could hardly get the words to form around the cry. "So, so soon."

"I love you bigger than the whole entire space," Ben responded quietly, sadly.

"I'm going to be thinking of you every second of every day—"

"Thank you for using GTL," said an automated voice, cutting off the call without warning.

* * *

The call was heavy, and I was selfishly glad for a reason to leave the house—to distract myself with facts and information.

Yesterday had been an onslaught of unsolicited advice and recommendations, from every corner of my life and Nikki's—friends of friends, Internet acquaintances, someone who knows a guy. I had a general idea of what was happening: Nikki had been arrested and was being detained; formal charges wouldn't come until she was indicted by a grand jury.

And she had been assigned public defenders: free, taxpayer-funded attorneys who work for the county.

Over the phone, she told me that she liked the public defenders she met, particularly one of the attorneys named Kara. But she also understood the general advice that overworked public defenders aren't ideal for this kind of life-threatening felony charge; she was open to considering other people. "I don't know who to trust, anyway," she said, sounding defeated. "Just ask Sarah and Elizabeth; I'll do whatever they think I should do."

Elizabeth and Wendy had begun making legal calls and setting up appointments, and Rachel and Laura reached out to their retired attorney friend. I brought people into the fold, too—a coworker with a long history advocating for women's rights and social change, who was also a former attorney. They all had information, which they relayed to me over the phone, as I scribbled in notebooks and on scrap paper to later pass to Nikki.

The consensus was clear: Step one was to find a private attorney who had taken murder cases before, and who, ideally, had represented victims of domestic violence and understood the unique criminal justice lane of sex trafficking and gender-based violence.

And we had to do it fast.

Prosecutors could present Nikki's case to a grand jury in a matter of days. Getting the right legal team in place was a crucial, immediate, panic-fueled need. And our family had to do this with no legal expertise, no connections to the criminal justice system, and no money. Even if we pooled all of our family resources, we couldn't afford a retainer fee, which some quoted as high as $100,000. That's probably why, according to the

Bureau of Justice Statistics, 82 percent of the felony defendants in state courts have public defenders,[2] and the American Bar Association states that as many as 90 percent of the people charged with a crime need publicly funded attorneys.[3]

What Nikki *did* have was a sister whose fear response was to learn as much as possible about a topic, whose stress response was to organize and project-manage, and who had the fortitude to fight rather than flee.

I was willing to sit in legal rooms and have uncomfortable conversations, and I also knew that my parents couldn't. Mom didn't have the capacity to get through a sentence without breaking into full-body sobs, and my dad had a narrow threshold before emotionally shutting down. Nikki had also asked me to shield him from the "sex stuff," as she called it, for as long as we could. *It's so disgusting*, she cried to me on the phone when I told her what I'd learned from Sarah and Lori. *It's all so disgusting.* But there was no way to have legal conversations without also talking about rape kit evidence, sex-trafficking experts, and porn sites. I stepped into the role as Nikki's "representative" immediately, without question. I was her next of kin.

There would be time for grappling with the crimes that had been committed against Nikki, but right now, our most urgent need was to get her out of jail for the crime she'd been accused of.

One of the connections passed along to us was a forensic scientist who worked as a criminal defense investigator. As it was explained to me, every defense attorney works closely with an investigator, akin to a private detective, who goes out and gathers information to feed back to the attorney. With a public defender, that investigator is a built-in part of the team, provided free of cost. With a private attorney, this is a separate expense on top of the attorney's fees. Typically, an attorney will recommend an investigator that he or she has worked with before, but in our case, we found the investigator first. He was a close family friend of one of the preschool moms on the "everyone knew" text thread, someone who had been concerned about

Nikki for a while; so the investigator was coming to us with a fair amount of knowledge about what people in the community had seen and heard about the abuse. He wanted to help. He said he knew the best local attorney for us to use.

Elizabeth and I planned to meet with this investigator at a local diner, before all of us would head to Sarah's office for another round of info-sharing and brainstorming, which the investigator would gather and present to the defense attorney he knew.

I had thirty minutes to get there, and I didn't want to keep Elizabeth waiting. I reached for my khaki trench coat, which had the ability of polishing any outfit, giving it the appearance of being put-together. I took a deep breath as I glanced in the mirror and softly exhaled. *I can do this.*

At the diner, I instinctively smiled at the hostess, pointing ahead at the far booth where I saw the back of Elizabeth's head. Facing her was a man with a round face, downturned eyes, and a collared shirt under a fleece. He looked to be around middle-age—his buzzed hair was slightly graying, and I knew he'd been working as a forensic scientist on criminal investigations since at least 2005.

I slid into the booth. An onlooker would have thought we were just a few friends catching up.

We exchanged pleasantries: *Wish we didn't have to meet in these circumstances... How are the kids?... How's Nikki?... What a terrible tragedy...*

The investigator ordered a full breakfast. Elizabeth had a mug of tea in front of her. "Nothing for me," I told the waitress, who had followed me over to the table. No part of my body could eat or drink. I was sustaining myself on adrenaline and cortisol. I feared that any amount of food would run right through me.

I did more listening than talking at the diner. As I sat next to her, I realized that, despite our near-constant talking over the past two days, I knew very little about Elizabeth's life. I knew she taught music, had two kids around Noah's age, and had a husband who taught at Vassar College. I knew she was very involved with her church, as deacon and church council president, and she led a children's choir at the local Boys & Girls Club—details that mostly came from Nikki, over the jail's monitored phone line, when she was telling me about Elizabeth's goodness, maybe as an explanation for why she had confided in her and not me.

I also knew Elizabeth was a fan of Glennon Doyle, because Nikki had mentioned Elizabeth's name when she'd loaned me a copy of Doyle's first memoir, *Carry On, Warrior*, about a year ago. It was a book that reminded women they're not alone, that life is "brutiful" (both brutal and beautiful), and that "we can do hard things." Nikki had latched on to that reminder like a mantra. She'd repeated it to the kids; she'd captioned Instagram posts with the quote. I knew Elizabeth had gifted her the book.

"I think I have a friend," Nikki had sheepishly confessed, excited about their budding relationship. I was happy to see her making a connection for herself, recognizing how important female friendships were in my own life. Even though she was only two years younger than me, our social circles had always been very separate.

Sitting there on the maroon vinyl booth, witnessing Elizabeth talk to the investigator, I took in just how "brutal" and "hard" their friendship really was.

"So I had a background in social work..." Elizabeth began, a fact I did not know, which helped explain why she'd seen the signs of abuse during Ben's second Music Together session toward the end of 2015. "I talked to the program owner about it, and decided to approach Nikki if she showed up to the next music session with injuries." Which she did, in the spring of 2016. Elizabeth was looking at the investigator as she spoke, and he slightly shook his head, taking it all in.

The amount that Elizabeth told us she had seen with her own eyes was startling. "One time, earlier this year, I went over to her house while she was actively miscarrying," she said, implying that the miscarriage happened after a vicious assault. I didn't even know Nikki had been pregnant for a third time. "I saw a pool of red blood on the bathroom floor. I helped her to the couch, and saw her wince in pain as she moved. I saw a giant black-and-blue contusion on her ribs. These were not injuries she could have done to herself," Elizabeth added, anticipating whatever skepticism the investigator might have.

He didn't look skeptical. He looked sick and furious. "I just keep thinking about if this were my daughter..." he said, shaking his head.

Elizabeth told us that Sarah, Nikki's former therapist and ongoing confidante, had encouraged Nikki to talk to Elizabeth about what was going on. Even though it took some time, Elizabeth had slowly gained her trust, and Nikki put Elizabeth and Sarah in touch.

"As I understand it, Sarah encouraged Nikki to keep opening up to me, and my main role was to try and build up her self-esteem, to let her know she deserved more. Sarah helped me understand that there was no way to make Nikki leave; she had to be ready. And Sarah also helped me understand that this was a really dangerous situation, and that victims know their abusers best and are the only ones who can gauge their safety." I didn't know that, in the United States, femicide is a consistent silent epidemic. Nearly three women are killed by an intimate partner every day, and the majority are killed while they're trying to leave, or after they've escaped the relationship.[4]

Elizabeth described Nikki's being unable to leave as a safety decision on Nikki's part. She saw that her job was to be a nonjudgmental friend, to check in with Nikki, and give her a safe place when she was ready to leave. "I was part of her safety plan," Elizabeth told us.

"When you say 'safety plan,'" the investigator said, fork in hand, "was there an actual plan in place?"

The safety plan, she explained, was a blueprint for how Nikki could best protect herself at home and what to do when she finally left. The idea, as she understood it, was for Nikki to leave with the children when Chris was at work—he was the head coach at a local gymnastics studio—and take the laptop and any other video evidence of his abuse that she could find. (Chris had a habit of periodically wiping his hard drive at the Apple Store.) Then she and the kids would go to Elizabeth's house, and they'd all call Sarah and strategize the next steps.

I was not a part of her plan.

"Did she ever try to leave?" he asked. I wondered the same thing.

Elizabeth nodded. "A couple of times Nikki was close." Her voice lowered. "I remember sitting on my couch in front of the living room window, watching her car drive by in a loop, knowing Ben and Faye were sleeping in the back seat. She never actually stopped. She always went back. And about a month ago, Chris found a bag Nikki had packed and he really hurt her that night. Nikki couldn't even tell me what he did, but it seemed bad." Elizabeth's heavy eyes blinked tears down her cheeks.

"Why do you think she went back?" the investigator asked.

"She was scared." She and Nikki would play out the scenarios—what would happen after she left? Where would she go, a secret shelter? Nikki reasoned that Chris was only hurting her, no one else; and to be truly free, she'd have to press charges against him, destroying the lives of countless young gymnasts who looked up to him as a mentor and coach, and obliterating her relationship with his family. And then if she *did* press charges, she worried she didn't have enough evidence to prosecute. It would always be his word against hers. He'd fight her for custody. He'd swear the porn was consensual and Nikki was just a "slut"—that the videos were *her* idea and she liked it. She'd always decide to endure it for just a little longer, for the sake of the family.

"I lived every day in fear of her being killed by Chris; it never occurred to me that a universe could exist in which she would have to kill him to save her own life," Elizabeth added.

"And there are videos?" he asked. "He was actually recording and posting himself raping her?"

"Yes, I think so, but Sarah has all of that information. We can all head over to her office now, if you want," she said, checking her watch. The investigator nodded, ready to go.

I steadied myself with comforting self-talk: *Whatever I'll learn at Sarah's office will just be more information. I can handle it.*

Before we stood up to leave, Elizabeth fiddled with a Zip drive in her hands and slid it across the table to the investigator. "So, on here, my husband helped me export all of the Facebook messages I had with Nikki, which is where we did most of our talking." She paused. "It's a lot. Like, a *lot*. And you'll notice that sometimes, late at night, the conversation would end abruptly, and I'd be holding my breath, knowing that something terrible was happening and I couldn't do anything to stop it." I could see the weight this woman was carrying, the terrible toll Nikki's situation had taken on her. I was just stepping into it, but she'd been navigating it for years.

"You're a really good friend," I told her. "I'm glad she had you."

my sister's sisters

I followed my phone GPS to Sarah's office, four miles into the Town of Poughkeepsie. Ben's preschool teacher was meeting us there, too. I had never met her, but like Elizabeth, I'd heard a lot about Miss Michelle; we shared a name and a love for Ben and Faye. When I'd first arranged this meeting with Elizabeth and Sarah, I had been most interested in gathering guidance from three professionals with expertise in child development. I wanted to talk about how to transition Ben back to preschool, how to explain why CPS workers were soon coming back to interview him, and to air my overall concerns about CPS's presence before and after the shooting. But the legal issues were urgent, and this investigator had the availability to join, so we had decided to have one big conversation. I knew Miss Michelle was an important piece of the puzzle and she might have witnessed something helpful for the investigator to know. After all, much of the whispered concern about Nikki was done around the "mom" community. I figured we'd talk a little about the evidence each of us had, and a little about the kids. I'd be home by lunch.

I had no way to prepare myself for how much I still didn't know.

Within minutes, I was pulling up to a commercial building down a narrow side road in Arlington Square, the pedestrian shopping district next to Vassar College. I knew the area well. Sarah's office was between the sushi place where I met friends for lunch and the smoothie shop where I used to take Noah after preschool. It was across the street from the bank that had given me my student loans, and around the corner from a restaurant where I had once waitressed. And there, in the middle of all this familiar terrain, was an inconspicuous glass door where Nikki had recently entered to devise a safety plan for her exit from Chris, a plan that had gone wildly off the rails. I went inside.

Sarah's door was slightly ajar, so I stepped into the cozy space, first a small waiting room and then a bigger, sunny office. I was the last to arrive. Sarah, standing next to the couch, looked up from the stack of papers in her hand to greet me. Another woman, who I presumed was Ben's teacher, was sitting on the couch next to the investigator. We introduced ourselves.

I sat down in an armless canvas chair next to Elizabeth and looked around. There was a small sand tray on the coffee table in front of me, and a bookshelf along one wall with jars of markers and toys. I wondered how many times Nikki had been in this room, and what kinds of secrets she'd shared. What had I been doing when she sat in this spot?

Sarah made it clear that Nikki had consented to her sharing confidential client information with us, and then she launched into her side of the story. Some of it I knew, but most was new to me. Once again, I sat like a shadow, listening to people tell me who my sister was.

In explaining the evolution of her client relationship with Nikki, Sarah made characterizations of her that were new to me. At one point, Sarah said, "Nikki has selective mutism,"[5] as nonchalantly as if she'd said, "Nikki is short and has small feet." I watched Elizabeth nod in recognition. They both told stories of times when Nikki was rendered unable to move or speak— for Sarah, it was when Nikki would try to say what Chris had done to her, often something humiliating or shameful, and she physically couldn't get the words out; for Elizabeth, it was in the parking lot of the hospital, deciding whether or not to be treated for a particularly severe injury (she didn't go in). In those specific trauma-induced moments, Nikki was frozen in silence.

I'd never seen this.

They both rattled off times they'd involved other people in helping Nikki— and not just friends, like Wendy and Lori, who I'd met the previous night at the jail—but people who worked within the system that, in theory, was here to protect people like Nikki. From Sarah, I learned that Nikki had been connected to our county's domestic violence services. For years. Police in two neighboring departments had records of Nikki as a victim of domestic violence. Sarah was one of several people who had gone to the DA's office over the years and spoken about Nikki's abuse, raising red flags, including a lethality assessment[6] administered multiple times, which showed that Nikki was at the highest level of risk for domestic homicide. She scored in the *extreme danger* category more than once. At Sarah's insistence, Nikki's case was conferenced by the county's Universal Response to Domestic Violence (URDV), which was a coordinated, multidisciplinary team including the District Attorney's Office, Family Services (where Sarah worked), the courts, probation, Legal Services of the Hudson Valley, local and state police, and several domestic violence shelters. There were records of this.

The investigator "liked" these facts. I didn't like that they had happened, but the evidence was undeniable.

The abuse was recorded and uploaded in videos that were so violent and disturbing that a police officer in our hometown had tracked the porn site where Chris had posted them, taken screen shots, and compiled a report for the DA's Office.

"He was ready to arrest Chris," Sarah said. But when he'd brought the affidavit over for Nikki to sign, she froze. She was terrified. Her numb hands weren't working well enough to hold a pen, so Sarah wrote down what Nikki said, while the officer and a domestic violence advocate waited. They waited five hours. They waited until Nikki finally said no.

A *why* hung in the air, and Sarah gave a list of reasons, including that Nikki didn't want Chris to be arrested at the gym, she didn't want to traumatize the gymnasts she loved and hurt the owners' business. She didn't want people to know. She was also scared he wouldn't be prosecuted in a way that actually kept her safe.

"The standard line I kept hearing was that nothing could be done if Nikki wouldn't cooperate with law enforcement," Sarah said. (When in reality, nothing was stopping Dutchess County from pursuing an evidence-based prosecution[7] without Nikki's participation.) Even still, the officer took it upon himself to bring a file of evidence to the DA and send out an alert to surrounding police stations, saying Nikki was in a high-risk domestic situation, there were two children, and there was a gun in the house. I'd later see that alert written in black and white: "The victim is Nicole Addimando, the perpetrator is Christopher Grover."

As I quickly learned, the burden to prove abuse is so high that most domestic violence cases never get prosecuted, and if they do, the sentences are insultingly short for abusers, putting the victims at risk of being killed.

The investigator shifted on the couch. "Can we talk about the spoon incident?" His eyes darted to me, then back to Sarah. "Is it okay to talk about it in front of everyone?" Clearly, there had been a conversation ahead of this meeting, because the temperature in the room changed. Sarah and Elizabeth stiffened.

I, on the other hand, loudly sighed. I felt insulted. *Don't you dare hold back information on me now.*

"I want to know," I said firmly.

Sarah cleared her throat and told another story she clearly didn't want to be telling: When Nikki was pregnant with Faye, Chris had heated up a metal spoon in the flame of their gas stove and held it to her vulva, burning her inside and out. The injury was so bad that Nikki had to meet Sarah at the hospital, where she agreed to undergo an invasive exam by a forensic nurse to document the injuries and collect evidence. It was done through the Department of Health's Sexual Assault Forensic Examiner (SAFE) Program, and there were records.

"I'm sure the forensic nurse remembers it," Sarah said. "She demonstrated how Chris had to have burned her to get those injuries, saying, 'He held the spoon to her like *this,*'" and she motioned an object being held to the skin for one, two, three seconds. "I was told that it would have been very hard for Nikki to self-inflict wounds like that, as her body's natural pain reflexes would've compelled her to pull her hand away."

"What the fuck!" I said, sitting up, spine straight, stomach clenched. "So we're talking about torture?" Heads nodded. "And she was pregnant?" More heads nodding.

Considering that the majority of the abuse was centered around sex trafficking and pornography, I first thought the "spoon incident" was a sadistic sexual kink. I'd soon learn from Sarah and Nikki that the burning, as well as most of the filmed videos, were a punishment. A punishment for talking back to Chris. A punishment for refusing sex. A punishment for disrespecting him, for not obeying. The name of his porn account, which was created using his email, included his last name with the word *Respect*, and the video captions detailed how he was teaching Nikki a lesson.

She also told me that, counter to what I would have thought, abuse is known to spike during pregnancy. It's one of the risk factors listed on the Danger Assessment[8] that Sarah had administered. In fact, homicide is the leading cause of death for pregnant women in the United States.[9]

"And the police knew. And the DA knew, *the DA who is now prosecuting her.*" I looked around, making sure I was understanding what they were telling me.

"Not only that, but I had direct conversations with Kristine about Nikki," Sarah said, referring to Kristine Whelan, the ADA who was now tasked with prosecuting. She said that she and Kristine had a good working relationship, and sometimes Kristine would check in about Nikki, asking *"How's the girl?"* This past spring, Sarah had let Kristine know that "the girl's" abuser was in the jury pool for a rape case. "He didn't stay on the jury," Sarah said.

From everything Sarah said, it seemed as though Nikki had been inching her way toward an escape while the violence was getting worse.

"Is this the worst I'm going to hear?" I asked the room.

Sarah shook her head no. Unbelievably there would be more horrors for me to learn in the days and weeks ahead. But that would be enough for today.

I felt sick.

I looked to the preschool teacher sitting across from me, the only other person in the room who hadn't heard these gruesome details before. Her eyes were cast down to the floor, her lips pursed. Her outsides looked the way my insides felt, as if I had to hold still, and breathe very slowly, to keep myself from exploding.

We didn't talk about the kids at all.

* * *

I don't remember how the meeting ended, only that, at some point, everyone else had left and I was sitting alone with Sarah. Now, I figured, was the time to ask about the blood and zip-ties incident. If anyone knew the full truth other than Nikki, it would have been Sarah. I needed her to help solve that looming mystery, and I knew Nikki had told Sarah to bring me up to speed on all I'd overlooked.

"So back when there was that *other* police investigation, before Ben was born..." I started.

Sarah nodded. "Yeah, I know about that."

"Okay, so was that Chris who was hurting her?"

"Yes and no," she said again. "There was actually someone else who raped her before Chris," she said, giving me the name of someone I recognized, a man who had been a maintenance worker at my mom's apartment complex and a family acquaintance at the time. I hadn't thought of him in years.

"Holy shit," I said, surprised that I still had the capacity to be shocked.

This was the person who Dave was looking for, way back when he was in my mom's living room. Sarah relayed the story: While Nikki was alone in the apartment, this man came in to do a work order, smelling like alcohol, and assaulted Nikki. It was during the beginning of her relationship with Chris, and Chris had been patiently waiting for nearly a full year for Nikki to be ready to have sex. When Chris learned that someone else "had her," and Nikki continued to deny him sex, he became increasingly aggressive, saying she must "like it rough." This man assaulted Nikki at least twice—Sarah said that Nikki's memories were fragmented, as trauma memories often are, and the rapes had happened years before she started talking about them in therapy. By the time Nikki was confessing these stories to Sarah, Nikki's memories of the rapes between the maintenance worker[10] and Chris had blurred together, and she had a lot of shame admitting that Chris had been hurting her, too.

"She already had Ben by the time that she was seeing me, and she blamed herself. She said that the abuse kept happening to her with different people, and Chris is a nice guy, so it must be her fault. A lot of our work together was getting Nikki to see what was and wasn't normal and acceptable, and that she didn't cause the abuse to happen."

Sarah went on to say that the science shows that rape victims tend to get revictimized[11] throughout their lives, especially if there was untreated childhood sexual assault.

"The real complicated part—and I think this played a big part in why Nikki didn't press charges and wanted the initial police investigation to go away—is that, you remember Dave?" Sarah shifted uncomfortably.

"Yes..." I said.

"Well, did you know Nikki was living there for a little while?"

I shook my head no. "I know she babysat for his daughter, but I didn't think she lived there."

"Yeah, it wasn't for long, but he was trying to keep her safe because all Nikki would say was that it happened in your mom's apartment, but she wouldn't say who it was. So he had her move in."

"Okay..."

"And then he started raping her," she said quickly, the words tumbling out of her mouth.

I stared blankly and blinked. Dave. The older guy, overweight, belly hanging over his pants? The married police officer who was twice Nikki's age?

"Rape is my word, not hers," Sarah was quick to clarify. "He was holding a roof and basic safety over her head. There was a built-in power imbalance; she could never really consent. But whenever Nikki talked about it, she said that she didn't want to have sex but didn't know what she owed him. And she said that, out of all the men who raped her—and again, Nikki never used that word—Dave was nice to her. He didn't hurt her like the others did. I just think she was really confused and vulnerable, and Dave absolutely took advantage of that."

"But—Dave?" I said, my mouth curled in disgust. I had a sudden urge to go hug my sister.

I had to sit for a minute and let this information settle in the little space

I had left to hold all these horrors. Nikki's story was more complex than I realized.

"But there's still plenty of evidence that Chris was hurting her, torturing her, broadcasting it online—there's no way she'll be charged with murder, right? With all this prosecutor knows, that's a good thing, right?" I was desperate for good news.

Sarah didn't look convinced.

"I've seen a lot, and rape cases are really hard to prove in court, especially in this county, with this jury pool." She told me about a case a few years before, where a woman was gang-raped at a college party. One of the guys filmed and shared it. On the video, they were identifiable, and the girl was slipping in and out of consciousness.

"One of the three offenders even flipped and testified against the other two. I listened to him lay out step-by-step how this had been a planned attack, and how they targeted her during the party for the purpose of assaulting her," she said. But the jury acquitted them all because, according to Sarah, there was a fundamental misunderstanding of consent.

I heard what she said, but I couldn't believe it. There was no way a jury could hear all that I just heard in her office and convict Nikki. There was just no way.

CHAPTER 14

a sexy story

October 1, 2017: Day 4

Nikki had the right to a counsel of her choice, written into the Sixth Amendment. And so legally this could only be Nikki's choice, no one else's. Yet Nikki was locked in a cell, alone, with no access to information or resources. No way to actually choose.

This left the choice of counsel up to those of us on the outside, which is why, on Sunday morning, Elizabeth and I sat in another room with another professional, retelling the same story. We were meeting with the attorney that the investigator recommended ("I only work with *this* guy," he said plainly). I could sign the retainer paperwork on Nikki's behalf.

The attorney's office was empty except for us. Elizabeth and I walked through a large open space past rows of cubicles, and into a conference room with windows facing out to the city sidewalk. Two men—the investigator, in baggy jeans, and the attorney in a crisp suit and shiny black shoes—stood to greet us. They had ordered three large pizzas, for the four of us. I politely took a piece and nibbled at it, but still had no appetite.

Energy had been seeping out of me, as if I had a small leak. Talking required so much effort. I had spent most of the thirty-minute drive looking out the window, and sat quietly through the two-hour meeting listening to their proposed trial-by-media strategy. Step one: Get national news coverage. Write the full story—including detailed descriptions of the abuse—in a GoFundMe campaign that would raise legal funds to pay our legal bills (i.e., them). They name-dropped connections at network and cable news shows, the kind of shows that run twenty-four-hour coverage of missing women, or a killed child, or a missing woman who'd killed a child. Shows that, to me, seemed exploitive and sensationalized for ratings.

"You'll have news cameras at your door, following you to your car," the investigator warned, with a hint of excitement. The more he talked, the less I trusted his motives. "This is going to be big. It's a sexy story."

I felt the room spin, like it was falling away under my feet. A sexy story?

But no words came out.

If we talked about anything else, I don't remember. My mind reeled, thinking of other women who had been skewered in the media and disbelieved—international cases like that of Amanda Knox, who despite being acquitted after a high-profile murder case, was still viewed as guilty by a large swath of the population. *Foxy Knoxy.*

I knew what the media did. I had a degree in journalism and had spent most of my professional life freelance writing on the Internet, working within a system that operated on a currency of clicks and shares, people's lives reduced to salacious headlines. What would Nikki's headline name be? Nikki had spent years carefully hiding the abuse in her life. I knew it brought her tremendous shame, so the idea of broadcasting it out into the world, in places her children would one day see—it felt like another form of torture.

I was in no state to be making decisions, but when the attorney asked me to sign a document retaining him for Nikki's representation, I went ahead. Before we left, the attorney delivered one last shock to my fragile system.

"The best-case scenario, Nikki is home by May."

Best-case scenario.

That was more than six months away.

It was a subdued drive home. I didn't play music. Elizabeth drove my car because my body couldn't stop shaking. At least six months? I'd now be taking care of Ben and Faye for the better part of a year. I'd need to register Ben for kindergarten. I'd need to somehow continue managing a relationship with the Grovers. I'd need to break the news to Noah that this temporary living situation now had an indefinite end date.

Noah. We had just fallen into a post-separation rhythm, he and I. It was more peaceful in the house, which put both of us at ease. And even though part of me was sad that I probably wouldn't have more kids, Noah had never wanted a sibling. He liked his space. He liked his alone time. He identified as an only child, and wanted to keep it that way.

And what about Ben and Faye? Six months is an eternity in kid time—a quarter of Faye's entire life.

I tried to keep it contained in front of Elizabeth, but my shoulders were trembling, and tears streamed down my cheeks. My body was operating on its own, and controlling its responses was impossible. My lungs felt tight, my heart was racing. I was not okay.

"Is this your intuition saying these lawyers are the wrong choice, or are you overwhelmed by all of it?" she gently asked.

I had no way to know. It could be either, or both. It was impossible to excavate my feelings from the rubble. It was impossible to trust myself to know anything.

She must have been able to see the fear on my face, because unprompted, she said, "Listen, I know you need to have these kids, but if you need someone to take them, I will."

I let her offer sit suspended between us. But despite the panic and grief and compounding ways this would alter my life, I knew that taking care of Nikki's children was my only choice.

I'd spent years saying *no* to reality—avoiding, denying, numbing. As my marriage fell apart, I caught myself fighting what was happening in front of me by escaping into daydreams of what life *could* be, or by intellectualizing what it *should* be. Through podcast teachings and retreat workshops and quiet meditation, I started a practice of saying *yes* to reality. To meet what is with a friendly attitude. *Yes* to the traffic. *Yes* to the headache. *Yes* to the irritation flooding my nervous system.

And through all of that practice, I was now facing the most glaring unchangeable reality in front of me. I knew, without a single doubt, what life was asking of me, and I was willing to say yes.

By morning, a new headline was published online: SERVICES SET FOR POUGHKEEPSIE MAN POLICE SAY WAS KILLED BY GIRLFRIEND. The article included a video of Chris and Nikki's apartment surrounded by crime scene tape.

Along with the article, news spread that we'd hired a new private defense team, the one we had retained the day before. Over the next hour, I heard from a number of trusted people, all saying that hiring these guys was a mistake. One local attorney even said that Nikki was sure to be convicted if we stayed with that attorney and investigator.

My first legal action for Nikki's defense, and I seemed to have blown it. And yet, at the same time, I also felt a little relieved. My intense physical reaction the day before felt like a signal from my body that something was wrong, and this warning reaction from the community reinforced it.

How is it possibly my job to make these choices? I thought to myself. But the responses kept coming, and were unanimous. So I did something I dreaded: I called up the attorney and the investigator and fired them, less than twenty-four hours after signing a document that retained their services. They weren't happy, but I needed to step up as an advocate—which meant finding a voice I wasn't used to using.

It was now clear which attorney we *shouldn't* hire, but no one who was part of our legal sounding board could tell us exactly who we should. There was no right way to go forward, no best person for the job. It all depended: depended on the county's politics, depended on the judge's disposition, depended on the facts of the case that were only beginning to be uncovered. Nikki's randomly assigned judge, a man named Edward McLoughlin, was recently elected to a ten-year term on the Republican Party line. He had a reputation for being tough, known for long sentences.

But everyone agreed, we needed to find Nikki a good defense, and fast. Everyone we consulted said some version of *you need to slow the timeline down so that Nikki's evidence can be gathered.*

Elizabeth and I went back to the public defenders, Nikki's first choice of representation, and apologized for pulling the case and blindsiding them. At their office situated on a floor high above the DMV, sandwiched between Family Court and Criminal Court, we asked them to take the case again, and they agreed.

Kara, the attorney whom Nikki had liked in the first place, assured me: Yes, public defenders are busy, she said, but she had a whole team committed to this case, including a female investigator and domestic violence liaison who understood the complexity of the situation. The people on Kara's team believed Nikki. The community believed her. "I've never had so many witnesses reach out for a client, ever," Kara said. Dozens of community members had called her office, explaining that they had seen Nikki's injuries and would testify for her.

With Kara back on board, I felt that Nikki was in capable hands, at least through the initial stage of grand jury.

Before now, I had assumed a trial jury and a *grand* jury were interchangeable terms. Now I learned that before a trial jury can decide if a person is innocent or guilty, a different kind of jury, a *grand jury*, decides whether a crime actually took place and what the charges should be. Not all states have grand juries, but in New York, a grand jury is used to set criminal felony charges. Trials often have twelve jurors selected for a specific case, while a grand jury consists of twenty-three randomly picked people who sit for however many felony cases happen within a set block of time. The prosecutor will present each case and the grand jury can ask questions, request evidence, and have people subpoenaed. In theory, a grand jury can even hear testimony from the accused person. But as I was told many times from many people, that was rare.

Then, the prosecutor will ask if there's enough evidence to proceed with a case. If there isn't, then the accused person is free. If there is, then the grand jury decides on the charge—in Nikki's case, it could be manslaughter, criminal possession of a weapon, or murder. The charges would then determine what kind of plea deal the prosecutor might negotiate, how much money a judge would set for bail (if it were offered), and what kind of sentence a guilty verdict might carry. The charges set by a grand jury have momentous consequences: They can be the difference between several years or a lifetime in prison.

The part that most people didn't know, including myself, is that the grand jury is conducted solely through the prosecutor, in the District Attorney's Office. There's no defense attorney, and most defendants never testify or present evidence. It's "the prosecutor's show," as it was described to me. Yet the DA's Office was allowing Nikki to prepare testimony and present a full picture to the grand jury. We saw this as an act of goodwill, a sign that Nikki would be given a fair chance at an acquittal.

The scales were still unbalanced—it was, after all, completely up to the prosecutors' discretion what a grand jury hears—but all signs pointed to an "open and fair" presentation, which is the term people kept using. As if the norm was for grand juries to be *closed* and *unfair*.

I also kept hearing the word *secret*, as if that were the appropriate legal definition. The grand jury happens without notice being given to the accused person's attorney or media—*in secret*. It happens without any testimony or evidence from defense witnesses being offered—*in secret*. Why did they keep using that word? Didn't everyone know that nothing good comes from keeping secrets?

I was also told, again and again, that it would be pretty easy for a group of people to charge Nikki with the bare-bones facts: *A man was found dead by a gunshot wound, his body was found lying on the couch, and his girlfriend admitted she pulled the trigger.* All true, and all would indicate a crime and a perpetrator.

But the public defenders felt they had a good working relationship with the District Attorney's Office that would allow them to make the grand jury a fair process at which Nikki could testify. They said they were already in discussion about allowing Nikki and her witnesses to make a case—which was almost unheard of, but these circumstances were extenuating.

If a grand jury chose not to indict her, this would all be over much sooner than May. My heart lifted.

We told the lawyers that we would stick with them through the grand jury, and if she were indicted, then we might have to consider hiring private counsel. They understood.

CHAPTER 15

DCJ

Early October 2017

Once Nikki was classified and taken off of twenty-four-hour sui-cide watch—a formality, the jail said, for the kinds of charges she faced—she was put into a unit with a group of women deemed the most dangerous in the jail, and she was given two 60-minute visits a week. These took place in a coed visiting room, which was often filled with loud male inmates in black-and-white-striped jumpsuits, reeking of body odor. It was one big open room with rows of wooden tables—each with a short wooden partition separating visitor from inmate, and a laminated list of rules: no candy, no open-mouth kissing, feet had to stay on the ground, only one short embrace.

The first visit with my mom had been the hardest. Mom carried herself in and out of the jail like an overfilled balloon, the smallest prick causing her to burst into tears. Nikki spoke softly, at times inaudibly, and the visiting room was one loud ruckus of voices.

"What did she say?" my mom said, eyes wide, panic in her voice, when-ever Nikki said something. "My heart's beating so loud, it's all I can hear." I got pretty good at reading Nikki's lips, and so I learned to pass messages back and forth across the table, like a translator in a foreign country.

Today it was just me, standing in the visiting room with the other visi-tors, waiting for them to assign us each a table before the room filled with prisoners.

"Addimando," a dark-haired man yelled out, nodding when I raised my hand.

I always bristled when they called the maiden name I shared with Nikki out into the room. I felt eyes on me. Her name sparked gossip. I made sure to smile, to say thank you, follow the rules.

I followed the guard's finger to a table in the far left corner, under an overhead camera, in front of a large frosted window.

I sat and waited. Men were brought in first, then women—including my Nikki, the shortest one in the line, walking sheepishly into the room. Her shoulders were pulled up, her twiglike arms hugged close to her body as she shuffled her way to the front of the line, where she handed a guard her ID and was led over to me.

I smiled at Nikki and leaned in for the hug—the one luxury we had in the visiting room. We had to stand on either side of the table and lean our bodies over the partition, so only our shoulders touched in the embrace. I could feel the guard watching us closely, making sure our hands weren't passing off contraband.

"Hi, sister," she breathed into my shoulder.

"Hi, sister," I repeated, wrapping my arms around her orange jumpsuit. She felt skeletal.

"How are the kids?" she said, sitting down on the circular steel stool.

That was always her first question. And there was never a good answer. If I said they went to school happily and were excited for Halloween (which was true), she'd worry that they were forgetting about her. If I said they'd cried out for her the night before and felt they couldn't have Halloween without her (also true), I would see the helplessness of a mother who couldn't get to her hurting children. It was always both, and it was always painful.

She needed to see them. They were desperate to see her. But looking around the room, at the one woman struggling to keep her grandson from sitting up on his knees, and at another toddler girl being reminded not to touch her father's hand—we knew that we couldn't bring Ben and Faye here. There was no way. They'd need to crawl on her lap, to feel her hug, to be reassured that she was safe. And it was loud here. Smelly. Intimidating. Subjecting them to this place—on top of everything else they were coping with—would feel cruel. We had to believe that her time here was limited, and they'd reunite soon. We had no capacity to imagine otherwise.

"This pain of being away from them, it's worse than anything I've felt before," she said quietly. "I put up with all of that so I wouldn't have to be away from them."

Nikki looked sicker than I'd seen her yet. Her skin was gray, her eyes dull, as if someone had drained all the color from her.

The food she described was all but inedible, especially for a vegetarian. Her choices were usually white rice and white bread, with some mushy microwaved vegetables that counted for the "one hot meal" the jail was required to serve.

"Have you been able to keep any food down?" I knew she'd been throwing up in the small toilet in her cell, which was also where she brushed her teeth. She told me she cleaned up the toilet with sanitary napkins, when she had them.

Nikki shook her head.

"How can they get away with this?" I asked, semi-rhetorically, but also genuinely thinking that the jail system must have to operate within some kind of human rights boundaries.

She changed the subject. "Did you hear anything from Kara?"

That was always her next question. She said it with a glimmer of hope, like maybe the Powers That Be had realized their mistake and I was there to whisk her home. But more realistically, she was hoping I'd have some kind of timeline. When would she be testifying in front of a grand jury?

I shook my head, indicating no news from Kara. I felt myself grasping for something good to tell her.

"You know, Nikki, I don't think there's a better time for this to be happening," I said. A few days earlier, a movement called #MeToo had begun to spread through my social media feeds. Just as I started to learn about the reality of Nikki's abuse, the entire world began talking about power imbalances and the pervasiveness of violence against women. "There's never been a moment in history when a jury would be more educated on issues like consent and intimate partner rape. Everyone is talking about this right now. People are feeling empowered to finally start sharing. This is going to help you."

A feeling swelled—something I thought had died in me; a kind of faith that maybe something would be served by all of Nikki's suffering, on the other side of this disruption and chaos. Lately I had become allergic to the kind of hyper-positivity that claimed, "The universe has your back." Things like, "God doesn't give people more than they can handle; it's all part of a bigger plan; all's well that ends well." But I couldn't help wondering: *Maybe.* Maybe what I was witnessing was a soul's calling, as my sister teetered on the precipice of facing her deepest fears in front of a grand jury. And maybe where I was, standing alongside her as she walked that spiritual gauntlet, was exactly where I was supposed to be, in service of whatever life was asking of me.

Nikki listened to what I had to say, but didn't respond. Did she not want to get her hopes up? Was she unable to understand the pervasiveness of this #MeToo phenomenon while locked away from social media? Or was she, like me, annoyed at the very idea that all of this could be for some mysterious higher purpose? Even I was slightly annoyed by what I was saying.

Well-meaning friends and my eighty-year-old therapist had tried to get me to see that maybe I was being handed this experience for a reason—for my own personal development. "It's like they say, another fucking growth experience," my therapist said at the end of our last session.

Nope. No way. I was not ready to see a single upside in this situation. My body was wholly fed up with my overintellectualizing, my tidying and shining up, my "look at the positives" optimism. That knee-jerk attitude was a function of my mom, without a doubt. She was a "glass half-full, accentuate the bright side" kind of woman. She'd taught us to seek out the good in an uncontrollable situation. Find the heart in a broken man. Focus on the silver linings.

I saw none of that here.

I certainly wasn't ready to accept that any of this could help in my own personal evolution. I was tired from the pain of stretching through growth. I'd done the hard work when I split from my husband. I'd specifically asked the universe for three concrete things: Lightness. Ease. Freedom. I'd prayed for these things. I'd trusted—against my better judgment and my conditioned control strategies—something greater than myself, and rested in that faith.

Now, the rage in me felt existential—it felt bigger than one person or one situation, directed at life itself. I felt dismissed. Attacked. Eternally pissed. I didn't want to have to jump through more hoops and prove myself through more hard things. I didn't want another *growth experience*; I wanted to be grown already.

I felt a similar resistance in Nikki when I brought up the #MeToo movement, and I respected it. How could we possibly find meaning in the midst of this wreckage, while we were both trapped in this unchangeable hell?

CHAPTER 16

we can handle the truth

Mid-October 2017

It had been more than two weeks, and Nikki still wasn't home. There was no hiding that something bad was happening from the kids. The grown-ups kept crying. Relatives and strangers funneled in and out of the house, wearing the kind of expressions you see at wakes. Lots of head-shaking, hugging. But it was an ambiguous kind of mourning, stacked with losses big and small. Loss of normalcy. Loss of innocence.

I was a living disruption, constantly running out of the room to take an important call. My most reliable routines, gone. I stopped watching the sunrise with Noah. My candle sat unlit. Some nights I slept on the couch; other nights I made a bed on Noah's floor, while he stayed up later than usual to catch up on our lost time together.

Ben oscillated between big bouts of anger—demanding that we TELL HIM THE TRUTH, running through the house like a whirlwind of pent-up energy, fists clenched and eyebrows furrowed—and pure despondency. He knew that Nikki was "at the police station," the same place he'd left her. Neither kid had asked about Chris yet, so we didn't bring him up.

At night, Ben slept with a picture of Nikki. It was the same picture that Nikki used on her Facebook and Instagram profile: The three of them were in tie-dyed shirts, smiling. Nikki was wearing big sunglasses. If you look closely, which I now did, you could see there was a bruise under her eye.

I was sure that lying to them was the wrong thing to do. I knew this from raising the child of someone who was addicted—kids need to understand the confusing things they're seeing and hearing.

But how do you tell a four- and a two-year-old that their dad is dead and their mom killed him? What's the best setting? What kind of psychological reinforcements did I need to have in place? This would be a crucial moment, a core memory, and the last thing I wanted to do was fuck it up. The stakes seemed impossibly high.

I needed help, and so I reached out to Sarah; to the kids' preschool teacher, Miss Michelle; and to the Internet. This is what they told me: Caregivers need to have an agreed-upon narrative for what we tell the kids about their parents, and it needs to ring true. We need to validate the kids' feelings, give them an outlet for creative expression—drawing, painting, playing, which is the natural language of kids. And we need as much professional support as humanly possible.

In my outreach, one name came up again and again: Dr. David Crenshaw. He was the most well-respected child psychologist in our area, and a world-renowned expert in play therapy, having worked with traumatized families for fifty years. He was currently the director of a local residential children's home, the kind of place where kids like Ben and Faye go to live when there's no family to care for them. It was some consolation that at least Nikki's children were with me, rather than in foster care or an institution. Recent statistics show that there are more than 380,000 children in foster care in the United States,[12] and while children often enter the system for multiple reasons, parental incarceration is estimated to account for around 40 percent of foster placements.[13]

If anyone could give us a blueprint for talking to children who've lost both of their parents in scary ways, it would be Dr. Crenshaw. *He's like Mr. Rogers*, said nearly every person who mentioned his name.

Sarah had worked closely with him through the years, presenting alongside him at conferences and coauthoring papers. She put us in touch.

"I'm way out of my depth," I wrote him in an email. "I'm prepared to allow whatever feelings come up to be what they are and not diminish them, and to hold Ben and Faye through their deep grief. But I just want to make sure we handle this without further traumatizing them."

We talked back and forth. His wisdom sparked hope. And within two weeks of the shooting, we met at Sarah's office for a face-to-face consultation.

I asked my mom to come with me, since she was currently spending almost all of her time around the kids. She was terrified of doing or saying the wrong thing. "I've messed up enough," she told me on the way to Sarah's office. She was willing to show up and have some hard conversations, look truth in the face.

It was something she was just starting to do—and over the previous two years, my mom and I *had* started having some direct conversations. My own self-reflective, marriage-ending period of time coincided with my mom's personal growth. Maybe it was the way her Crohn's disease was slowing her body down, as her stomach grew to the size of a second-trimester belly; she wore my old maternity jeans around the house, and spent a lot of time resting in bed. Maybe it was the introduction to guided meditation, which she'd play on a CD in her bedroom every day. She stopped caring as much about her clothes, only that they had to cover her growing stomach. She'd come to Omega in the middle of the day to lie in a hammock and meditate, and then take a walk with me on my lunch break.

Why were you so critical of the way we looked as kids? I asked her. *Did you know that a main message I internalized was to fit in and blend in with the crowd? Why did you put so much emphasis on our love lives during our teenage years, while giving some problematic messages: Men need sex, our role was to be desired, it's normal and okay for my seventeen-year-old boyfriend to live with us when his mom kicked him out, because some boys need to be saved. What were you thinking?*

She couldn't say, only that it felt right at the time. "I would do things differently," she had recently admitted. "I was always trying to protect you, to make your life better and easier than mine was."

Being likable and marriageable was an insurance policy for finding men to take care of us, and keeping them. She didn't want us to get picked on or rejected. She had done the best she could at the time, and had some regrets. Yet she had also been proud of the women Nikki and I were, and often said that her one true purpose in life was to birth us into life.

Now she was seeing that all of her misguided instincts and choices had led us *here*, with her younger baby in jail and her older baby saddled with a life she didn't choose...

She was dripping in something thicker than guilt. Her face looked permanently confused, deep worry lines stacked on her forehead; she couldn't stop crying. No one was more upset with her than herself.

We sat on Sarah's couch, our thighs pressed against each other for stability. Dr. Crenshaw and Sarah sat across from us.

He was an older man with trim white hair, spectacles, and a warm demeanor. I could understand why kids liked him.

"I've been called on to intervene in many heartbreaking tragedies," he started, "but not this kind of devastating experience."

My heart sank. I was hoping for a well-worn path to follow. With Noah, there were Al-Anon meetings he could attend as the child of an addict, but clearly there were no support groups for kids whose mother killed their father, the double whammy of incarceration and death in one fell swoop.

Still, Dr. Crenshaw had a clear perspective. "In the aftermath of trauma, children can usually deal with reality no matter how awful. What they don't cope well with is mystery; when they sense that adults are not telling them the full story," he said. Kids will use their imaginations to fill in the blanks, he explained, and what they come up with is most often worse than reality. Instead of the truth—that Nikki had protected them—they might internalize a belief that Nikki and Chris chose to leave them: that Ben and Faye were bad and to blame. Kids' own stories, he said, almost always involved blaming themselves.

He was concerned about Ben's repeated pleas to be told the truth. "It's crucial that the kids feel that the adults they are relying on now can be fully trusted." *That ship may have sailed,* I thought. Had we already done the damage we were trying to avoid?

"Ben will eventually learn the truth," he continued. "And when he does, there will arise the question of what harm has been done to his relationships with those who love him and, with the best of intentions, tried to protect him from the painful reality."

I glanced over at my mom. Her arms were wrapped around her waist. She rocked slightly, forward and back, nodding her head. I knew this was a paradigm shift for her. Hiding the truth was what my mother knew how to do.

"But *how* do we tell them?" I asked. I felt frozen in the face of this; I needed a script.

"There is no way to protect Ben from the horrific pain of this tragedy." Dr. Crenshaw spoke empathetically. "No carefully chosen words, no perfect timing. What you do have control over is how and when he finds out. If he doesn't hear the painful truth from those who love him the most and surround him with support, there will always be the risk that he will hear it from someone else. And *that* would be devastating on so many levels."

Right. Okay. That, too, made sense.

"And what about Faye?" my mom asked.

Dr. Crenshaw smiled. "The main thing she needs to know for the immediate future is that she is surrounded by family who love her and will take good care of her."

That part was easy.

Sarah chimed in. "Faye will take her cues from Ben, and the two of them are so connected that, as he starts to feel more secure with what's happening, she will, too." She suggested that when we were ready for the initial conversation with Ben, we should create an environment that felt safe so he could better take in the information, including soothing sensory elements—like rocking him, or playing music, or having some soft stuffed animals around. If possible, avoid the imagery of Mom shooting Dad, they suggested. Allow him space to ask questions and answer them as honestly as possible (while still being age-appropriate). More than anything, reinforce that we were all in this together as a family, and that we would make sure they'd have everything they needed until their mom could come back.

Our conversation veered in different directions—including how to handle the Child Protective Services case that was still open. They were scheduled to interview Ben in the coming days, and had warned that they'd drop by for random home visits to make sure the kids were safe.

Not only did CPS have to finish their initial investigation, but since a gun had been fired in the home in a room next to the kids' bedroom, they were now considering indicting *Nikki* for child abuse. The injustice was maddening. I ranted to Sarah and Dr. Crenshaw about my frustrations, asking them if this was normal for the agency, wondering if CPS were culpable for mishandling the investigation—and instigating a violent, desperate response.

Dr. Crenshaw and Sarah exchanged looks, indicating they'd navigated these questions before.

"Yeah, this is what happens with CPS sometimes," Dr. Crenshaw said, shaking his head. *Yes! I wasn't crazy for thinking they'd fumbled this.*

"When I had talked to her initially, she was really scared that the kids would be taken away by CPS," I said. "Could they have done that?"

Sarah shrugged a shoulder, then nodded. "It is true that domestic violence victims can and do get charged with child endangerment or failure to protect if there's violence in the home that the kids are exposed to."

That was exactly what Nikki had told me before I filed for an order of protection against my ex-husband. I now understood that this knowledge had come from Sarah.

"It's not that CPS has bad intentions and wants to punish women for being victims of domestic violence, but they expect victims to leave. If they don't, or can't, and stay in the home knowing that the kids are exposed to violence, they can be charged. It doesn't always happen this way, but it happens enough that it's a problem for DV victims."[14]

"I did call CPS, with an abundance of caution, after Nikki told me about the burns," she continued. The "spoon" story came back to me, with a shudder. I glanced over at my mom, who hadn't heard about that yet. She didn't ask for more information.

"I suspected they wouldn't take the case because, as I learned from the mandated reporter training, pregnancy is 'outside of their jurisdiction,'" Sarah said with air quotes. I knew that mandated reporters were often people who worked with kids, sworn to report any suspected abuse. "However,

I had consulted with my supervisor and she felt I needed to call anyway. When I did, they told me that they couldn't do anything until the baby was on the outside."

My mouth hung open. "I'm sorry, what? There *was* a baby on the outside, Ben. He was living in that house."

"Because Ben had been asleep, there was no information suggesting he was exposed to it," she said.

Fury bubbled in my stomach. I knew next to nothing about the intricacies of highly lethal domestic violence, but I knew that domestic violence isn't a one-time event that a kid might sleep through. It's a constant, ongoing, patterned threat. I couldn't grasp why an agency designed to protect children was only considering it abuse if it happened *to* them or in their line of sight, not around them.

"Nikki always told me that the kids weren't exposed to violence. That if they were, she would leave," Sarah continued. "But even if they didn't see violence, there were definitely things Ben picked up on. If nothing else, he is very protective of his mom, and sensed the tension and fear when she was around Chris. I know he's gone through phases where he cried when Chris would come home from work—"

I remembered that, too. I had chalked it up to a phase, where he only wanted his mom.

"There was also a period of time when he became worried that Nikki was going to die, and had a series of nightmares about this," she recalled from her sessions with Nikki. "He's a very smart, observant kid, and may be able to piece together more of the details than we're expecting."

Dr. Crenshaw left us with one more piece of advice: "The kids will ask for the truth when they're ready to hear it." When they asked for their dad—which, in nearly two weeks, they still hadn't—then we would know it was time to have this difficult talk.

That felt like a solid action item. When they asked, I'd answer. Until then, I didn't have to worry about dropping this bombshell into our everyday conversation.

CHAPTER 17

ready or not

Later that night, as if on cue from the meeting with Dr. Crenshaw, Noah came to me. We were in the safety of his room during our before-bed alone time. He looked alert, like he had something he needed to say.

He told me his older friend from the neighborhood had read the newspaper and had a crazy theory: *What if your aunt killed your uncle, and she's in jail?*

Noah was now in a school that went up to fifth grade. I wasn't surprised that some of the children had caught wind of our family's situation. The *Poughkeepsie Journal* had become relentless about splashing Nikki's name online and in the paper, with headlines like, POUGHKEEPSIE MAN KILLED BY GIRLFRIEND and ADDIMANDO MURDER CASE. But I hoped Noah's different last name would shield him from the gossip.

"So, is it true?" he asked plainly.

"Yes," I responded. Instantly. It turned out the truth was easy to tell.

His face and shoulders fell in one dejected motion. His hands gripped the edge of his mattress. "Why?" he asked.

I took a deep breath and said what I knew to be true: "He'd been hurting her for a long time, and that night she was scared he was going to hurt her so bad that she would die, and she protected herself."

My words drew a line across his childhood, a Before and an After.

Silence.

"Did *you* know he was hurting her?" I asked him, realizing that I didn't know what he'd seen or heard when he'd slept over. I had been wondering how much Ben and Faye saw, but Noah had been there hundreds of times. What had he been exposed to that I didn't know about?

"No," he said, shaking his head. "But she did have a lot of bruises." I could feel his innocence peel away.

He didn't hesitate before asking another blunt question. "How did she kill him?"

Again, I trusted in the truth. "Uncle Chris had a gun."

His expression didn't change, but I could tell he was thinking, putting together his own string of hindsight memories. "Did you know he had a gun when you let me go over there?"

Oof. Like a punch to the gut. I was taken aback by how quickly his mind pinpointed the source of my guilt and fear.

"I didn't," I said. "I didn't know a lot of things. And I'm still learning. I don't have all the answers yet. But I can promise you that no matter what happens, we'll get through this together."

I held his hand and squeezed three times; our signal for *I love you.*

He squeezed four times back, *I love you, too.*

"Can you just answer me this?" he asked, still holding my hand.

What couldn't I answer at this point?

"Will Aunt Nikki be home by the time I'm in middle school?"

I smiled. Middle school felt like an eternity away. Here I was worried about six months, and he was thinking three years in the future. "My God, yes. I can't imagine a world where she isn't home by then."

He nodded. Then we turned on the TV and zoned out into a reality other than our own.

I kept waiting, but weeks passed, and Ben and Faye didn't ask where their dad was. Not even after seeing the Grovers on Sunday visits. Not even when they'd talk about "the red house," the brick apartment building where they'd all lived.

Bit by bit, Ben and Faye watched us carry remnants of their old lives into my apartment—their beds and blankies; their play kitchen (which Nikki had refurbished by hand); Ben's instruments and Faye's stuffed animals. Their books showed up on my bookshelf. Their clothes were suddenly in their dresser. Little by little, their lives were stitched into my home.

And they still didn't ask where their dad was.

I wondered if they assumed Chris was with Nikki, as I had at first. I simultaneously wanted them to ask so I could get it over with, and wished that would never happen. I both hoped that Ben would ask me instead of someone else in the family—I knew I was the most equipped to handle it— and hated that I was the one who had to break the news.

Then, finally, the day came. A full month had passed since the shooting. It was a Wednesday, the one day a week that Ben didn't have preschool and joined Faye at home, and the three of us would have special time for art projects and playground playdates.

I'd planned our afternoon errands for Faye's nap time—get diapers, then pick up our dinner from the meal train that had been feeding us for weeks. I took the long way home, hoping she'd take a snooze in the car.

Luckily, both kids did. After our standard nap loop through town, I sat in my driveway listening to the soothing lullaby music playing through the stereo, hesitant to cut off the hum of the engine. Then, in my rearview mirror, I noticed Ben was wide awake, staring out the window.

I turned off the ignition and opened the driver's side door, leaving the bags of food on the passenger seat. I had a routine down: Carry in the kids one at a time, then run back to the car for the rest.

Just as I unbuckled the chest latch on his car seat, he perked up, as if he'd had a sudden epiphany. "Wait, where's Dad? Is he at work?"

At work? I thought. *At work?! For an entire month?*

What was it about this day, at this moment, that made him ask? I'd never know. He asked, which meant it was time I answered.

"Let's go inside and we'll talk about it," I said, leading him out of the car and making my way over to Faye's side. I hoisted her sleeping body on my shoulder and followed Ben up the sidewalk into my apartment—*our* apartment—and up the stairs, adrenaline ramping up in my body.

"Go on into Grandma's room," I whispered, nodding to the room down the hall. "I'm just going to lay Faye down and I'll be right in." I searched my brain for the script I'd been practicing in the shower, with phrases like *his body stopped working* and *he isn't coming home.*

I settled Faye in her toddler bed and steadied myself. *Feel your feet against the floor. Breathe.* It was time.

Ben was lying on the bed, holding the teddy bear that the police officers had given him that night at the police station, sometime between Nikki saying *I'll be right back* and Grandma coming to get them.

I remembered Sarah's suggestions—*go someplace comfortable,* check, *have cozy items like stuffed animals,* check. I sat down next to him, cross-legged on the bed.

Here we go.

"Do you remember the 'Bad Night'?" I asked, which is the language he used to talk about the night his mom was taken away. Ben nodded. "What do you remember?"

He remembered the police car. He remembered his mom crying. He remembered Elizabeth coming and officers bringing him McDonald's pancakes for breakfast.

"Did you see anything before you went in the car with Mom? Or hear anything?" I had held back on asking him this directly until now. I guess I hadn't felt ready for the truth, either. But he shook his head no; he didn't see or hear anything.

"Well, that night something bad happened, and your dad's body stopped working. He died. Do you know what that means?"

The words had left my mouth and entered his body. I held my breath, waiting for a reaction.

He didn't answer, just looked in my eyes. "It means he isn't going to come home," I said.

His face was devoid of emotion. He said nothing. After a few excruciatingly long beats, he said, "That's weird." Then he slid off the bed and lay on the floor with his teddy bear.

"It is weird," I said, stretching out on my stomach to look down where he lay. "And it's sad. I'm so sorry, Ben." The words felt empty, not enough.

He didn't say anything back. The two of us stayed there for what felt like an eternity. I didn't want to fill the space with more words, only my presence. I would wait for as long as he needed.

When he was ready, he stood up. "I don't like this teddy bear," he said, handing it to me.

He walked out of the room, down the hall, past the room where Faye was asleep, and out into the living room. As I was following him down the hall, I heard him talking to my mom.

"My dad died," he said. "Now I need a new daddy."

He never picked up that teddy bear again.

Days later, we collided with a fresh crisis: Mom walked into the kitchen crying, the left side of her face frozen.

She was having a stroke.

Her body had decided that she could not, in fact, handle all of this truth.

I was the one to bring her to the hospital. It was nearly midnight, and the air was cold. The sky was clear. *The stars are so bright tonight*, I thought, looking up through the windshield while Mom whimpered a slur of words I couldn't understand.

"Shhh, it's okay, Mom, we'll be at the hospital soon." Calm radiated over me. I was the grown-up steering us to the doctor; she was the scared girl in the passenger seat, leaning on my optimism. There was no space in that car for two people to freak out. No need to spin into mental catastrophizing. The worst was already happening.

PART II

reality

"We must always take sides. Neutrality helps the oppressor, never the victim. Silence encourages the tormentor, never the tormented. Sometimes we must interfere."

—Elie Wiesel

CHAPTER 18

new normal

November 2017

It's astonishing how quickly the mind can regroup and recategorize, how effortless it is for the brain to label something as "normal." It takes far less energy to acclimate to whatever circumstances are around us than to argue with an unchangeable reality. I saw it in the kids, too, this ability to move forward despite it all.

And my version of "normal" now involved roughly three hours a day of school runs. Noah was dropped off first, then we'd head across the river and over to the preschool—a thirty-minute ride each way. I could have found Ben and Faye a different preschool closer to me, but I wanted to keep as much continuity for the kids as possible. The preschool community was a ready-made source of support, not just for the kids but for me.

I also loved the drive, all of us strapped in, listening to the new children's albums I downloaded to my iTunes. We belted out silly songs from deep in our bellies, our voices layered together, our laughs bouncing between the windows: *Buzz buzz-b-buzz buzz*, we sang like bees, playfully dancing in our seats. Something about being in the car felt like a physical recalibration. Most days Ben brought a ukulele with him to play along with the music, and he'd always offer Faye a turn.

"No thanks," Faye said sweetly one day, her little hand on her chest. "You play so beautifully, and my heart sings, so I'm going to sing the song." In moments like that I could feel my whole body smile from the inside out. I considered myself lucky to be there to catch that exchange and witness the innate resilience and love between them. Her heart *did* sing. And so, it turned out, did mine. The warmth of gratitude felt like a salve, a reminder that better feelings were possible.

The hour-long school commute tracked a complete circle—up one side of the Poughkeepsie arterial, over the bridge, back down the other side. Around and around, every day. And on the way there, we drove past North Hamilton Street, a place they didn't know held the jail—and their mom. I wondered if they could feel it somewhere, the way something in me quivered as I drove past.

Today I had a tight window to drop off Ben and Faye, and rush back across the river to the jail. We pulled up to the preschool on the cul-de-sac of a quiet residential neighborhood. I gathered up the backpacks and water bottles, unbuckled each car seat, and followed the two of them inside to their cubbies, where I gave them hugs, kisses, and promises to return.

Ben quickly disappeared into the small and cozy classroom in the basement of the teacher's home. But Faye clung to the bottom of my shirt as I tried to head back up the stairs. *One more hug.* I knew about separation anxiety, especially in preschool—Noah was the kid who cried at drop-off every single day for the first few months of a new school year. But there was something deeper about Faye's angst, a panic I had recognized in Ben, too—a fear that the grown-up who says she'll be right back, won't.

But I had minutes to make it to see Nikki for a visit at the jail; I could feel the adrenaline simmering. I had to get into the visiting room before officers would turn me away.

Their teacher, Miss Michelle, who I'd met at Sarah's office, rounded the corner to help distract Faye.

"Oh, Faye! I just got this brand-new book on bunnies, I was thinking you'd love it! Do you want to sit on my lap while I read?"

Faye gave me one last hug and waddled after the teacher—leaving me on the stairs, feeling the tug between wanting to make sure Faye was okay and needing to get to my sister. I quietly slipped out the front door and made the mad dash to North Hamilton and Nikki. I would need to hit every green light and not get caught behind a construction vehicle in order to make it.

CHAPTER 19

sister visits

*O*ne green light. I mentally flipped through the items I had been asked to discuss. Kara, who was still wrapping her head around the complexities of the case, had texted me a bunch of *next time you talk to Nikki* questions.

Any kind of legal query was dispatched with an urgency that interrupted my day and required me to physically go to the jail and pass messages back and forth like a courier pigeon—the safest way to give information without it being intercepted. Kara visited Nikki when she could, but no one could get to the jail as frequently as me.

Three more green lights, no bridge traffic. I would make it; now it would be a straight shot to North Hamilton. As soon as I pulled into a space, I threw my car into park and speed-walked toward the jail, hearing the beep of my lock behind me.

Pulling open the heavy glass doors, I reenacted the routine I did once, usually twice, a week: Walk up to the officer's desk in the front of the room and write my sister's name down on a clipboard. Wait for her name to be called and exchange my driver's license for a small locker key. *What's your relation?* they'd ask, even when they knew. *Sister.* Match the number on the small key chain to the number on a rusted green locker. Hope that it opens. Put in my coat and bag. Make sure my phone is completely turned off. Nothing in my pockets. No hair tie around my wrist. No jewelry. Double-check that I'm not wearing an underwire bra. Make sure there's no metal on my shoes, no rips in my clothes. (Even the smallest hole could be reason enough to be turned away, out of fear that we'd sneak in drugs, or out of sheer disobedience to the rules—I'd seen it happen.) Ten minutes before the visit is set to start, walk over to the hallway leading to the metal detector and stand behind the red line. Some weeks, the line would extend all the way to the back of the building, alongside the two run-down bathrooms and broken vending machines.

On this day I was in with only seconds to spare. The woman behind the desk looked behind her to the clock and smiled. "Yeah, you made it, you're good." My lungs unclenched and I exhaled. She was one of the guards who could be compassionate and kind, or snappy and irritable; I never knew. She seemed to be in a good mood today, another green light.

Visitors were already standing behind the red line. I smiled at a few familiar faces I recognized from past visits—a young Black woman with a small pregnant belly and a quick friendliness, a gray-haired woman in a Mickey Mouse sweatshirt whose three-year-old grandson was twirling in the middle of the hall. I passed them all and stood in the back, leaning against the painted cinderblock walls and hoping that everyone else in the line was as prepared as I was. At least one of them would probably be turned away at the whim of the guard in charge. It happened all the time. Restriction lists were laminated and taped to the walls, strictly enforced. Even if someone had driven a long way and taken the day off work to visit. Even if they genuinely didn't know that a salmon-colored shirt could be mistaken for orange—a restricted color—or that the heel of their boot contained metal. And sometimes the machine would beep for no discernible reason, and the visit would be denied just because.

Nikki asked to see me every week and told me that my visits were the high points of her day, events to look forward to. And if someone else was planning to visit her, she usually asked if I could come, too.

Usually, I went with Elizabeth during Nikki's visiting hours, now that my mom was too sick to endure an hour-long visit without access to a bathroom. Some days I coordinated a visit with someone Nikki wanted to see—like Lisa, the friend who had first connected her to a domestic violence agency years earlier. While waiting for the visit to start, Lisa told me about seeing Nikki beat up with bruises. "I met her in the hospital once, and I was there when the doctors told Nikki she was pregnant with Ben. I almost fainted." *Lisa had been there for Nikki in that milestone moment; where was I?* I thought.

I was never shy about confronting the elephant-size question in the room with these strangers: *How didn't I see it?* I was just as flabbergasted as anyone else. I was less forthcoming about asking the question caught in my throat: *Why didn't you tell me?*

Sometimes I felt like a chaperone, ushering strangers to Nikki in that room with its rows of partitioned tables, and sitting in silence while they reconnected, privy to conversations from a life I didn't know. At no time was that more apparent than the day I brought Caitlin, the friend who had once lived in Butch's house across the street.

She was one of the many people who had reentered our lives during this fresh crisis as a source of love and support—but there also seemed to be something raw in Caitlin, something else that brought her. I knew that she'd lived a hard life after we all grew up. Nikki and Caitlin stayed close through our childhood, both of them moving away from our neighboring houses to the same Hyde Park school district. In our college days, Nikki sometimes talked about Caitlin, saying how hard it was to watch her disappear into an escalating drug addiction.

I heard less about her through our twenties, only passing details of her being arrested or unhoused, and Nikki's struggle with losing her friend.

More recently, I'd wondered if the *something that maybe happened* to Nikki at the sleepover with Butch also happened to Caitlin, who lived with him; maybe that would explain the path her life took.

"This is fucking surreal, bro," Caitlin had said at the visit, leaning toward Nikki and looking around the room. She told us how she'd turned her life around—she had gotten clean in jail, and she was now going to a methadone clinic, leading AA meetings, in a happy relationship, and pregnant with her first baby, a girl.

During the visit, I watched the two of them re-create the floor plan of Unit 11, where Caitlin had recently lived—arrested for multiple petit larceny charges, since stealing had been how she had financially supported her drug addiction. I saw them figure out that, had Caitlin not been released two weeks earlier, they would have been neighbors.

"We always wanted to be roommates," Nikki joked in an attempt to lighten the mood. Caitlin laughed. But there was also a heaviness between them. Caitlin was the only person we knew who had literally sat where Nikki was now, in that same jail. And as I suspected, she was the only person on the planet who understood how Nikki had gotten there.

I don't know who brought up Butch first; I only remember how it felt to sit at that table and watch Caitlin on my right, her once-blond hair darkened with age, pulled back in a low bun; and Nikki, her normally tamed hair now loose and long (since hair ties and haircare products were banned), sitting across from her. They were both in their late twenties, but I saw two little girls sitting on those stools, saying the words they'd kept hidden for a lifetime: *It happened to me, too.* Time seemed to slow to a standstill as they unpacked their memories: the crawl spaces they used to hide in, the games they'd played to distract themselves from the man who scared them. Caitlin hadn't been ready to talk about it before, but now she was willing to testify, she said, and to bring it all out into the light. I saw Caitlin with fresh eyes—not as my sister's little friend across the street, but as a young woman holding up a wound that fit alongside Nikki's like a friendship necklace.

"Addimando!" the guard called, snapping me back to the present moment. I was alone today—no ushering or witnessing. We were just two sisters reconciling our ideas of who we thought the other was, seeing one other anew. We called these kinds of days a *Sister Visit.*

She'd tell me about the filthy conditions outside the visiting room—shit smeared on walls, screaming and fighting between cellmates, the dog-eat-dog reality where no one could be trusted and connections were dangerous. How she'd play spades all weekend with the girls in her unit, but refused to mingle with the rest of the jail population at "rec" time, and about how her timid and reclusive nature was confused for stuck-up bitchiness. She described the constant surveillance from guards, who shone a light in her cell through the night and could, at any time, come in and trash her few belongings at whim.

She also told me about her stress dreams—particularly one that recurred on a loop for weeks. She'd be out walking in public when her knee would give out, and she'd fall. No one would stop to help. No one seemed to notice. Then she'd go on limping until her other leg gave out, too.

"It seems like a pretty clear metaphor," I said. "You were always out in public injured, and people didn't say anything." She nodded. "What was that like for you?" I asked slowly.

She hesitated before she spoke. "Honestly that was the loneliest part, I think. After years of hiding it, being told by Chris no one would believe me, eventually I stopped covering it up. I'd go out with black eyes and clear injuries, and no one would say anything. That felt more isolating than staying home and hiding. It felt like I was invisible." She spoke with her eyes cast down, looking at the table, maybe because she knew that she was implicating me, too.

I swallowed hard but didn't look away. I nodded and listened. "That must have been really hard, Nik."

"All of these people are coming out of the woodwork now, and that's great," she said, looking up. "I'm so grateful, really. But it's also like, 'Where were you?'"

I felt embarrassment flood to my face.

"I think a lot of people were too scared to say something and be wrong. They second-guessed themselves and didn't want to pry into someone else's business," I said, passing on a common reaction I heard through meal train handoffs and direct messages on social media. "Some didn't know what they were seeing and live with a lot of guilt for what they *didn't* do."

I had reflected on my own not seeing, too. In the wake of separating from Justin, I had been in a new stage of life where I was actively trying not to get into other people's business. It felt very *evolved* of me, to stay in my own lane and know that I couldn't fix or save other people, especially if they weren't asking for it. This had come from the previous two years of codependent recovery—meaning Al-Anon meetings, therapy sessions, and stacks of self-help books—which told me that people get the help they need when they're ready to ask for it. The words *give people the dignity of their process* were written on a Post-it Note on my bedroom mirror, a reminder from my years loving and trying to save an addict. There, in that visiting room, I couldn't help but wonder if my *let it be* attitude had gone too far.

I paused. "You know, I would have believed you, if you'd told me." I tried to keep my voice from breaking. "I'm sorry I didn't see it."

She looked at me and nodded. "I know that now. I do. I don't know why I didn't know it then. I thought you loved Chris, *everyone* loved Chris. I never thought anyone would believe me."

Clearly, now there was a team of people around her who had immediately and undoubtedly believed her and were rearranging their lives to support her—including both her attorney, Kara, and me. It seemed to genuinely stun her; her own version of a blind spot, of "Why didn't I see this before?"

"Well, *he* told me no one would believe me. A lot. He said that if I tried to leave him, he'd take me to family court and fight for custody and say that the porn stuff was my idea and I was a slut," she added. "I believed him."

I imagined how Chris repeatedly telling her *no one will believe you* would have been paralyzing, and I couldn't help but wonder if he was perhaps not the first man to whisper that into her ear. I wondered if the original *no one will believe you* voice belonged to Butch, but I didn't ask. I listened.

"If I had known all these people would help me..." Nikki continued, her voice trailing off. She shook her head and blinked as tears ran down her cheeks.

She cried at nearly every Sister Visit now. She cried for the kids. For our mom's anguish. For my burden. She even, at times, cried for Chris. "I just want to call him," she said through tears. "I just need to know that he forgives me."

And sitting between us every time, like a ball of yarn, was this confounding mess of *How didn't I see?* and *Why didn't I tell you?* Over time, we started unraveling it, pulling at memories and reflections through the partition, monitored by a camera above our heads.

At the visiting room table, we unpacked the experience of being the daughters of a woman who, at fourteen years old, was raped by her friend's older brother. She wanted him to like her, she once told me, but she didn't want *that*. She said he never spoke to her again.

We were the daughters of a woman who, in her early twenties, was dating a man named Nicky, who burned her with cigarettes and choked her. I'd heard my mom tell the story in the past, in pieces, and I vaguely remembered that she was living next door to my Aunt Kathy, one of my mom's sisters, during that time of her life—I recalled stories about Mom being thrown against walls, and how she romanticized the relationship, framing it as young passion. (My Aunt Kathy had her own history of abuse at the hands of an alcoholic, and had spent years as a director to a domestic violence agency. Even with all of her knowledge and experience, she was too close to Nikki to see the full scope of what was happening to her.)

"But isn't it weird that she named you *Nikki*?" I said one day. "Wouldn't you not want a daily, life-long reminder of the man who brutalized you?"

I wondered if that in itself was evidence that Mom didn't carry the kind of seething hatred for her abusive ex-boyfriend as she maybe should have. How much did her past experiences influence the way she saw the world, and rewire her alarm system, handicapping her ability to detect threats—not only for herself, but for her girls? How did it inform the lessons she taught us?

But now wasn't the time to confront Mom with all she could have done differently—what good could it do to pour salt into her gaping open wounds? She was barely hanging on, at constant risk of another stroke. And my love for her was bigger than her mistakes.

Nikki and I spent other visits tracing our lineage back even further, finding evidence of all the women in our maternal line who deferred in their lives to abusive men, who gave up their identities and autonomy to "keep the peace" and "stay in their place."

Our grandma, someone I only knew through stories and black-and-white photographs, died in her fifties of lung cancer. And as the story went, she had never smoked a day in her life. But she worked in an office with no windows while her mostly male coworkers smoked cigarettes. There was something emblematic about her death—breathing in other people's toxic habits, until it killed her. How long had this maternal line of women sacrificed ourselves for the comfort and compulsions of the men around us?

One hour was coming to a close. Officers started walking around the room, handing out white ID cards and initiating the end-of-visit hug.

"I think another reason why I didn't say anything," she said quickly, knowing our time was limited, "was that, if I said it out loud, it would be real. And part of me didn't want it to be real. Does that make sense?"

I nodded. Of course it made sense. I'd avoided acknowledging painful truths in my own life because, on some level, I knew I'd then have to deal with them. It's always easier to ignore something than it is to face it. But now I was choosing to sit in the uncomfortable experience, to look at Nikki's hollowed-out face, her eyes brimming with despair, and listen to the hard facts in front of me—and to keep showing up for it, week after week.

A man in a white button-up shirt with rolled-up sleeves extended out Nikki's ID card. I saw a large tattoo of the Statue of Liberty holding a rifle. He smiled at us and seemed apologetic to end our visit. "Go on and give her a hug," he said. I stood up and opened my arms.

"Bye, sister," she whispered.

"Bye, sister." I pulled away and smiled.

I walked to the other side of the room and into the holding area, which opened like a double-sided elevator, bringing us back to the outside world. The area was almost full, and I squeezed in, toes behind the red line, and looked back out into the room. I waved to Nikki, she waved back, and as the heavy metal door slowly clanged shut, I watched her pull her feet up on the stool and wrap her arms around her shins, curling into herself. I felt an animal-like instinct to run back into the room and take her with me.

CHAPTER 20

recusal

As we moved through a gray November, the weather outside matched my internal system: cold and stormy, with less discernible light each day.

I held on to the stubborn faith that Nikki would speak in front of a grand jury, and she would be believed. I also knew, in more grounded terms, that I had absolutely no control over when and how this went. I continued to live with a buzzing feeling that, at any moment, my life could be completely up-ended. I couldn't make plans further out than a week—between grand jury, family court dates to finalize temporary custody of the kids, and the one-in-three chance that someone would wake up sick and have to stay home from school, my schedule wasn't mine to set.

And so I lived in a perpetual transition—a forced experience of being completely and totally present.

Before all this happened, I'd been praying to see the capital-T Truth around me, and I'd also been working on living in the moment. And now here I was, with my past suddenly unimportant—even the big stuff, like the end of my marriage. None of it mattered. At the same time, I didn't have a future to plan, no goals to set. Everything hinged on whether or not Nikki would be indicted for murder. Either I would be handed back my old life or I'd have to forge a new path. The only rational way to live in that pressure cooker of uncertainty was to *be* and to *wait*, red-light freeze.

Meanwhile, the rest of the world was zipping by.

I couldn't imagine many workplaces being as understanding as mine was, as "take the week" turned into two months, with no end in sight. I did what I could to keep the department afloat, and my coworkers stretched themselves to the far edges of compassion. They filled in for me at weekend conferences I had already committed to working months earlier. They bought me a new company laptop when mine flew off the roof of my car—forgotten in the early-morning rush to preschool, when I didn't have enough hands to carry all of the things, and enough brain space to hold all of the thoughts. My coworkers were understanding and kind, rallying resources and connections to help me navigate those early weeks, but I knew this was an untenable situation.

Yet by some stroke of luck, or as I preferred to think of it, fate, New York's Paid Family Leave was finally to be enacted on January 1, 2018. So in less than two months, I'd be able to take additional time off work while getting paid half of my salary. Until then, I'd have to keep pushing myself to fit this wobbly existence; racing from drop-offs to jail to work to pickups, using every second of allowable company time.

I was also feeling a building panic as each day passed—Nikki's birthday was around the corner, on November 19. Then came Thanksgiving, and then Christmas, and then, finishing out the year, was Ben's fifth birthday on New Year's Eve. How could Nikki miss all of that?

While I understood that there was a process for something as serious as a gun fatality, I also knew that self-defense wasn't a crime. Enough was enough. We needed her back.

And then, one day in mid-November, Kara texted me. The Dutchess County DA's Office had finally made a decision.

"What does this mean?" Nikki's voice was crackly on the recorded jail line.

"The Dutchess County DA's Office are recusing themselves, which means they're removing themselves from prosecuting you," I said, regurgitating everything I'd gathered from Kara, and then Sarah, and every other person I'd frantically called in the past hour. "They're saying there was a conflict of interest, and so they can't ethically prosecute you."

"Did they say what that conflict is?" Nikki asked.

"I mean—apparently the conflict is that they had records that you're a victim, and they can't prosecute a victim." I waited a beat. "But no, they haven't publicly said what the conflict is."

"Okay..." Her voice carried a flicker of hope. "So they're going to let me go?"

"No, a different prosecutor is taking the case, from Putnam County." The Dutchess County public defenders would still represent Nikki, but Putnam County district attorneys would be the ones to prosecute, on our county's behalf.

I held my breath. Nikki was smart. She knew what this meant: more time, more waiting, more uncertainty.

"But you know, I've talked to a lot of people..." I could hear my tone brighten. "Kara thinks that this might be a good thing because, if Dutchess County were to investigate and find you not guilty, then they'd have to hold themselves accountable for some of the blame, considering they didn't do their jobs when they had evidence of a crime being committed." I was talking fast, aware that my comments were being monitored. I wanted them to hear me, I wanted *everyone* to hear me. "Maybe an impartial prosecutor, someone with no skin in the game, will be able to see things clearly," I added.

The phone line was silent.

"And you know that attorney I talk to sometimes—the one whose wife's personal trainer used to buy baby slippers from you?" That's how almost all our connections were established nowadays—someone who knew someone who used to know Nikki.

This attorney couldn't take Nikki as a client because he was tied up with a high-profile pro bono case, but he seemed to care about the injustice and wanted to help. He had become part of my sounding board.

"Well, he knows Chana—Chana Krauss is the new Putnam County prosecutor—and he said she's reasonable and fair. He actually thinks this is a good thing..." My voice trailed off.

"Chana? She's a woman?"

"Yes," I said, "and when I looked her up, I saw she was the chief of the Sex

Crimes Bureau down in the Bronx, so she should be able to recognize what Chris did to you. In this day and age, with the #MeToo movement, she's not going to want to prosecute a victim."

Silence.

"I'm sorry, Nikki, I'll be there to see you in a few hours."

"Yep."

The line went dead.

We barely talked about the prosecution handover in the visiting room that day. Nikki had a more pressing crisis on her mind.

"Am I killing Mom?" Nikki asked me across the visiting table. Another afternoon, another hour-long conversation. While some days she was hopeful and chatty, today was not one of those days. She looked terrible. She didn't have to tell me that she'd spent the day vomiting—I could tell.

The shift in prosecution felt like small potatoes compared to the other cataclysmic news I had to pass on that week: Our mom was now in the Intensive Care Unit at Vassar Brothers Medical Center, on the other side of Poughkeepsie, less than two miles away from the jail.

The stress of Nikki's situation was too much on her already-fraught body. She had been in and out of doctors' offices for the past two years, perplexing the specialists with her disparate symptoms. *Is it MS?* one neurologist wondered, sending her for inconclusive testing. *It's just your Crohn's,* said her gastroenterologist before upping her steroids prescription, masking and minimizing the symptoms, keeping her comfortable. No one saw the underlying roots of her pain—cancer, hiding behind her stomach—until multiple strokes and an unquantifiable amount of stress led to a bowel perforation, sending her to emergency surgery. Out came the cancer, spreading through her body like ink in water.

She was now in a medically induced coma. We had no idea if she'd ever wake up.

"What if I never get to hug her again?" Nikki cried. "Oh, Michelle, what if she never knows how sorry I am?"

I sat across from her, stoic, letting my baby sister shed the tears she'd spent so long holding in, while my own emotions stayed compartmentalized and locked away. It wasn't until I was back in my car that I allowed myself to silently cry into my steering wheel, unable to breathe. Some of it was preemptive grief, knowing our mom would soon be gone, and some of it was a deep heirloom sadness, knowing that what Nikki and I were experiencing was the result of seeds planted long ago, by women hurting, shrinking, suffocating in a society that never helped them.

CHAPTER 21

fragile peace

Four days after a new prosecutor was assigned, Nikki turned twenty-nine years old.

I bought a cake—carrot cake, Faye's choice. We lit candles and sang to her over the phone. It sounded slow and sad. Ben and Faye blew out the candles and made a wish. Afterward, I went into the bathroom to cry.

Six days after that came Thanksgiving—a day of gratitude, a time to pause and reflect on the sheer frequency that I'd been saying the words *thank you* lately. And I had. Despite the heavy and hard loss that our family carried around, there had also been a steady outpouring of empathy since Nikki's arrest.

A local family, complete strangers to us, cooked us an entire Thanksgiving dinner so that we would have one less thing to plan and execute. And as we neared the month of December, I received text after text requesting Christmas wish lists. A photographer friend of Nikki's offered a free photo session for Christmas cards. Other friends held fundraisers and "adopted" us in gift drives, recognizing the toll on our family in a way that the system never did.

I've always had trouble accepting gifts, but I got the sense that people *needed* to help, not to earn do-gooder points, but to be able to sleep at night. It was enough to bring a fragile sort of peace to the season, the knowledge that this kind of goodness lived around us.

As more people in our community were paying attention to the case, wanting to help, the subject of bail started to come up. People seemed to assume, as I had, that bail is a right for someone accused of a crime, and money is the only obstacle. But in reality, defendants typically get only one shot at making a bail application; the prosecutor can oppose and the judge can deny it. The new prosecutor said she needed some time to understand the case before agreeing to bail, and would consider it if Nikki got indicted by a grand jury.

And so, while we waited some more, we started the process of raising money. We had no way to know what bail the judge would set—it's arbitrary and at his discretion—but Kara guessed we'd need around $100,000. She said we could email out a synopsis of Nikki's story to people who might be willing to donate, but we couldn't post anything on social media or initiate any kind of public crowdfunding; that wouldn't look good to the prosecutor or judge.

By the second week of December, a group of us—me, Elizabeth, Sarah, Wendy, Nikki's two childhood friends Rachel and Laura, and a colleague of mine named Carla—discreetly began collecting pledges. I also emailed out a message urging people to read Nikki's story and email it out to their networks. I detailed the bail process—we would collect money to give the court, and then, as long as Nikki didn't miss court dates or skip town, the money would be returned once Nikki was either acquitted or convicted. I promised to take full responsibility for any bail money that was lost to the court, even though I had only a few thousand in my bank account and was about to go on leave from my job. I had no backup plan.

My contacts emailed it out to their networks and we quietly gathered $50,000 in two days.

The generosity was stunning. I couldn't believe that there were real live human beings out there who would loan $1,000, $5,000—we even had a couple of five-digit amounts—out of their sheer belief in my sister, in our family. I had no idea that there was this underground branch of (mostly women) philanthropists who quietly used their wealth to do good in the community, insisting on being anonymous. All in the hope of bringing Nikki home for Christmas.

CHAPTER 22

lights

At the top of his Christmas list, Ben wrote, "MOM."

"Santa will help," he said confidently, handing me a list that also included a costume of his favorite superhero, the Flash. Starting from nearly the very beginning of Ben's time living with me, he would frequently disappear into a superhero disguise, finding strength and power where he had none. He especially liked the Flash, who would transform him into a speedster—prompting him to run around the house and yard at top speed, pretending to fight a bad guy, his fight-or-flight trauma response playing out before my eyes.

We had stuffed the lists into envelopes, which I was supposed to mail to the North Pole. Instead, I opened them after bedtime and hid the letters in my closet. I had started obsessively collecting all the things Nikki was missing, neatly organized and filed away, so she could later read them.

Each day the kids opened a small drawer on a wooden advent calendar and pulled out a piece of paper naming a different Christmas activity. It was a tradition I'd had with Noah every year—one day we would write letters to Santa, the next we'd go on a drive to see Christmas decorations, with hot cocoa for the ride. It was all much easier to manage with one kid.

Today the little slip of paper said, "Decorate the tree."

Just as I wanted to retain as much normalcy as I could for Ben and Faye, I felt the same about Noah. He wanted a real tree, which meant asking one of my few male friends to come with us to a local Christmas tree farm to help carry it.

I pulled totes of Christmas decorations from the bowels of my overstuffed garage. It was filled to the brim with the contents of Nikki's apartment, old memorabilia and furniture that had once belonged to my parents, tools and clothes that Justin had never picked up. Opening the garage door and staring at this mess of other people's literal baggage, now mine to deal with, felt symbolic.

I ended up carrying six containers back into the house, mix-matched between three different lives: I had my own ornaments, which I'd been using to decorate a tree with Noah and his dad for eight years. I had Ben and Faye's ornaments, which included Nikki and Chris's childhood ornaments and evidence of their relationship together. And I had my parents' ornaments, since my dad wouldn't put up a tree this year just for himself. All of our childhood was there, visible in Precious Moments and Crayola ornaments from the nineties, as well as handmade pieces with our school pictures on them. I had become not just my sister's keeper, but my family's keeper. There, right in front of us, was evidence of the lives we had lost.

I saw Nikki, smiling in her third grade class picture behind a ceramic wreath she had painted in art class. I'd looked at it every year for as long as I could remember: her crooked bangs, her forced smile. We had just moved to Hyde Park. I gazed at the photo, thinking of all that little girl was holding by the time she was nine years old. I wondered if she'd seen Hyde Park as a fresh start, a chance to run away from her ghosts, to be new.

I wish I had been a better sister. I wish I had known.

"Ben, can you just stop," Noah snapped as Ben ran around the room, knocking over a container of ornaments.

Ben reminded me of Nikki, internally coping with a storm of feelings too big for such a small body, looking up to an older sibling and being rejected. Noah reminded me of myself, annoyed and intolerant of a small person's trauma responses—the difficult behaviors that are easy to mistake for personality traits, especially to a kid who doesn't understand why someone grabs for control when they feel powerless, or pushes people away so they don't get rejected first. It's not easy to live with someone whose nervous system is stuck in fight-or-flight mode.

I fought the urge to correct their behaviors, letting them work it out between them.

Ben pulled me back to the moment. To the Christmas tree. To the Christmas music. He was holding an ornament: #1 Coach Chris.

"Dad was so strong," Ben remembered, hanging it on the tree. He wanted to be strong like his dad, too, and loved to climb up doorframes like a ninja and do karate moves around the house. Nikki was still grieving for Chris, too. I had spent a recent visit sitting across from her as she openly cried, unable to hold in her sadness. These ornaments were a reminder of the people we used to love, in all of their complexity, separate from the way I saw and viewed them now.

Chris was a beloved coach. Nikki was a #1 Teacher. My mom had adored us so much that she saved every ornament we ever made in school. Life would be so much easier if people were only one thing: good, bad, right, wrong. Tonight, in the glow of the Christmas lights, I tried to make space for those multitudes—to remember that all of their parts were real and valuable, and belonged on the tree.

By the middle of December, the courts were about to shut down for the holidays and all cases were left at a standstill. We began to lose hope that Nikki would be home for Christmas.

The case itself wasn't exactly progressing, but every message that Kara passed on about Chana, the new prosecutor, was positive. She said they were being "collaborative," and there appeared to be a mutual agreement between the prosecution and the defense that a victim fearing for her life shouldn't be tried for murder.

The attorney I knew kept his promise to talk to Chana. He ran into her in court a number of times and mentioned that he was a friend of Nikki's family. After each encounter, he'd relay their conversations—saying things like, *She wants to investigate to make sure she's doing right by Nikki* and, eventually, *Chana says that she wants to meet Nikki and feel her energy; she says she's a good judge of character and feels spiritually called to take this case.* When I'd googled Chana's name, which I had done immediately, the only recent article was about how she'd won an award honoring her "honesty, integrity, and commitment to the fair and ethical administration of justice." She was quoted as calling it a "career defining" moment, and her boss, the elected district attorney, said it was "an honor that district attorneys daydream about." Maybe this woman was an answered prayer. Maybe she was a key character in Nikki's story of being believed.

Kara shared that Chana wanted to depose Nikki, which meant meeting her before trial and getting her testimony. If Chana believed her, then she could drop the charges altogether. But it also was a major risk, because anything Nikki said could be plucked out of the record and used against her on the stand. Any small discrepancy between what a stenographer recorded before trial and her testimony in front of a jury could be weaponized, weakening her defense. Kara struggled with the decision, and also considered allowing some of Nikki's key witnesses to sit for an interview with Chana: Sarah and Elizabeth, the medical professionals who had documented injuries, Dave the police officer, and me.

Ultimately, Kara chose to allow all of us, besides Nikki, to sit for depositions. It was a complicated case, but on a gut level, I think Kara found the witness testimony to be compelling, and the amount of documented evidence to be overwhelming. Kara leaned on two domestic violence experts who regularly advised the court, and it was clear that Nikki had more documented evidence of abuse than 99 percent of the victims in the county: Three professionals witnessed Nikki being raped on camera—two therapists and a police officer; dozens of witnesses saw injuries; and a handful of people could testify that they lost sleep thinking Nikki would be killed overnight. She had multiple lethality assessments, forensic nurse photographs, detailed medical records. I imagine that Kara, like all of us, believed that any reasonable person looking at the evidence—especially a woman, a mother, a seasoned professional who made a career out of prosecuting sex crimes—would believe Nikki, too.

* * *

Christmas came and went. The kids woke up to the kind of Christmas morning miracle they'd only seen in movies. Wrapped gifts extended out from under the tree, across the carpeted living room, and piled up on the couch and rocking chair. I'd prepared them that there were many "Santas" in the community, people with giving hearts, who wanted to show how much they cared about our family.

It wasn't just for Ben and Faye; perfect strangers wrapped gifts for Noah, and for me. There were even a few for Nikki, gestures of hope that she'd be home soon to receive them.

People from all corners and times of my life—and *their* friends, too— wanted to make sure that we were cared for. Cards had come in all through December: "I know the holidays in my own life are hard, here's something to alleviate the burden," with a check for $200. "You don't know me, but I know Elizabeth, and I think you're doing an incredible job," $500. There was $1,000 in an envelope from an old boss; $20 from a girl I played handbells with in church as a kid.

It wasn't the gifts themselves that lifted me up. It was the human impulse to help. The magic of my holiday season came in the form of people, igniting a kind of hope I hadn't known I could feel again.

do you swear to tell the truth?

I triple-checked my planner for the time I had to be down in Putnam County. In the square marked JANUARY 19, I'd scrawled "11:30 a.m."

Today I was going to meet with Chana, for the first time, two months after she'd been assigned to the case.

I had an hour to change out of the pajamas I'd worn to drop the kids at preschool and get on the road. I raked my hand over the clothes hanging in my closet, debating which was the right outfit to wear to meet the woman who wielded sole power over the direction of our lives—when I could return to work, when the kids could hug their mom, when we could all start healing. How do you dress for such an event?

We'd started 2018 with an update emailed out to our networks of donors. We now had $100,000 sitting in a bank account that Elizabeth and I had opened, ready and waiting for a bail application—as soon as Chana allowed it.

I wondered if she'd judge me as a stand-in for my sister. Nikki and I look alike and have similar mannerisms and speech patterns; there's no one on earth closer to her genetically. Would Chana be watching me, imagining how Nikki might appear to a jury? Did I need to impress her? Convince her? Maybe I could save the people around me if only I said and did the right things. As long as I wore the right clothes.

I chose a green V-neck sweater and dark blue jeans, jumped into my car, and typed the Putnam County District Attorney's Office address into my phone's GPS. *Starting route to 40 Gleneida Avenue, 40 minutes, 33 miles.*

I wound down the Taconic's narrow, hilly roads and into the mountains leading to Putnam County. I'd been traveling on these roads for as long as I could remember, since I was small enough to look out the window and see the overhead power lines stretching across the sky.

This was the same route my family took driving from our condo in Brewster to my Aunt Kathy's house in Poughkeepsie on the weekends, before we moved north. We lived in Brewster for only two years, but they were happy years. I was about Ben's age, and Nikki was around Faye's. We had a big hill outside our condo, where my dad took us sledding, Nikki and I piled onto a big inflatable tube, thick snow mittens gripping the plastic handles, knowing my dad would be there to help us walk back up.

As I crossed the county border, the undercurrent of anxiety, an ever-present companion over these last four months, kicked up. My back muscles started to tense and shake. My hands felt tingly. What if my brain turned to mush and I said the wrong thing? What if I single-handedly fucked everything up, and got my sister taken away forever?

I fought the urge to take the exit to Brewster and drive the streets of a life that could have been. *What if we had stayed here, and Nikki had never met Butch or crossed paths with Chris? Where would I be right now? Who would I be?*

I wondered if Chana would want to hear about our time living in Putnam County. Would it matter?

I pulled into the crowded parking lot outside the District Attorney's Office, which had a massive snowbank on one side, climbed out, and made my way upstairs into an ordinary waiting room. It was a small, dark space; the room was empty. No lawyers were meeting me here. I wasn't prepped. "Just tell her the truth," Kara had told me earlier that day.

I sat on a chair, legs crossed, top leg shaking. I texted Elizabeth, "I'm here, nervous." I breathed deep into the seat underneath me, trying to ground myself.

* * *

I didn't have to wait long. Within a few minutes, a secretary was leading me down a hallway into an office, where three people were waiting. Chana shook my hand; her smile wide on a round face. She was a short, compact woman propped up on heels. Her hair looked as if it had been loosely set with hot rollers, sprayed into place. "Nice to meet you," she said. Next, a tall, pale, white-haired man introduced himself as Michael, the private investigator who worked for Chana. It was his job, he said, to put the pieces together for the prosecution, so he'd be taking notes. A woman in the corner of the room smiled and waved when Chana introduced her as Amy, the county stenographer. Chana explained that Amy was recording my statement, along with those of Nikki's other witnesses, because they'd been talking to so many people that it was turning into a game of telephone. They were typing it all out to reference what I knew on my own versus what I'd heard from other people, the latter being less reliable information.

That made sense. I felt my guard coming down. They seemed to want to understand.

"Well, I'm confident that you'll see this for what it really was," I said. Chana told me she was a good judge of character, and I knew that my character, along with Nikki's, was good. I couldn't be sure of much, but I knew that.

The clock on the wall said eleven forty, and I was instructed to raise my right hand and swear to tell the truth.

"Everybody who's been coming in has such an enormous amount of information that they want to share," Chana began. I knew Elizabeth had come in already, but I wasn't sure who else *everybody* entailed. "What seems to be working best, because there's such a big time period we are going to need to talk about, is starting with the CPS visit and moving forward. After that, we can go all the way back to childhood and anything you want to tell me about."

"Okay," I replied.

"This is an opportunity for *you*," Chana said. "I'm here to listen."

* * *

"So, she is the one who told you how to do it [get a restraining order], and she thought you had to do it to protect yourself and kid, okay." She said *okay* with a small smile, and scribbled on the paper in front of her. I couldn't decipher why, but I felt a shift in the room.

I kept trying to explain, to give context so that Chana would see that Nikki's abuse and her response to it weren't an isolated event. It had deep roots. Like how Nikki was scared to go on sleepovers after the one with Butch, and my mom encouraged her to make up lies so that she wouldn't look weird to her peers. (I thought that would show how appearances and being accepted were high values to our mom, but *oh God, does that make Nikki look like a liar?*) I started second-guessing everything I was saying, but I was unable to stop the words from spilling out, desperate for her to understand.

For a time, I forgot there was a stenographer, only remembering when the woman in the corner asked to take a bathroom break.

As soon as she walked out of the room, Chana turned to me and leaned back in her chair. She brought up the name of the attorney I knew who'd run into her and asked about Nikki, the one who had reported that Chana had felt spiritually called to the case. She wanted to know how I knew him.

"He's a family friend," I said.

"He's a *really* good attorney," she said slowly, with that same hard-to-read smile on her face.

I tried to keep my face neutral, but inside my brain was screaming, *What is going on?* What did she mean by that statement—was she encouraging us to hire him? Did the two have a deal going on behind my back? Why did my stomach feel so sick? *What wasn't I seeing here?*

My alarms starting going off, and I couldn't place why. I had a hard time concentrating for the rest of the interview, as part of my brain flipped into a hypervigilant assessment on who and what was safe here. I added a few comments about Nikki grieving for Chris, saying that she really did love him and hadn't wanted it to end this way—but now every comment I said was met with my inner paranoia of *Does this make sense? Does she believe me?*

I told her that the kids were suffering without their mom, and a speedy timeline would mean everything to them.

And then it was over.

Chana walked me out into the narrow hallway and stopped me before the exit. There was no stenographer to take down our words or document the interaction. She looked me in the eyes and said, "I spent years prosecuting domestic violence cases. I know how hard it is to leave an abusive relationship. You should be really proud of yourself." I smiled, nodded, and she pulled me into a stiff hug. To an outsider, the interaction might seem warm and caring, but the hairs stood up on the back of my neck. My body knew something was wrong before my mind could figure out what.

a sign of spring

W hen is spring going to get here?" Faye asked from the back seat, watching a whirl of grays and browns outside her window. "I'm so tired of waiting," she sighed.

It was March in New York, a time when the cold grips and threatens to never let go.

We were all tired of waiting.

We were about to enter the sixth month. Six months was the original attorney's *best-case scenario* estimate for Nikki's release that had sent me into a panic. Yet here we were. Life felt less like a red-hot emergency now and more like an endurance test. We were in limbo between seasons, yearning for warmth just out of reach.

Six months, and the kids still hadn't seen their mom's face in person. Sometimes they happily chatted with her on the phone; other times her call disrupted a fun moment when they had momentarily forgotten their pain. Both scenarios were hard on Nikki and the kids.

I clung to shreds of hope, but I was becoming increasingly frustrated. Clearly something had shifted for the prosecution, and it wasn't looking good.

After Chana had taken our depositions and spoken to witnesses on both sides—friends of Chris's, friends of hers—I started hearing about alternative narratives she was starting to spin from Nikki's attorneys: Maybe Nikki made all of the abuse up, she said, spouting theories that people who loved Chris had told her. Chris was too nice, too easygoing; it was *Nikki* who was controlling, not letting anyone else drive the kids, not wanting them to eat junk food, and only buying organic and natural baby products. Nikki had a tight grasp on her kids (the only part of her life she could control, I rea-soned), and therefore she was the abuser and Chris the innocent victim. But it appeared to be the "multiple abuser" part of the story—the brief period of time when Chris, Dave, and the maintenance worker were having sex with her against her will; the part where Nikki's memory was fragmented and muddy—that seemed to be the hardest for the prosecution to grasp. "Light-ning doesn't strike twice," Chana was quoted as saying.

"This isn't lightning, it's sexual assault," Sarah had said, "and sexual assault absolutely strikes more than once." The research supported that—something that I would have thought Chana, someone who had spent years prosecuting sex crimes—would know. Numerous studies suggest that sexual victimization in childhood and adolescence significantly increases the like-lihood of sexual victimization in adulthood. Similarly, of those injured by domestic violence, over 75 percent continue to experience abuse. According to the CDC, when childhood abuse goes untreated, especially sexual abuse like Nikki's, violence usually recurs and escalates in frequency and severity.[1]

Still—it seemed that Chana was entertaining every other possible theory, including that Nikki was constructing an elaborate lie to get away with mur-der. (*For what reason?* we all lamented.)

Chana was insisting that she still needed more time to investigate, but it seemed to me each day she became less convinced of Nikki's innocence.

I had routine phone calls with Kara, when she'd tell me that the grand jury date was moved—again.

"This feels like a human rights violation," I said to Kara one day. "What more does Nikki possibly have to prove? If Chana truly wants a community with less crime," I vented into my cell phone, pacing around the kitchen, "she needs to at least not be *causing* childhood trauma."

Kara's outlook was the same as that of every attorney I knew and talked to: This is the way the system is, and there was nothing we could do but play the game. The underlying strategy was always the same:

1. Don't do anything to upset Chana.
2. Don't do anything to embarrass Judge McLoughlin.

After I'd hung up the phone with no more information or clarity than before, I picked up an envelope stamped with DUTCHESS COUNTY JAIL and reread the letter inside:

dear ben and faye,

it's a cold, snowy day. the wind is harsh, howling against the windowpane.

  and i stand up—
  pressing my face against the glass.
  i squint through the cracks and it's difficult to see too far
ahead—but still, i know the snowfall will get lighter,
  white mountains will melt away.
  the sun will soak the earth, and roots that are frozen,
preserved underground, will be nourished, and the flowers—
  "where flowers bloom, so does hope."
  warmer days are coming. i'll be home soon.
  i miss you every day. i love you always.

                              love and hope,
                              mommy

"I'll be home soon." *Soon.* It was a word said so many times that we'd forgotten what it meant.

We followed Nikki's lead. As the snow began to melt, we all delighted at seeing the "signs of spring," as Faye called them. The bees and the crocuses, proof that everything comes back once again. Faye was pure sunshine, leaving preschool every day with dirt smeared on her face and twigs in her hair.

"Remember the butterflies, Ben?" Faye leaned her head out from her car seat to look at her brother. Last Spring, Nikki had bought a butterfly kit and the kids had watched their life cycle in real time, eventually releasing them in their backyard.

Faye had been reminiscing a lot more lately, starting sentences with, "Remember when...," as if she was desperate not to forget. Six months to someone who has only lived two years is a fourth of her entire life, a significant span of time.

"Yes, I remember," I'd say, even when I didn't. The least I could do was join in with her, to validate the idea that those memories were real and important.

"I remember," Ben responded without looking over at her. I noticed that Ben had been reminiscing more, too, wanting to look at Nikki's old Instagram page nearly every morning. They were striving to keep those memories fresh.

Physically, we were all struggling. Two rounds of strep throat. A ruthless stomach bug that jumped from one to another of us, producing a steady rotation of vomit-soaked laundry and constant visits to doctors' offices. Ben was hit the hardest, suffering the highest fevers and the most painful symptoms.

One night, after a long day spent in urgent care, Ben was sitting on the couch. My dad sat next to him, coaxing him to choke down the liquid medicine he really didn't want to take. Ben's shoulders slumped, an expression of misery on his face. I was climbing up and down the stairs with a laundry basket, cleaning and sanitizing as I went.

I watched Ben swallow and shudder. His shudder turned into a shaking sob. The sob turned into sounds and the sounds formed words, wrapping around a feeling so big the room reverberated: "I...lost...everything."

I stopped where I was. Three words that melted away his armor and my fix-it instincts. These three words hung in the silence between us. His body sank into the couch, cushioned by a flood of sadness.

"Well, you didn't lose everything—" my dad started to say, which was a script I could have followed. He didn't lose his sister; he didn't lose the rest of his family; most of his things had migrated from the red house to here.

"No." I held up my hand to my dad. "No, Ben, you're right. You lost everything."

Ben looked between me and my dad, anguish painted on his face. He was so small and vulnerable, and I felt as though I was seeing his truest child self out in the open, the kind of scared inner child that could get trapped inside him as his body kept growing, the kind of original pain that some take decades to uncover in therapy. There he was, sitting on my couch, wearing his raw despair on his outsides.

And then he started a list.

"I lost my mom." He screamed.

"I lost my dad." Tears welled in his eyes, his words caught in his throat.

"I lost my home?" The end of the sentence curved up like a question.

He let out a cry and looked at me, like he wanted me to *see*. To witness these truths.

I dropped the laundry basket on the stairs and went to his side. I held his hand.

"You lost so much," I said. No bright sides. What I'd learned from all the people who'd witnessed my own pain is that sometimes all we need is to be heard.

"I lost my stage," his voice crescendoed, breaking into a cry, thinking of the raised platform my dad had built for him at home to perform music on. The rest came out faster, with urgency, through tears.

"I lost my guitar stands, I lost my things, I lost my room, I lost my piano—" I could feel my heart swell with each item. These were things that couldn't fit into this new space; things I'd left behind or boxed up in my garage.

"I lost the trees I used to climb—" He was fully sobbing now.

"I lost the hill I used to run down!"

"I lost EVERYTHING." He threw himself onto my lap, and cried.

It wasn't the kind of loss that had a name. It was too big. It was *everything*.

CHAPTER 25

purging

The springtime sun didn't bring much warmth to my inner world.

On April 16, three months after I'd sat in Chana's office for a deposition, nearly seven months of Nikki being in jail, it was abundantly clear to Nikki's legal team that the prosecution wasn't going to drop the charges. Kara "waived the case for the action of the grand jury," as it was called, meaning that they were reactivating Nikki's right to a speedy trial and the prosecutors had forty-five days to get an indictment.

On April 24, days before the grand jury was scheduled, Chana put in a motion to remove Kara and the entire Public Defender's Office from Nikki's case, insisting that Nikki's lawyers had to be replaced. This was *outrageous* to us. Did Chana know how deeply bonded Nikki felt to Kara—did she listen to the jail calls where Nikki told me things like, "Kara actually believes me, and not only that, but she wants to fight like hell for me. It's like I've been waiting my whole life for this."? Did Chana see Kara as a threat to winning the case? Or was this a Hail Mary play at the buzzer, designed to stop the clock and give her more time?

The prosecutor's reasoning was equally perplexing: Chana had spent months trying to track down the maintenance worker who appeared in Sarah's therapy notes, apparently to ask if he ever violently raped Nikki. And after the DA's Office found him, living out of state, they came to realize that he'd previously been represented by the Dutchess County Public Defender's Office. They hadn't represented him for rape, or for anything connected to Nikki, but for drunk driving. And so because of this prior representation, Chana argued in writing to the judge, Kara's office had a conflict of interest.

She characterized this maintenance worker as a crucial material witness, someone who could get on the stand and show that Nikki had a history of falsely accusing innocent men.

"There's no conflict," Kara had said when she passed on the news. She was more than confident. Kara hadn't even been working there when her office represented him, and they're assigned thousands of cases a year.

Our collective general consensus was that this appeared to be an act of desperation, a delay tactic, because the prosecution didn't have a case. "But now we have to wait for Judge McLoughlin to review the motion."

Of course, this could easily be resolved in a quick phone call or email exchange, but like everything in the legal system, it was a formal process that took time. The motion had to be written in legal-speak on oversized paper and mailed with a stamp. Then weeks would have to be allotted for the judge to read and respond. Grand jury dates were wiped off the calendar.

We waited.

My three-month family leave was coming to an end soon. I had to make a decision: Go back to work full-time, or let them fill my position. My life didn't afford me the choice of what I *wanted*. I knew where I had to be. The grand jury wasn't even on the schedule. The kids needed me. I knew I'd have to let go of a job I wanted to keep, and somehow figure out how to live on the kids' monthly social security payments, the dribbles of child support I got from Justin, and my dwindling savings account.

But when I finally decided to quit my job, an incredible thing happened: The friends of friends of friends who had been willing to donate to Nikki's bail fund started to send *me* money. All of the time and work it took to support my sister and her kids was being acknowledged by people I didn't even know. And the people who did know and love me reached out to their networks of family and friends, offering whatever they could. It felt like every drop of goodwill I had put out in the world—including my decision to take in Ben and Faye—was coming back to me. Every hard and right decision I had made was met with unforeseen support. When I finally chose to leave my job and the financial security it provided me, a colleague reached out to her influential network—a community of activists and donors—and handed me a year's worth of rent money, so at least I didn't have to worry about keeping a roof over our heads. As scared as I was for my future and my ability to take care of three kids, I also felt as if I was in an active trust-fall with the universe, and so far, there had been a safety net.

And yet I couldn't stop throwing up.

By May, the kids' springtime sickness was long gone but I was still struggling to recover. I was burned out, in a perpetual state of unwellness. Just when I thought I was feeling okay, I'd be retching over the toilet again.

It went on for so many weeks that I wondered if there was something more going on than just physical illness. It felt as though the emotional compartments inside me were overflowing, blowing the doors off their hinges.

Maybe it was pure anger wanting to be purged. My fury had been building over the past few weeks. Nikki had steeled herself to testify. She had written her story. She'd imagined saying the words in her head. I had seen her courage growing throughout the spring; now she was ready to speak. But we were still waiting for the grand jury to start—dates were constantly moved due to conflicting court dates, vacations, illness.

Anger simmered under the surface of my everyday life, and I could see it in the people around me, too. The women who had been closest to me and helped me digest the developments, who had gotten to peek through the veiled legal system, were similarly gobsmacked that something like this could happen. We had absorbed the shock of what Nikki had endured for years at home; now, together, we processed the shock of how cold and ruthless the system was in responding to it. Ours was a righteous anger that said, We aren't angry because we are hurt or sad; we are angry because *this is wrong.*

Nikki's team was cautioned that we couldn't talk to the press about how long it was taking. We couldn't post about it on social media, because the power of the State is real, and if we upset or embarrassed The System, it could easily railroad Nikki into a conviction. We were warned that this happened all the time. But that seemed like an exaggeration, an extreme act of caution.

I had a constant dull ache in the center of my torso, right below my ribs, deep in my solar plexus. I had been throwing up nearly every day for the better part of a month, when people began offering help—names of doctors and Eastern practitioners, some in fields of healing I'd never tried before.

Medical doctors affirmed that someone with a situation as complicated as mine was more likely to have a stress-related stomach ulcer, and wrote a referral for an endoscopy that I didn't have the time to schedule. Instead I leaned into the holistic practitioners—many of whom reached out to offer their own services, or who were gifted to me through certificates tucked in sympathy cards. These practitioners recognized the grief of it all; they helped.

A naturopath prescribed a simple meal plan, a dropper bottle of flower essence, and a vial of small white pellets labeled IGNATIA. I used it all.

An acupuncturist felt my wrist and asked if I knew that my body was stuck in fight-or-flight response. "You're running on adrenaline," she said, while putting a hair-thin needle in my torso. "And adrenaline is important to get us away from acute danger, a tiger or a threatening person. But we're not meant to run on adrenaline for months at a time," she said, sticking needles in my forehead. I had guessed that I was living in survival mode, but it was helpful to have that confirmed by my body.

And during a ninety-minute energy healing session, the practitioner—a woman draped in layers of fabric, with a thick Australian accent—gave me language for the persistent pain in my solar plexus. "That's your third chakra, your personal power center," she said while I lay on a warmed massage table under thick blankets, smelling frankincense and hearing the sounds of a singing bowl. I *was* feeling perpetually, relentlessly helpless. It was no wonder that my energy center was a throbbing void.

She concluded the session with a final clarifying message, identifying the root of it all: "You have a deeply broken heart."

I recognized the truth immediately. I was so completely, hopelessly, gut-wrenchingly heartbroken.

CHAPTER 26

a big cry in me

I anticipated that Mother's Day would be rough. I saw it sitting on my calendar like a land mine. And here we were, standing right on top of it. I woke up irritated.

After coming out of her month-long coma with a new diagnosis of Stage 4 cancer, my mom was transferred to a specialized New York City hospital to start treatment. Her bones were so brittle from a lifetime of steroids prescribed for her Crohn's that she had recently fractured her spine when she'd coughed. She was in constant pain and required around-the-clock care between chemo sessions, so she had moved in with her oldest sister—who was retired, and lived closer to New York City.

My Aunt Debbie rearranged her entire life to take my mom. Sisters show up. Sisters stay.

We would gather for Mother's Day at my dad's apartment, which he'd moved into three months earlier to give us all a little more space. He'd picked up my mom from my aunt's condo in Westchester that morning, and the two of them were waiting for us. It would only be a short visit, but still, my dad had been talking as if my mom would move back in with him after she'd made a full recovery. The doctors were talking in terms of *life extension*, never of cure.

Her most recent scans did show that the cancer treatment was working: The tumors were shrinking. The doctors were hopeful about the next three-month treatment. But would she live for another Mother's Day? The pressure of making this one memorable—it weighed me down to near paralysis.

The interesting thing I learned about these big, overarching feelings of grief and fear and anxiety: I had to open up the places where I held these feelings carefully, as if I were twisting the cap on a shaken-up bottle of soda so the liquid wouldn't all come spilling out. And not just whatever pertained to what I was thinking about in that moment, but *all of the grief*—the losses stacked on top of each other. Even the ordinary grief—like watching Noah grow up, and being unable to hold on to that little boy. Even the less acknowledged grief—like the loss of my personal autonomy, and the plans I had for my future. Out would spill the very many reasons my heart was broken.

When I checked in with my body and had the courage to dip into the deep well inside me, it felt like a cave of dark water, bottomless. I didn't think I could survive that depth of sadness. And I certainly didn't have time for that today. I could feel myself papering over the sadness with anger: layers of frustration and annoyance. Sadness was paralyzing. Anger had a momentum to it.

From the outside, I didn't look like a person who was sad; I looked like a woman running late to an event she didn't want to go to, sighing as she made breakfast, tossing clean silverware in the drawer loudly, hollering for the kids to pick their clothes up off the floor and get the cards they'd made for Grandma, huffing around saying that no one helped me and *for one day* I'd like to just have everyone listen to me.

I found the car keys under a mess of art supplies on the kitchen table, stepped over a bag of garbage I needed to lug out to the dumpster, and snapped at everyone to get their shoes on. We filed out like a mama duck leading her ducklings, past the wrapped Mother's Day gifts that Ben and Faye had made for Nikki in preschool and wouldn't be able to give her until she came home. Past the vase of flowers that a former boss had sent me, wanting me to feel recognized for all the unique ways I was mothering the people around me. Under the flowers was a card from Noah, a piece of red construction paper folded in half, with a big heart drawn on the front. Inside he wrote:

Dear Mom, No one can ever replace you in my heart. Love, me.

He was nine years old, with the emotional intelligence of someone far older. I could feel him watching me as I led them all down the stairs. I knew he needed me to be okay, but I wasn't.

I let Noah pick the music as I put the car in reverse. Imagine Dragons started playing through the speakers and the thump of anger got bigger as I drove ahead. I settled into my seat, hands gripping the steering wheel. It wasn't just my anger at being rapidly robbed of my mother, of having to smile and *make the best* of a Mother's Day that could be our last; it was also my anger that Nikki couldn't be here, that and the unfairness that *this* was our story.

I was angry that my mom, after a lifetime of being a good, present parent, whose overriding identity was *mother*, might have to leave this earth without rescuing the daughter she hadn't known needed saving.

I was angry that I was being asked to mother everyone, without anyone to take care of *me*. At Justin, for abandoning me and Noah. At the world, for piling so much on top of me that I couldn't even finish processing the pain and confusion of my marriage falling apart.

And somewhere at the center of this litany of rage, a deep realization came to the surface: I was mad at myself for not spending more time with my mom. My mom had been *everything* to me. Before all of this happened, I'd seen her every single day. I'd called and texted with her constantly. Yet now it felt as if she was away in the distance, floating aimlessly in the wake of my constant motion. I could already foresee the future anger I'd feel at not having taken advantage of what were potentially my last days with her, now that she was out of her coma, home from the hospital, and well enough to be driven an hour and a half to visit us. Was I using all of my compounding responsibilities as an excuse to ignore the truth that my mother was dying?

The thoughts piled up higher, pushing out tears like a release valve.

No one in the car said a word.

Two and a half songs later, I was pulling into my dad's parking lot. My mom sat on a foldout chair outside the door, two big planter pots full of soil at her feet. She was a shell of herself, emptied out by the onslaught of illness.

She wore loose pajama clothes. Her left arm was wrapped in gauze covering the TPN port in her arm, which was how she had to get her nutrients. She had a dazed look in her eyes from the medication, but a smile spread across her face when she saw us.

I felt fury rise from my chest into my throat, coming out as three little words: *Hop out, guys.* I couldn't get out myself. Not right then. I needed a little space to let this anger out before it came hurling toward the person who was in the worst position to receive it: my mom.

Ben unbuckled his car seat and leaned over to help Faye with hers. Noah climbed over and helped the others jump out. I kept my eyes on the steering wheel.

"Mom, I'm going to be right back," I said out my window, holding back tears. I saw a flash of her eyes following my car in my rearview mirror before she turned her attention to the kids.

"Who wants to plant flowers?" I heard her new, slurred voice fade as I drove away.

I pulled into an abandoned parking lot. My breathing felt shaky. Doubled over the steering wheel, I let out a ragged scream that turned into a cry, an attempt to drain the deep well of sadness.

After around ten minutes, I drove back and pulled up to the apartment with swollen eyes and a softer body. I noticed the freshly planted bright purple flowers, smiling up at the sun. I noticed the kids playing tag and laughing and had the urge to apologize. But before I did, I had to find Mom.

She was resting in bed, staring at the TV, watching housewives bicker on a reality show. She looked over at me and smiled, reaching out.

I crawled into bed next to her and held her hand. We lay in a calm silence until she looked over at me.

"I have a big cry in me," she said with a childlike simplicity. Like Ben detailing his list of losses, there was a stark vulnerability in her words. *I have a big cry in me.*

I knew that feeling. The kids knew that feeling.

But instead of releasing that cry in fits of rage or tearful tantrums, all of

Mom's sadness was stuck in her body, numbed by medication. Her mouth could hardly form words to express what was inside.

Like Nikki, she was trapped.

"Are you having a good Mother's Day?" Noah sweetly asked later that night, lying in his bed, one arm wrapped around my body. He wanted the day to be special. He wanted to be the one to make it so.

"I am, honey, thank you," I said. "It's just a hard day, with Grandma being sick and Aunt Nikki still gone." I was getting better at finding the truth under my knee-jerk instinct to sugarcoat.

"At least you got to see your mom?" Hyper-positivity was a family trait, apparently. I nodded and smiled.

"Did you like your card?" His eyes looked up at me.

"Yes!" I told him again, with as much enthusiasm as the three other times he had asked.

"I'm not always going to feel happy, even when I'm supposed to," I said gently, thinking about what Nikki would say. "There's nothing you can do to make me feel happy right now, because the sad is really big. But now that I've calmed down, I can also feel really grateful that you wanted to give me a happy day."

"You're doing a really good job," Noah said.

No part of me felt like that was true, but I accepted his love anyway.

CHAPTER 27

we stand with nikki

Forty-five days had come and gone. It was now the end of May, and there'd been no grand jury, *and* no answer from Judge McLoughlin on the motion to remove Kara from the case. And so, the morning after Nikki's 244th day of allowable jail time, Kara walked from her office down the street and into the courthouse to file a motion for Nikki's release.

I had just dropped off Ben and Faye at preschool and was sitting in my car when the phone rang.

"We've been taken off the case," Kara said, a bite to her words. I could hear her heels on the sidewalk; she was breathing hard. She sounded outraged.

"What?" I said, feeling my body deflate.

"I can't believe it! He made the decision days ago and snail-mailed it to the office. He could have called or emailed. I stood in front of him yesterday for another case, and he didn't mention anything."

"So, are you saying that Nikki has been unrepresented for days?"

"Yes," she said.

"And could Chana go to grand jury with this before Nikki has an attorney?"

"She could go to grand jury today," Kara said.

"Shit," I said. "So now what?"

"So now the State is going to assign a replacement public defender from a different county, someone who doesn't live around here and doesn't know anything about Nikki's case." Kara had by now spent eight months on preparation, Chana five months. Nikki's next attorney, whoever that might be, would be coming in cold, at a severe disadvantage.

The motion to remove Kara seemed like a strategic move on Chana's part, but she had argued, in a motion submitted to the court, that it was in Nikki's best interest for a fair trial. She acted as if she were just following the letter of the law; it was out of her hands.

"There's a hearing scheduled for tomorrow to transfer the case to the new PDs, and Nikki is going to be produced from court," Kara continued. This meant that the correctional officers would strip-search, shackle, and transport Nikki in the back of a long white police van, chained down like a stray dog going to the pound.

"The replacement attorney will file a writ for habeas corpus," Kara explained, which I knew meant that Nikki was being held unlawfully and needed to be released. It wouldn't prevent Chana from getting an indictment from the grand jury, but it would mean Nikki couldn't be kept in jail until charges were set.

"Can we show up?"

"Bring as many people as you can. Have them pack the court. Tell them to wear purple; it's the color of domestic violence."

So that's what we did.

It was a warm sunny Tuesday in early June, no rain in the forecast. That was one bit of good luck on our side; we didn't need bad weather deterring people from showing up.

I had updated a small group of people about the hearing: those who had donated, offered support, or were in positions of power and had reached out privately to be kept in the loop. Most wanted to be anonymous; very few of those with local influence would speak out in public. No domestic violence shelter or nonprofit relying on State funding, no professional PR firm or elected official, wanted visibility for fear of repercussions. But people were watching, and I emailed them all.

A growing number of activists and advocacy groups were also paying attention to the case from a distance. Over the course of a few months, I had been introduced to a grassroots network of people who'd been liberating domestic violence survivors from the carceral system for a long, long time. I downloaded their toolkits[2] about forming community defense committees and helping incarcerated people from the outside. My list of contacts had swelled to include executive directors, published authors, and celebrity activists.

The women around me who had been my legal decision sounding board and bail-fundraising helpers—Elizabeth, Sarah, Wendy, and four other friends of mine and Nikki's—started calling ourselves a committee. We had our first in-person meeting to plan the gathering. Elizabeth offered to lead the crowd in a song. We imagined what it would be like for Nikki to pull onto Market Street and hear our voices.

Although we'd often talked through text or private social media messaging, we planned this in-person gathering even more quietly. Word of mouth only—the women on the committee spent an afternoon calling their friends to give the information, along with the explicit direction not to post the information anywhere. Chris had a large family, and the gymnastics community Chris had worked with were starting to be vocal that Chris *could never* have hurt Nikki—not the man who they trusted with their young daughters. We didn't want a counter-group to show up.

Getting people to come into the City of Poughkeepsie on a Tuesday afternoon was tough. Standing in public on a street corner, aligning themselves with someone accused of murder? It was a risk.

But now was when we needed people. Not their texts or prayers or even their money; we needed bodies. The press would likely be there. The judge and the prosecutor definitely would be. More than anything, I needed Nikki to *see* that we would show up and stand together, for her.

CHAPTER 28

stand by me

I'm here," I texted the committee, women who'd grown to be my closest confidants. We were together in the trenches, bonded by trauma. I knew they were as nervous as I was.

I looked around at the quiet street. Some of the structures had been standing since the 1700s, like the courthouse on the corner, built in the Federalist style and commanding reverence and respect. You could feel that important things had happened on this ground.

This felt important, too.

Because it was all organized verbally, we had no way to know how many people would actually come. We'd had a few dozen "I'll be there" commitments, but I was worried no one would show up, and we'd be embarrassed in front of whatever media presence came to report on the scene. So far, only one news outlet had been paying consistent attention, the *Poughkeepsie Journal*, reporting a *woman shoots boyfriend for no apparent reason* narrative. The journalist assigned to Nikki's story had reached out a few times, but the cardinal legal rule I had to follow, according to every single lawyer I'd spoken to, was to never give a comment. Give the judge a chance to make a ruling before it's tried by the court of public opinion. The truth would come out in time; we just had to be patient.

Here we were, six months and forty-five days later; our patience was all dried up.

One of the first decisions we made as a committee was who would be our media spokesperson. No professional was willing to put their reputation on the line and make waves in the community by speaking publicly on Nikki's behalf. Not yet, at least. It had to be one of us.

We decided on Elizabeth. She'd scripted a statement and had sent it around to the text group, looking to find the right concise language for what we needed to say.

But would anyone be around to hear it?

I walked up and down the street, past babies being strolled and fast-walking business suits carrying cups of coffee. Gradually, I started to spot purple clothes—two people over in the far corner of Market Street, another crossing in front of the DMV. I saw Elizabeth and her husband walking toward me, holding a big cardboard box. It was filled with purple T-shirts straight from the print shop. In bold white letters they read, WE STAND WITH NIKKI.

We gravitated to the courthouse, hugged, prepared. More dots of purple moved into my periphery, making their way toward us. People started to see familiar faces and congregated in small circles lining the sidewalk. Most wanted to come find me—to say hello, to say they were sorry, to introduce themselves as a friend. I found myself moving from group to group like a hostess. My smile was genuine; I was relieved that people had come. The gathering had the energy of a funeral, where you're sorry for the circumstance that brought you here but so heartened to be together nonetheless.

Our committee was ready. Wendy passed around a clipboard to collect emails. Nearly a hundred people signed up. We gave out a sheet of paper with song lyrics on one side and a brief description of Nikki on the other. We included a drawing that Nikki had made in jail. It was the shape of a woman portrayed as a tree, with winding interconnected branches that attached to roots deep beneath her.

In front of me, I was witnessing seedlings born of those roots, a community sprouting up around her.

Elizabeth stood at the top of the stairs leading up to the courthouse, about to speak to the crowd. Most of us were in purple, ranging from deep royal to shades of lilac and mauve. Some carried signs saying, I BELIEVE NIKKI.

I was desperate for Nikki to turn the corner and see the way we brightened up the sidewalk, noticeably distinct from the drab professionals cutting their way through our group to get inside the courthouse.

The journalist from the *Poughkeepsie Journal* took photos. This was the narrative shift we needed. Instead of the papers reporting dully that *no motive has been found for the killing*, they could show the truth in vibrant color.

On top of the stairs, Elizabeth cleared her throat and began speaking without the aid of a microphone, stretching her voice louder than the roar of the cars barreling down the one-way road behind us.

"We are here for Nicole Addimando, Nikki—a mom, friend, and beloved community member to so many of us here," she started, thanking everyone for coming.

"As a community we need to keep an eye on what's happening with Nikki's case, and the injustice that's happening to her." Elizabeth spoke with a steady voice. "She's held in Dutchess County Jail without bail, without adequate representation, and she has been held now past the time when she can be held without indictment. So, we have a real reason to be gathering here today, and we have important work to do."

She went on to use phrases like *abuse of power* and *failure of our system*—words I'd wanted to scream from the rooftop for months. I nodded. It felt good to hear it all said out loud.

Toward the corner of the building, my mom was sitting in a wheelchair with my aunts—her sisters—standing on either side. She was wearing an oversized purple T-shirt with my aunt's handwriting in Sharpie: I STAND WITH NIKKI. A baseball cap covered her balding head and a mask on her face shielded her from germs, but I could see her eyes smiling.

"We are a small town in one tiny part of America," Elizabeth continued. "But this is happening all over. For many of us, this is our first exposure to the injustice of the system—"

Suddenly two officers bolted out the front doors of the courthouse.

"Whoa, whoa, whoa," they said, cutting Elizabeth off.

"Ma'am, you can't be blocking the door. You need to keep this area clear," said a woman in a dark blue uniform with a shiny gold badge, her hair pulled back tight.

Elizabeth was polite. We were all accommodating, shuffling over to the side of the building to finish.

A white-haired officer pulled me aside with a smile. "Listen, let me give you some advice to keep you out of trouble," he said. "Never block doors or entrances, stay out of the road, and get a permit next time. Oh. And you wouldn't be able to wear that shirt inside," he added, pointing to my purple I STAND WITH NIKKI tee. "You can't wear any public statements of support in front of the judge."

Noted. I still had so much to learn.

Nikki's replacement attorney, a younger guy with thick brown eyebrows, came out the door, flashed me a smile, and motioned for me to stand to the side. I had never met him before. I could hear Elizabeth regrouping with the crowd, directing them to the song sheet on their handout.

"She won't be produced today," he said. "The hearing has been taken off the docket."

Unbelievable. No explanation given, all of this support and Nikki would never see it.

The singing started, the words to the song "Stand by Me." We had hoped she'd hear it from the courthouse, to feel less alone up there.

But she wasn't coming.

"When the night has come."

"I filed the writ of habeas corpus," the attorney added. "There will be a hearing tomorrow. It's a long shot. Judges, especially around here, tend to side with the prosecution." I nodded my head. I had already seen this happen.

"Speaking of that, let me ask you a question," I said. "Before Judge McLoughlin was a judge, he was the bureau chief of the Dutchess County DA's Office, during the time when the DA's office had evidence that Nikki was a victim of abuse. So if the DA's Office had to recuse themselves because of a conflict, then how is it not a conflict for Judge McLoughlin to be her trial judge? And clearly he's biased against Nikki, considering his crazy ruling to remove Kara."

He nodded as I talked, as most attorneys did when I pointed out blatant inconsistencies. So often, my comments were met with a dismissive "This is just the way things are."

The attorney considered my question. "There are a lot of protections for judges when it comes to conflicts of interest, because so many judges used to be prosecutors," he said. "I can file a motion, but it's likely not going to be approved. Judge McLoughlin would need to decide for himself whether or not there's a conflict.

"I can continue to be your sister's lawyer," he continued, "but you should know that I'm transferring to another county, so I won't be able to keep the case for long. I'd need to move you to another replacement attorney."

"I think we're going to just hire a private attorney," I replied, exhausted.

"That's a good idea." He nodded. "I have some people I recommend; I'll send you a text. And I'll give you more details about tomorrow soon."

"No, I won't be afraid."

I watched him walk away and turned my attention back to the music sheet in my hand. I could only listen, staring at the paper as a blank screen for the thoughts jumping across my mind.

The voices pressed around me, stretching down the sidewalk out of view. All these people had shown up, not knowing that Nikki wasn't up in the top window of the courthouse, but streets and concrete walls away from their song.

Looking around at the crowd, I felt myself fill up with a love that was intended for my sister. If she couldn't be here to feel it, I'd feel it for the both of us. All these people! And they weren't just here for her, or for me. We were all here for each other.

The next lyrics in the song were changed. All around me I heard voices sing:

"So sister, sister, stand by me."

CHAPTER 29

immediate release

Just as the replacement attorney had promised, the next day there was a hearing, and his replacement—another brand-new attorney—was assigned to represent Nikki.

Many of the same crowd showed up to the same sidewalk, again wearing shades of purple—and, as instructed, minus the slogans of support. I entered the courtroom with the attendees, while some stayed outside to protest. Wendy stood with a clipboard, directing people like an usher—*third floor, you'll need to empty your pockets, keep your phone turned off.*

Because this was a habeas corpus hearing, it got kicked up to a higher court, and we were now going to a different courtroom on a different floor, the name HONORABLE MARIA G. ROSA on the door.

I followed my body up the stairs into an unfamiliar room and sat down next to Elizabeth. She was wearing a plum purple wraparound dress with matching leggings, and she scooted over to make room for me on the wooden bench. I didn't have any purple clothes clean—my laundry baskets were overspilling with more clothes than I'd ever had to wash—so instead I wore the closest I could find: light pink pants with a white top, and a purple sports bra underneath. I had pinned a purple ribbon above my heart.

People had been posting photos with the hashtag "#WeStandWithNikki" on social media, and the journalist who had shown up the day before had written an article with the title MURDER SUSPECT NICOLE ADDIMANDO SUFFERED "HORRIFIC ABUSE," LAWYER SAYS. The journalist had also posted a clip of our "Stand by Me" rendition to her personal Facebook page.

On the way over earlier, I had wondered if a counterprotest would erupt.

I wondered whether Chris's family would come to the courthouse. Neither happened. That gave me hope.

There was what felt like an endless span of delays: The new defense attorney was late, Chana was late—and before producing Nikki (who I knew was sitting somewhere in the building, scared and alone), the judge gave Nikki and her new attorney time to meet each other in the jury room. He had never set eyes on Nikki before and likely had little time to read her file. That gave me less hope.

I experienced the day in sensations: sheets of anxiety falling like rain from my head down to my feet; my throat tight from all the words I couldn't say—*let her go, please help her, please please please.* I eyed the door, wondering how far the nearest bathroom was in case my bowels suddenly decided to empty.

There was a waist-high divider separating us and Nikki, who now stood at the defendant table on the right, next to her towering attorney in a gray suit. Her feet were shackled together, and the chain around her waist was wrapped around twice, her hands cuffed in front of her.

The new defense attorney started.

"Your Honor, Defendant acknowledges that there has been a change in counsel recently and that might have contributed to some confusion in the procedural status of this case—" *An understatement*, I thought. *Was it normal for a case to be passed around like a hot potato? No wonder Nikki was confused.* "However, there was no confusion that the Dutchess County Public Defender waived this case to the grand jury," meaning that Nikki didn't consent to more delays. "The People had the responsibility to present this case and obtain an indictment within forty-five days pursuant to Criminal Procedure Law 190.80." The attorney spoke clearly and confidently. I looked over to Kara, who was sitting in the front row behind Chana's table, and she nodded along in agreement. "At my count it is now fifty-one days since that date."

To the left of the room, standing behind another table, was Chana, wearing a skirt suit and kitten heels. The judge asked her why the prosecution couldn't get the case to the grand jury within the forty-five-day time frame, and Chana launched into a monologue, her brown hair bobbing in time with her fast-talking arguments—she claimed the lengthy investigation was done at the request of the defense.

"We secured documents that *they* couldn't, we interviewed witnesses because *they* asked us to—" she said, her face was red.

She continued: "Defense was unable to get her CPS reports. We knocked on doors until we finally got the CPS records and provided them to the defense." I watched the back of Kara's head from the first row, furiously shaking her head no.

"Defense was unable to get her therapy notes that predated her relationship with Mr. Grover...we received those records. We knocked on doors until we got those records." I glanced over at Sarah, who shot me an *Is she kidding me?* look. Sarah voluntarily sat for a deposition and had made herself more than available to both the defense and the prosecution from day one. What doors was she knocking on?

"We conducted every bit of investigation and then some that *they* asked us to do because it was important," she concluded.

She detailed the defense's case from her perspective, despite that not being part of the judge's question:

"*They* outlined to me allegations that their client had said she had a history of sexual and physical abuse starting at the age of seven—"

Five, I thought, again stunned that facts could be rewritten in real time.

"*They* indicated that there was sexual and physical abuse by another individual when she was a teenager"—meaning the maintenance worker, while Nikki was in college—"and then proceeded to outline a very serious and horrific allegation of sexual and physical abuse by someone other than Mr. Grover who is not here to defend himself," she said, referring again to the maintenance worker, but making it sound like she was talking about different people.

I could see what she was doing, clear as day. Laying the foundation for slut shaming, victim blaming, and lying.

"I had a full confession from the Defendant and I had a young man that was dead. This case could have proceeded to the grand jury very quickly," she said, emphasizing that the delay was at the defense's urging request.

I watched the judge's impassioned face through the long rant. "Okay. This was all before the April 11, 2018, Notice to Produce to the grand jury? So, what happened since then?"

I'd learned to hear through the legal-speak, and I understood what she meant: *Okay, so you did a long investigation at the defense's request—but then once the defense asked for the case to move to the grand jury, why didn't you?*

"Grand jury was set for May second"—nearly a month earlier—"and the Defendant was told she would be the first one to testify," Chana said, explaining that Nikki's testimony would lay the foundation for the rest of the witnesses.

"So why didn't it proceed on May second?" Judge Rosa asked, to which Chana and Judge Rosa went back and forth about the attorney replacement debacle, and that Chana couldn't produce Nikki to testify in front of a grand jury before she'd spoken to Nikki's new counsel—which, even up to that day in court, was still in flux. It was like watching a Ping-Pong match, as the two women paddled arguments back and forth, and all of us in the audience watched in hushed silence. Nikki's new attorney simply offered that nothing was stopping Chana from presenting the case without Nikki's testimony, starting with different witnesses while the attorney situation was sorted out (*a situation created by Chana*, I thought).

I was desperate to know what the judge was thinking. Was she buying Chana's rhetoric?

The judge left the chamber to make a decision. We all sat and waited, whispering quietly among ourselves.

Nikki sat still, her arms wrapped around her pale, slight body. I stared at the back of her dark hair, willing her to look back at me, to see the faces of all those present who loved and supported her; she never did.

I don't know how long it took for the judge to walk back in, *all rise*, but I could feel the silence ringing in my ears, the air thick with anticipation. I held my breath while the judge began.

"I've considered the arguments made here today and of course I've considered the law, and just to summarize, it is clear that once someone is arraigned, held without bail, they are supposed to be indicted or released within forty-five days, but there's a number of circumstances under which that release does not take place, including what happened here—"

My heart sank. Her words became muffled in my loud brain, as I steeled myself for the stomach-drop disappointment.

And then suddenly—"There's no proof offered that Ms. Addimando consented after April sixteenth to have those grand jury proceedings delayed any further..."

Elizabeth and I looked at each other; our knees pressed together, an unspoken *is this really happening?* between us.

"...So therefore I find there was not good cause to exceed the statutory deadline and I'm granting the writ and ordering Ms. Addimando released."

Released.

There was an uproar, a great, loud cheer. People began applauding.

I sat completely still, watching the faces around me—happy tears, big smiles. Chana strode out of the room, her face wearing a look of fury that shot right through me. The judge had a slight smile on her face before retreating back to her chambers. None of the stone-faced guards quieted us down, and if they did, I didn't hear them. *Oh my God*, I thought, *Ben and Faye are going to see their mom!*

ghosts

I had known this was a possibility, but until Judge Rosa actually said the words, no part of me had truly believed that Nikki would be released. I hadn't allowed myself to imagine it. We'd endured one worst-case scenario after another; a series of injustices dismissed, downplayed, and unreported— why would this be any different?

And yet, it was. She was coming home. That night.

All of us in the courtroom made our way down the white marble staircase, our loud celebratory voices echoing around us. My legs felt like jelly.

We walked out to a sunny afternoon on the same sidewalk where we'd stood the day before, demanding justice. Around twenty or so people stuck around to hug one another and digest what we'd just witnessed. A smaller group of us broke away to start serious next-step planning: How do we get Nikki? What do we need to bring? Where do we take her?

I was riding a surge of vindication. We exchanged *Did you see Chana's face?* banter, dissecting what her expression had said about her state of mind and ability to argue a case. Was she humiliated? Would she retaliate? Nikki's release didn't change the fact that the grand jury would be fully in Chana's control. It was going to happen, and seeing how mad Chana was, it would likely happen fast.

Nikki would need lawyers, *good* lawyers, immediately.

Sarah offered to call two local attorneys and try to get appointments. Elizabeth texted Kara to get information on when and how to pick Nikki up. Even though she was no longer Nikki's attorney, Kara continued to offer help and support. She had become attached to this case—and to Nikki. She was mad as hell not to be the one up against Chana.

Nikki's childhood friend Caitlin had been in the courtroom, too. Since that first visit at the jail, she and Nikki had reconnected through letters and visits. And because she knew the discharge process from firsthand experience, she joined us on the sidewalk to pass on protocol. "Someone will have to get clothes for her. All of the clothes she was arrested in will have been bagged for evidence in the New York State Crime Lab, so she needs something new to wear home."

I never would have thought of that. All of Nikki's clothes were boxed up in my garage, but I did have one pair of her shoes in my car trunk. Caitlin offered to go to the Family Dollar on Main Street to buy Nikki a new outfit, and regroup with me and Elizabeth at the jail.

I went straight to DCJ. Elizabeth was already in the visiting room, standing with another childhood friend of Nikki's still wearing her purple I STAND WITH NIKKI shirt. Within minutes, Caitlin showed up with a bag of clothes, which she handed off to a correctional officer.

We seemed to wait for an eternity. Everything felt surreal, like a dream inside a nightmare. Then suddenly the heavy metal door opened, and there she was. My Nikki. My sister. Her body was emaciated, even smaller than I had realized during our visits. The baggy orange jumpsuit she typically wore had always hung on her, obscuring her figure. Now she wore a thin white T-shirt that Caitlin found at the Family Dollar, and the purple leggings that Elizabeth had been wearing in the courtroom—taken right off her body in the jail's parking lot. I could see Nikki's hips protrude over her stick-thin legs. I could have wrapped my thumb and pointer finger around her ankle.

"Hi, sister," she said, opening her arms.

"Hi, hi, hi," I whispered, hugging her back tightly.

We pulled apart and looked at each other in stunned amazement, her expression mirroring what my brain was repeating on a loop: *Is this really happening?*

We all took turns embracing, reminding one another that we were real, that this was all real. Caitlin's hug lasted longer than the rest, until their whispered greetings turned into sobs, slowly subsiding.

Nikki walked over to me with news. "Butch died," she said with an air of disbelief. "It feels like a ghost just left my body."

As she spoke, I noticed men with cameras outside the large window, and saw that there was no way for life to snap back to normal. "Let me pull my car up," I announced, "and let's get ready to go before more news cameras show up."

Minutes later, Nikki, supported by Elizabeth on one side and two of her oldest friends on the other, walked out into a day of freedom.

No bail terms.

No ankle monitor.

Hell, she didn't even have a lawyer.

For a moment, she was free.

Caitlin waved goodbye as Nikki climbed into the back seat and squeezed between the kids' car seats. As Elizabeth got in the passenger seat, I watched through my rearview mirror: Nikki pulled out the books her babies had been reading, the crayons they'd been holding—evidence of a life she missed. She touched their car seats, like she had been air-dropped into this life that looked familiar but was unrecognizable.

I felt like that, too.

Nikki wanted to go straight to Ben and Faye, who were home with my dad, but their reunion had to wait. An attorney named John was available to meet with Nikki that same night, and time was of the essence. So, with Elizabeth and Nikki in the car, I pulled out of the jail parking lot, and I set my GPS to John's Newburgh office, a forty-minute ride across the Hudson River. We picked up Sarah on the way. We were four free women on an open road.

We didn't know much about this attorney other than over the past week his name had been recommended more than any other. We'd already been down the path of trying to find a private attorney with a New York license who had successfully represented women like Nikki—those who'd fought back and killed their abusers in order to defend themselves. That had been a short ride down a dead-end street.

This was strange to me, considering that Nikki's situation was not a once-in-a-generation phenomenon. A quick Google search showed a long history of documented cases, spanning back to the 1960s and '70s. One, from 1977, nearly a decade before I was born, set a legal and cultural precedent when a woman named Francine Hughes set her abusive ex-husband's bed on fire while he slept, and she was acquitted by a jury. The case was memorialized in a book, *The Burning Bed*, in 1980, then made into a TV movie starring Farrah Fawcett, one of the biggest stars of the time. According to the think-pieces I read, the notoriety of the Burning Bed case created a national conversation on the realities of intimate partner violence and how law enforcement responds to it, and helped create a new legal defense that would later be described as the "battered woman syndrome."

Yet the number of attorneys practicing in New York who had found success in using that defense was exactly one—a man the *New York Times* profiled in 2011 with the headline: QUEENS LAWYER'S NICHE: DEFENDING ABUSED WOMEN WHO KILL. He'd spent more than thirty years representing wives who'd killed their husbands, and helped juries understand that the post-traumatic stress of living in a violent home, especially ones with a high level of lethality, is like living in a combat zone. The battered-woman defense, as I understood it, aimed to show that the killing wasn't an isolated event—but rather a long process, a trackable escalation, that ends in someone being dead (usually the woman)—and it was reasonable for her to have feared for her life.

I don't even know how I got hold of that man's phone number, but I did. I called him, and found out that, at eighty years old, he had just taken his last case. It was well beyond time for him to retire, and as he told me, these kinds of cases take time and an emotional toll that he couldn't sustain anymore. Even if he could have taken the case, there were also very real political considerations to factor in. It wasn't simply, *Who is the best person to represent Nikki*, but also, *Who will perform best for this particular judge in this specific county?* John was pitched to us along with the explanation that Judge McLoughlin didn't like big New York City lawyers coming in and peacocking in his courtroom. The jury pool, I was told, was also a conservative-thinking bunch, and a homegrown defense attorney would likely play better than an "elite" outsider.

But it was impossible to find a practicing attorney with a battered-woman-defense background within a twenty-five-mile radius. As one lawyer on a free consult phone call told me: "The person you're looking for doesn't exist."

But John existed. He was a Hudson Valley staple in the courthouse, well liked and respected, known to do a good job and not ruffle feathers. He was also available, and we were running out of time.

I pulled off the highway and into the large shopping hub of Newburgh. John's office was tucked behind a row of fast-food drive-throughs and gas stations.

I stepped out into an empty parking lot, and Nikki followed me. She hadn't been in any building other than the jail and courthouse in almost nine months. It was now early June. She'd missed fall and winter entirely. Her skin was almost translucent, deprived of sunlight. Another committee member pulled in next to us, and John came out of the darkened building, a middle-aged man wearing wire-framed glasses and a button-down shirt.

As he greeted us, his eyes landed on Nikki. "You look like you're fifteen!" he said, as if this was a good thing.

We all followed him into the eerily quiet office, motion-sensored lights guiding the way.

"Here we go," he said, dragging two more chairs into his office, and the five of us crammed together in front of a desk stacked high with file folders. On the wall was a newspaper clipping of a smiling woman walking out of a courthouse, a victim who had stabbed her abuser. John had helped get her acquitted on a retrial.

"She was this really pathetic woman..." he started, launching into the story of how she stabbed her abuser. I bristled at his description; it was clear, through context, that he was using the word to mean *pitiful,* but the word was jarring.

I watched Nikki taking it all in. After countless meetings I'd sat in just like this, sitting in front of Very Important professional people discussing Nikki's past and future, finally Nikki had a seat in the room. I wouldn't need to relay this information like a game of telephone; she was *here.* The surreality lingered.

We all took turns talking, with Sarah doing most of the heavy lifting on Nikki's story—the escalation that she had become aware of during therapy sessions, specific assaults that sent Nikki to the hospital, and what happened the night of the shooting. When Nikki spoke, her voice was small, her sentences short.

"I like the facts of this case," John told us, just like the original investigator had said. He liked that she had shot Chris only once. He liked all the evidence of abuse, the abundance of witnesses who stepped forward. We told him we'd have to fundraise the legal costs, and so he suggested teaming up with another local attorney—a man named Ben, who had been recommended to us with almost as much frequency as John. They'd do it for a reduced rate: They'd cut their retainer fees down to $30,000 each.

We discussed the meeting on the ride home. None of us were wowed by John, but we were also exhausted by decisions. We rationalized his paternalistic language. *He's a man from another era*, we said. *He seems to believe you, Nikki*, we agreed. We needed him to be Nikki's attorney, and we left his office that night prepared to move onto the next step: the legal fight for Nikki's life.

reunion

Nikki had called my parents on the way home, and I heard my mom openly weep on speakerphone. My dad was more composed, saying, "I can't wait to see you, honey, sleep well." It was long past the kids' bedtime once we got back into Poughkeepsie, so Nikki had decided to sleep at Elizabeth's for the night, then surprise the kids first thing in the morning.

I woke up happy.

"Someone's coming to visit," I said in a singsong voice after feeding and dressing the kids. I had put them in clothes I thought Nikki would like—Ben's favorite blue whale T-shirt, and a summery floral dress for Faye. Elizabeth had just texted that they were pulling into the complex.

"Is it Mom?" Ben's eyes were wide and eager.

I smiled as my phone flashed with a text from Elizabeth's phone. "We're here."

"Wait, Aunt Nikki is back?" Noah's head poked out from his lofted bedroom like a meerkat popping out of a hole.

"She's not back for good, but she's allowed to visit for a few days." I wanted to manage their expectations. But the kids had stopped listening; I might as well have told them that Santa and his reindeer were parked outside. Their bodies brightened and unfurled like flowers rising to the sun.

Their excitement was contagious: "And she's pulling into the parking lot right about...now," I added playfully.

The three of them bolted down the stairs and threw open the door. I followed close behind.

Nikki climbed out of the passenger side of Elizabeth's sedan, and immediately ran toward us, arms open. She was wearing the same white shirt as yesterday, but with a clean pair of Elizabeth's old faded blue jeans.

Faye was in the lead, curls bouncing, arms outstretched, little pink rubber shoes slapping the sidewalk. "MOMMY!"

"Hi, baby girl," she cried as Faye jumped into her arms. Nikki pulled her up onto her shoulder, somehow finding strength. Ben was a millisecond behind and leapt up onto Nikki's other shoulder, legs dangling next to Faye. Nikki held them both to her face, one baby on either side, as she knelt down in the shade of a tree. The sun was high, and a warm, brilliant light was filtering through the leaves overhead.

"Hi," she cried, kneeling down to their level, pulling back to look at them, at Ben's new height, Faye's longer hair. She kissed both of their faces, repeating, "Oh I love you, oh I love you."

They had spent eight months and sixteen days apart, wishing for this moment. I watched her breathe in their necks, their hair. She was crying. Their body language looked primal, expressing a deep hunger for physical connection after so much time apart.

Noah ran over to join the group hug. Ben looked up from his mom's embrace and over at me and Elizabeth, watching through tears. "You two are mean," he said, eyebrows furrowed.

Neither of us took it personally. We knew he was feeling a mess of emotions all at once, and it was safer for him to be mad at us than at some invisible force that had kept them apart. He certainly wasn't willing to be mad at Nikki.

"They're not mean; they just brought Mommy home to see you," Nikki said, and Ben threw himself back into another hug. Faye stayed wrapped around Nikki's shoulders, a big smile on her face.

Noah leaned over and stuck his head into Nikki's sightline, waving and smiling, with a look that said, *I'm here, too!*

I watched Nikki's eyes scan my baby, taking in his changing face, his longer arms. Tears spilled down her cheeks, past her smile.

"Oh my God! Noah! You're so big!" She wiped her tears away and brightened at the little boy who had grown inches since she'd last seen him.

I stood in the background, watching it all unfold on my phone's camera, knowing this was something that needed to be documented, and also giving myself a buffer between watching the emotions on the screen and feeling them myself.

"We're all different ages," Ben announced proudly. "I'm five, Faye's three, and Noah is nine."

They were welcoming her back to a life that had taken shape in her absence, to a home that had stretched to fit us all.

In a blur of excitement, Ben and Faye ran inside to "get something," squealing up and down the stairs. They bounded back toward her holding the wrapped Mother's Day gifts they'd been keeping, painted wooden picture frames, with a photo of each of them at preschool.

My camera panned to Nikki on the lawn, her bony hands pressing down into the earth, reuniting with the natural world, as her kids clambered on and off her lap.

My camera captured Nikki picking up Faye under her arms and spinning her in circles, Faye's legs billowing out, her laugh calling up to the treetops; Ben and Noah showing off their speed skills, as if to say, *Look at me! See how big and strong I am now? Aren't you impressed?*"—and Nikki, getting up to run with them, racing across an imaginary finish line with Faye in her arms. I didn't know how she was running, let alone walking. She looked like she hadn't eaten a real meal in months. She'd been existing inside a cage. She'd told me she was barely sleeping from the night terrors.

But there, under that warm sun, she was happy. Radiant. Whole.

I felt it, too—something like grace.

Of all the days Nikki could have been reunited with her kids, today was a good one: It was the day of their preschool's annual art show. And there was no court restriction preventing Nikki from going.

We decided to wait until the art show was *just* about to end, in the hope of avoiding uncomfortable run-ins with other parents. It also gave Nikki time to reunite with our mom and dad, who showed up within thirty minutes of her homecoming. My mom—wearing one of the tie-dye shirts that Nikki had made—practically collapsed in Nikki's arms, crying into her neck. Nikki hugged her back, cradling the back of Mom's head. Faye toddled over and reached up, wrapping her small arms around Nikki's waist, and I stood back to take a picture of three generations of women tangled together in grief and love.

Around four thirty, we headed out to the art show. Noah stayed back with my parents, and the rest of us piled into my car and took the familiar route to preschool. The front seat was empty; Nikki chose to sit between Ben and Faye's car seats. Ben tied himself to his mom with a thin red scarf, unwilling to let her go. He'd brought his ukulele to play for her, just like he used to. I hadn't seen him pick it up in months.

"I used to go this route in my mind every day," Nikki said. I could hear what she was saying underneath: *God, I've missed taking them to school.*

The classroom was in the basement of the teacher's house. On the left of the room was a row of small windows, on the right, a painting center. Book and play areas were tucked in the corners. Today, every available inch of wall space was used to display the kids' artwork, each piece mounted on larger colored paper that included their names, self-written titles, and a brief description.

Faye led Nikki by the hand, introducing her to a part of her life that her mom had not yet seen—pointing out the dress-up area, bringing her to the book rug, telling stories about things that happened in those places.

Nikki's eyes stopped in front of one of Faye's paintings, and she gestured for me to look.

Title: My Mom in her House All These golden dots Are to Keep Her Safe

By: Faye

It was a picture of a smiling Nikki, stick hands stretched outward, surrounded by bright gold dots. The title said "in her House," but there was no house. Just the earth—tall blades of green grass, a high yellow sun. The other families had cleared out pretty quickly, leaving the four of us to our private art show. We traveled from one picture to the next.

After wandering through the artwork and the surroundings, Ben wrapped his arms around his mom's waist. "Let's go home," he said, looking up at her through his long eyelashes. "I've been wanting to say that for a long time."

"Me too." Nikki smiled.

surrender

With Nikki home, we all relaxed into freedom. Freedom from confinement, freedom from constant worry about whether she was okay. Freedom from the grip of a strange and terrible reality. Her homecoming was a great loosening, a long-held breath exhaled, but we weren't able to enjoy the feeling for long. Within a day of her return, her time was swallowed up by meetings with attorneys, logistics, and the sobering reality that her release had a time limit.

Ben and Faye could finally be rocked to sleep, but they fought sleep—we all did—as if we weren't quite sure if this would all be gone when we opened our eyes again.

And so most nights Nikki and I found a reason to drive the kids around the neighborhood before bedtime, giving all of us space to settle our nervous systems before facing the end of another day.

I enjoyed driving under a setting sun on the country roads of upper Dutchess County. There was a particular route I liked to take, up past the Christmas tree farm and pumpkin patch, over toward the open fields of Hyde Park, where our former high school selves had congregated around bonfires with kegs, and looping back to one particular west-facing road with hundreds of acres of unused flat land on either side stretching out to the sky like a canvas. And if I timed it just right, we could drive under a panoramic sunset, a mesmerizing light show.

I liked hearing the little gasps of awe from the back seat; having an excuse to point out the beauty and wonder. I liked the way I could feel the kids falling asleep without looking at the back seat—the way my body settled into their calm. And I liked it so much more with Nikki in the passenger seat, sharing these intimate moments. I looked over at her, her eyes focused on the sky, watching the colors fade like a paintbrush dipped in water. A dark night would slowly bleed through, the moon illuminating what had always been true: We were two sisters driving on a spinning rock in space, unsure of how much more time we'd have together.

It was our own private bubble. We could forget for a moment that any day it could and would be popped by forces bigger and more powerful than us. But inevitably, a detail would come careening toward us, puncturing that fragile sense of safety. One such detail was the attorneys' $60,000 non-refundable retainer fee which we'd need to wrangle right away in order to hire them.

It was an unfathomable amount of money—$60,000 was more than I made in a year, and more than any assets or savings that I, Nikki, and our parents had combined. Our online crowdfunding efforts were only beginning, and we had raised less than half of what we needed. Most of the philanthropists we knew had already pledged to give money to the bail fund, which was just as important as this retainer, and we were stretching our networks thin with a continuous plea for donations.

Two women stepped up to pay it—Elizabeth's mom and my Aunt Debbie. Neither of them was wealthy—and so we promised to return the funds—but they both gave willingly.

Elizabeth's mom had never met Nikki, but she was a surrogate sister to Elizabeth, and that was enough.

My aunt, who was now my mom's full-time caregiver, didn't have children of her own and had always supported her sisters and their children. She was a retired New York City schoolteacher who lived on a pension. Yet she didn't think twice about depleting a significant chunk of her savings. "This is why I have this money," she told me. "To help my family."

Getting that retainer fee together produced a collective sigh of relief—and set another chain of events into motion. As soon as the attorneys were on board, negotiations started with the DA's Office. But Chana's tone was markedly different than how she had started her communication with Kara at the beginning. Instead of words like *collaborative* and *hopeful*, John was using words like *contentious* and *furious* to describe their back-and-forth, assumed to be a by-product of the humiliation Chana had felt at the habeas corpus hearing. John told us that Chana wanted Nikki back in jail immediately, *or else*—*or else* she'd rush to the grand jury without any defense witnesses and easily secure a murder charge; *or else* she'd fight for Nikki to be remanded with no bail, *or else* Nikki would be arrested as soon as the grand jury indicted her, at any time, and likely in front of her kids.

I worried that Nikki wouldn't physically survive another stint in jail. My sister vomited up any kind of food we gave her. Her body was collapsing under the stress. After debating whether Nikki needed to go to a hospital for severe malnourishment, an RN we knew from high school risked her license to bring over a bag of fluids in an IV drip, which seemed to bring some vitality back to her face.

I continued shuttling the kids to school and activities, and now began driving Nikki back and forth to John's office forty minutes away. Plus, she had so many appointments to get to. She needed her newly graying hair cut and colored in case we couldn't get her out of jail again before trial. (No amount of *"fuck you"* energy would change the fact that a jury would be more sympathetic toward an attractive, younger-looking defendant.) I took her to an acupuncturist and a chiropractor to help ease the compounded stress and trauma she held in her body.

Our committee meetings increased in frequency, and we explored fundraising and press strategies. There was no way for me to do all of it, so I delegated to-dos—like finding a crowdfunding platform that allowed for open legal cases, setting up a We Stand With Nikki website and email list, and sending thank-you notes to donors.

As the days ticked by, calls with Nikki's attorneys began to reveal a quality we hadn't recognized from the outset: their deferential attitude toward the prosecution. They appeared to be playing a chess game, arguing that the move of giving the DA what she wanted now would result in a more favorable win in the end. They wanted Nikki to voluntarily surrender herself and return to jail before Chana convened a grand jury. It would look good to the judge in a bail application, they said, showing Nikki wasn't a flight risk. It would keep the lines of communication open with the prosecution, something that was important to the attorneys because they were operating under such a severe time disadvantage. It would also "extend an olive branch," as John said, a sign that Nikki was willing to cooperate with the system.

This wasn't something I could push back on—not without being met with the same "*This is just how it is*" kind of attitude I was now accustomed to hearing from anyone connected to the justice system. So Nikki agreed to play their game in the hope that it would get her back home faster—except she was the pawn, being asked to forfeit her freedom, her health, her *children*, the most unnatural thing to ask of her. And the game, I feared, felt eternally rigged against her.

It was a Wednesday. Nikki had been home a week. "We were able to negotiate for a surrender on Monday," John said over the speakerphone in Nikki's hand. We were sitting in my car, about to drive to preschool pickup. She lowered the phone to her lap; her eyes found mine. Monday. That left us only five more days of togetherness.

He delivered the news as if it were a gift. "She really wanted you back by the end of last week, but we got you a few more days."

Knowing the official countdown had begun caused us to slow down. Rather than rushing from one appointment to the next, we hunkered down at my dad's apartment for long stretches. My mom hadn't gone back downstate to my aunt's after Mother's Day. Instead, she slept in her familiar bed with my dad, and we all helped with the complicated intravenous nutritional system given to her through the port in her arm. Her gaze was still a bit faraway, a side effect of her pain medication and stroke damage. She spent most days sitting on the couch, looking out at her daughters and grandkids, a childlike smile spread unevenly across her bloated face, pulling on a vape pen that she'd gotten at a medical cannabis dispensary. She needed a cane to move from one place to another, but when Nikki was around, they often walked arm in arm, their diminutive bodies holding each other up. Their eyes scanned each other's faces, taking in every detail, brimming with tears.

Ben's music filled the space around us, a familiar sound from a past life. While my parents and Nikki sat on the couch, the kids put on performances, twirling, laughing, and dancing. It was too beautiful—and devastating—to fully take in.

At intervals, I'd exit through the screened back door, taking calls, answering texts, sending out group emails with next-step updates. Go, go, go.

And yet something in me knew enough to sink below the turbulence and pause, to sit on the folding chairs propped outside the back door, next to a grill no one used and a towering tree canopied over a small plot of grass. After one performance had wrapped up, the kids came out to climb the tree. Eventually, Nikki's inner tree-climbing child came out, too, and joined them.

"Do you think I can just stay up here?" Nikki smiled down from the branches, sunlight streaming from behind, casting a glow on the lush green leaves around her. The kids had scattered to play on the grass and it felt as if the weather was conspiring in our favor, giving us a bright blue sky as a backdrop to these moments. I sat on one folding chair, my mom next to me, and craned my neck to see Nikki's face. She looked so peaceful, so happy, so *normal*.

"Do you think they'll find me?" she teased.

She could have run. Nothing was stopping her. No ankle bracelet. No warrant for her arrest. No travel restrictions. She could have taken those kids and got the hell out of the country, if that's what she'd wanted to do.

But running hadn't ever been an option—not from Chris, not by suicide, and not even from the police officer who, on that dark September morning, pulled up behind her at a green light and blew his air horn for her to go. She chose to stop. To stay. Didn't that count for anything?

"Come down from there, you silly!" Faye stood at the base of the tree trunk, looking up at her mom, radiant in the afternoon light.

"That's my Nik-nik," my mom slurred, her voice melodic and wistful. I wondered if she was looking up at Nikki and seeing the adventurous little girl we once knew.

Nikki climbed down the branches, jumping to solid ground.

Over on the grass, a squabble broke out between Ben and Noah over the bounds of their race and the rightful winner. While I stood up to referee, Nikki crouched down next to our mom. By the time I got back to my seat, Nikki was standing behind our mom's chair with a pair of tweezers in her hand. With one hand on Mom's forehead, she leaned over and tenderly groomed her eyebrows.

I felt a swell of a feeling too complex to name rise in my chest. Something like awe mingled with grief wrapped in gratitude. I felt the urge to slow the earth to a standstill, to freeze time exactly as we were—Nikki caring for our mom's rapidly dying body in ways she might never get to do again; the kids shrieking and laughing and my dad walking toward us, both hands behind his back, a big smile on his face.

"I have a surprise for my girls," he said, and pulled out the most gigantic box of Russell Stover chocolates I'd ever seen.

We all burst out laughing. "Daddy!" He laughed back. It wouldn't be Valentine's Day for another eight months. Where did he even find a box? It had never mattered if we were six or twenty-six, if we had partners and children of our own, our dad had been faithfully showing up with these gifts every February fourteenth.

We all gathered around the open box of chocolates, so big it stretched across both of our folding chairs. We didn't think about the finality of the sweetness. We just ate and smiled, ignoring the slowly setting sun behind us.

Two nights before she was due to surrender, on a warm, cloudless evening, we were driving through the heart of Poughkeepsie; Nikki was next to me, the three kids strapped in behind us. We drove toward Spackenkill, a hamlet under the City of Poughkeepsie (the Town wraps around them like a crescent); that's where Elizabeth lived. I pulled up in front of her stone house in a quiet cul-de-sac neighborhood, wondering if Ben and Faye remembered the times Nikki had driven past this spot in a loop.

But today I was in the driver's seat. Today we were stopping.

We got out of the car, greeted by Elizabeth's family, who were waiting for us with folding chairs and benches around their fire pit in the center of a backyard outfitted with twinkly lights, a netted trampoline, and a slackline set up between towering trees. It was the kind of life I wished for myself, shared with a nice husband and two kids, in the peaceful quiet of my own backyard, in a good school district with steady jobs. Her husband, Allan, was a quiet professor, spectacled and polite. He came in and out of the house, making sure we had enough chocolate for s'mores and that the fire was well stoked. Their two elementary-aged kids, just slightly older than Noah, took all three children under their wings and spent the next hour playing, laughing, hiding, seeking. Before long, Faye fell asleep in Nikki's lap. I watched Nikki stand up and carry Faye toward the covered porch as if she were cradling a precious porcelain doll. Fireflies lit their way—golden dots of light, like Faye's painting.

I sat in front of the fire alone. I could hear the kids jumping and laughing on the trampoline behind me. The fire was a blaze of light, crackling life, stretching toward the dark sky, spitting up sparks. I breathed it in, imagining the fire was filling up the vacant pit in my stomach, reigniting a dimmed flame, right below my rib cage. It felt something like hope.

Nikki's shadowed figure walked toward me and sat down on the bench.

"I don't want to go back to that place," she said, pulling her sweatshirt over her thumbs. She knew what was ahead for her—the correctional officers who would have loud opinions within earshot, the degradation of strip searches, the showers, the food, the deep ache of separation. I opened my arms and she sank onto my shoulder. I wrapped my arms around her and closed my eyes, imagining that all the warmth I felt around and inside me could surround her like a force field, a flood of golden light. If only I could keep her safe.

But when I opened my eyes, we were just two sisters with three exhausted children. It was time to go. We thanked Elizabeth's family for having us, and got back into our car. The moon led the way home.

* * *

Nikki was born twenty-seven months after me. I don't remember a time before she was in my life.

Sisterhood is a long thread in our family, weaving through generations. Our mom (left) and her two older sisters in the early 1960s.

Nikki and I became friends through motherhood. Here we are in 2008, during my second trimester, months after graduating college. My mom and sister were excited about my young pregnancy; I was mostly terrified. Nikki and Chris had recently met.

When my son, Noah, was born, Nikki became his second maternal figure, taking him on special "Aunt Days" while I built an editorial career.

By 2017, Ben and Faye were here too. This was a typical scene from the "before" time, when we saw each other nearly every day: Ben, Faye, Mom, and Dad.

The morning before the shooting. Noah and I finally had a peaceful space: He was happy to be an only child, and I felt a sense of freedom as a newly single mom. We had no idea what the next day would bring.

After the "Bad Night," Ben kept this photo by his bed as a reminder of the life he'd lost. He sometimes slept with Nikki's shirt over his face.

Nikki Addimando
August 6 · 👥

b: "mommy, I didn't like not being with you today. I missed you too much.. what would I do in my life without you?"
me: "I missed you so much, too. You don't have to worry about life without me. I'm with you, always."
b: "because our hearts have an invisible string that connect us no matter what, right mom?"
Yes. That. 💚 #theinvisiblestring

Nikki Addimando
May 14, 2017 · 🌐

My purpose in this life. My reason for today and for tomorrow. 💚

Ben and Faye stayed connected to their old life by looking through Nikki's social media accounts. I scrolled too—not to remember, like Ben and Faye, but to re-see: to look for signs I missed, like bruises hiding under sunglasses or strategic poses that covered her body.

A community rushed in to help after the shocking news broke, including a photographer who offered us free family photos. *(Karissa Dudzinski Photography)*

Meanwhile, Nikki sat alone in a jail cell. She created art by ripping up magazine pages and gluing them with toothpaste. This was the mantra she recited to herself while enduring strip searches at the jail.

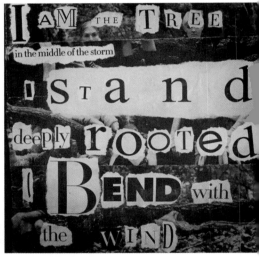

At home, we decorated the Christmas tree for the first time without her.

We spent our days driving back and forth from school, finding reasons to smile, sing, and laugh together.

We stayed connected to Nikki through phone calls and letters. Some envelopes were filled with letters and art for the kids to color, while some envelopes were just for me.

Meanwhile, we started organizing. Elizabeth addressed a crowd of purple shirts, the color of domestic violence awareness, declaring "We Stand with Nikki."

The next day, Nikki was released on a writ of habeas corpus. This is me, Nikki, and Elizabeth in the parking lot of the Dutchess County jail. Nikki is wearing a shirt from a nearby dollar store and Elizabeth's purple leggings.

After nine months without seeing their mother's face or feeling her hugs, the kids' reunion with Nikki was magic.

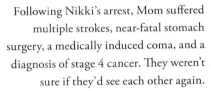

Following Nikki's arrest, Mom suffered multiple strokes, near-fatal stomach surgery, a medically induced coma, and a diagnosis of stage 4 cancer. They weren't sure if they'd see each other again.

One afternoon, we brought Nikki to her kids' preschool art show. Ben tied his body to hers with a scarf, hoping to keep them together forever.

And I got my sister back.

During twelve days we had with Nikki, we gave her sunshine, laughter, music, love.

And for a brief moment, we were free.

The goodbye was agony.

We spent the summer of 2018 counting down the days until the kids' play therapy visits at the Dutchess County jail—

...and making memories as a brand new family of four.

Nikki sent home a jail-made gift for my thirty-second birthday.

Six months after Nikki had surrendered and returned to jail, and fifteen months after her arrest, we finally secured bail and brought her home. An electronic monitoring device was required—

...but we gave Ben and Faye the only thing they wanted for Christmas.

A month later, our mom died.

Despite the stress and trauma of the trial, Nikki was somehow completely present and loving with her children.

To cope, Nikki made art. She painted this for the circle of sisters around her, which became a symbol for our "purple" community. We changed our social media profile pictures to this image, each of us vowing to "Stand with Nikki."

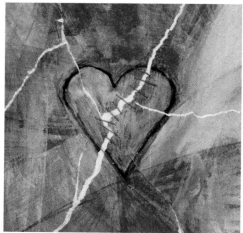

Ben joined in making art with his mom. He made this picture, ripped and glued it back together, then stitched it with thread and titled it "Together, Again."

I bought Reiki-infused candles and intentionally prayed every day of the trial. One day the blue candle, for "justice," filled with smoke, leaving a black film on the glass votive.

The morning of the verdict, Nikki's purple flower died. Was it a sign?

After the verdict at Wendy's house, sitting on the sofa between Elizabeth and Dr. Crenshaw. We felt shock, disbelief, and pulsating anger.

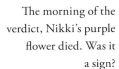

Life went on. We continued to be offered family photo sessions, while others offered their services as well: haircuts, chiropractor appointments, therapy, energy healing, dentist visits, free meals. The generosity of our community had no limits. *(Karissa Dudzinski Photography)*

The community also showed up for events that our committee put on: candlelight vigils, fundraising gatherings, and public protests.

In September 2019, we began advocating for Nikki to have a reduced sentence under the new DVSJA law.

Play therapy continued at the jail. Faye often brought her stuffed animal friends, Skye and Rockstar.

Faye sometimes came out with love notes from Nikki written in marker. We all held on to the hope that the judge would use the DVSJA and allow Nikki to return home sooner.

But the worst happened: Nikki was sentenced to nineteen years to life in a maximum-security women's prison.

Nikki's appeal was filed in the summer of 2020 by Nikki's pro bono appellate attorney, Garrard Beeney, standing here with most of our current committee: Caitlin, Wendy, me, Kate, Rachel, Linsey, Kellyann, Elizabeth, Larissa, Nicole, and Laura (Sarah and Rebecca are missing).

A year after the appeal was filed, a higher court resentenced Nikki to 7.5 years, including time served, meaning she still had three more years to her sentence. Despite a national campaign, New York Governor Kathy Hochul did not respond to our appeals for clemency.

And so Ben and Faye continued to wait, sing, and wish to the moon, waiting...

Before long, it was Sunday night. The kids knew it was the end of her visit, and we all steeled ourselves for a goodbye in the morning.

"Can I stay up late?" I heard Ben ask Nikki. The two of them were relaxing on the living room floor, Ben's head in Nikki's lap. Her fingers stroked his hair. Faye was sleeping next to them on the couch, unable to keep her eyes open despite our collective effort to will this day never to end.

Nikki smiled down into Ben's eyes. "Of course," she said. "Let's go for a walk."

They were gone a long while—so long that I went to the kids' bedroom and opened the blinds, wondering if I could spot them in the backyard. My reflection looked back at me in the glass, my face long, my skin pale. I pressed my forehead closer to the dark window and squinted out into the yard, where a bright moon was spilling silver light onto the grass. And there, lying face-up on a big blanket, were two shadowy figures—one big, one small—their feet crossed at the ankles. They were holding hands. I couldn't hear what they were saying or make out their facial expressions, but the way their bodies folded into each other took my breath away.

This is possible, too, I thought. Here, in this new reality that not only felt unsafe but *was* unsafe; here, suspended in endless uncertainty, where bad things kept happening and people I loved kept leaving—beauty and love and awe were possible.

I closed the blinds and let them have their moment. I knew enough to recognize something sacred when I saw it.

She had to be at the courthouse at 9 a.m. I set my alarm for 7.

I don't remember their goodbye. I must have blocked it out, as well as the moment of dropping Nikki off. I do remember how hot it was, and Nikki saying ruefully she'd be going back to a world without air-conditioning.

I returned to the house feeling heavier. Nikki's absence carried its own weight. Ben was curled up on the couch, asleep for a rare nap. "He cried himself to exhaustion," said my dad, who had stayed behind to manage the fallout. Ben was wearing the shirt Nikki had slept in the night before. On one side of him was his ukulele, which he'd later pack away. It hurt too much to play without her. On his other side was a note written in blue crayon: "I LOVE YOU MOMMY."

The papers would later report that Nikki "surrendered herself to the authorities," as if she were a fugitive on the run, rather than a lawfully free woman voluntarily cooperating to prove she was a "good girl" who could follow the rules.

She surrendered because there was no better choice.

PART III

hope

"Hope is a discipline."

—Mariame Kaba

invisible string

Hello, this is a prepaid call from *Nicole Addimando*, an inmate at Dutchess County Jail. This call is subject to monitoring and recording. To accept charges press 1 . . ."

Nikki was calling. I pressed 1 and put the call on speakerphone, propping up my cell phone at the dining room table, where Ben was intently drawing the Flash in his sketchbook. He briefly looked up, his dark, expressive eyebrows crinkling at the sound of the familiar automated voice.

"Mama's calling!" Faye sang from across the room, her eyes brightening. Her hair was growing into longer curls—matching her bouncy personality. Every day she was looking more like my sister.

Faye climbed onto a chair and perched next to her big brother. Together they watched the phone, waiting to connect, reenacting the daily routine. They knew they'd usually have fifteen minutes before another mommy needed the phone to call her babies. They didn't know where their mom lived, we never used the word *jail*, but they knew she wasn't alone. They could hear the yelling and ruckus in the background over the phone.

Sometimes Nikki could talk longer, some days she called more than once. It was an inconsistent connection, a not-enough connection, but it was the only mother-child connection they had.

Most days the three of them took advantage of the short calls, catching up about their day. Ben sent his kindergarten chapter books to Nikki in the mail so they could talk about them. Faye sent photos of her preschool friends so that her mom could know them, too. Nikki would tell them about a new mouse that was living with her, and Faye would excitedly say, "Oh, that's my friend! I sent him to you!" They'd name the mouse, pretending it was a friendly magical messenger rather than what it actually was, one of many rodents in a jail cell eating its way through Nikki's limited stash of food.

Every now and then one of the kids would need "alone time with Mom," which meant taking her off speakerphone and disappearing into a bathroom or closet. She held their secrets, their righteous anger, their unanswerable and consistent question, *Mama, when are you coming home?*

They knew she couldn't say when, they knew it was being decided by forces bigger than us all, but they asked anyway.

"If I could be anywhere in the world, I'd be right there with you," she told them.

Toward the end of each call, they'd plan where they'd meet in their dreams—to play in Candy Land, or picnic on the moon, or go back to "the red house," the brick apartment where they'd last lived as a family. Sometimes they'd plan to meet at 560 Together Lane, their future fantasy home, where Ben decided they'd grow a garden and Faye would design a door with plenty of locks to keep them safe. They'd close their eyes and will their dream-selves to find one another.

It was another ordinary conversation that ended with all of us piled on the couch, Nikki on speakerphone in my hand. The call was about to end and Faye could sense it. She slumped her shoulders toward the phone and lowered her voice to a whisper. "Mommy, when I dream, I don't go where we say," she said, as if confessing. "I have nightmares."

The line went quiet for a moment.

Then Nikki said, "Me too. What are your nightmares about?"

"You being taken away," Faye said.

"Yeah, you going away forever," Ben chimed in.

"Me too. I have those dreams, too," Nikki said quietly. "Those are hard dreams."

A silence hung on the phone line. I imagined that the correctional officers monitoring the call could feel the weight. I know I could.

Nikki spoke up, "Here, blow me your bad dreams and I'll hold them for you."

Faye closed her eyes, puffed up her body, and blew straight toward her mom's voice with a determined ferocity, exhaling everything she couldn't bear to hold.

"Sent." Faye nodded confidently and smiled.

"I have them here with me. I'll hold your nightmares," Nikki promised.

I felt Faye's body relax in my arms. "I miss you," she squeaked.

"Oh, I miss you, too, sweet girl, so much. Do you feel that tug on your heart?" Nikki asked, her own voice shrinking.

Faye put her small hand on her heart and closed her eyes. "Yes."

Ben did the same.

"That's our heartstring tugging back and forth. That's the invisible string that connects us."

"You have one minute left," said the robotic voice.

Everyone sighed.

Both kids stretched their arms toward the phone, hands open to catch the kisses they knew she'd blow. Then they sent kisses back in an identical cadence, in a crescendoing melody, *mwah-mwah-mwah!!* They did this at the end of every phone call, catching and swallowing her kisses, like some kind of emotional nourishment.

"Thank you, babies—"

Her voice cut off mid-sentence.

I knew that she hung up the phone and cried, knowing that her children would soon be bathed, cuddled, and put to bed by someone else—by me.

Ben and Faye were aware that we were working on getting them to visit their mom. Keeping them apart wasn't an option, even if it had to be in the crowded and heavily restricted visiting room. A hug once a week was better than nothing at all.

Before resorting to the less than ideal visiting room, Dr. Crenshaw—the child psychologist who had told me that *kids can handle the truth*—offered to facilitate private family therapy sessions at the jail. This kind of rupture of the children's primary attachment could have detrimental, long-lasting effects—particularly for Ben, who was affected the most severely. It was rare for incarcerated parents in DCJ to have private visits, but we had to try. Dr. Crenshaw filed a petition through a public defender he knew at the Dutchess County Family Court.

Dr. Crenshaw had a good reputation and a decades-long history in the community, so his recommendation held some weight. Even still, we were told to be prepared for a judge to deny it.

We waited.

Nights were the hardest.

I couldn't continue to spend the time or gas driving Ben and Faye around our neighborhood every night, just to avoid their cries. Cries that were unfixable. Cries that needed to come up and out, and not be stifled by the lull of a car engine.

So in the weeks after Nikki's surrender, I often spent evenings rocking and swaying around in a darkened bedroom, holding toddler-size bodies of raw emotion tucked inside feetsy pajamas, their wet hair pressed against my face. It was as if their baths had washed away their armor, too. I'd hold them while they screamed out into the darkness of their shared bedroom—*I want my ma-ma*—over and over like a beating drum, a primal plea.

I was depleted, yet somehow I still split myself in two, moving between Ben's twin-size bed—placed in the spot my queen-size mattress used to be—and Faye's white wooden toddler bed tucked in the corner, a hand-me-down from Noah.

And while I comforted the two children screaming, there was another one upstairs, quiet and alone, waiting for me to read him a book.

Noah was about to start fourth grade. He didn't need me to rock him to sleep, like he used to, but our bedtime routine had been the source of some of my most tender and intimate mother-child experiences. We'd read every night, and then he'd ask me to lie down next to him as he drifted off to sleep. It was there, in the safety of the dark, that he could burrow under my arm and ask deep, vulnerable questions: *Why are we here? What's the point of being alive?* That brief transition from awake to asleep was when the good stuff would spill out—stories from school, insights into his feelings and fears.

These nights, I sometimes spent *hours* in Ben and Faye's room—different arms needed me. And lately I wasn't having sweet conversations or fielding big questions; I was simply enduring piercing screams. There was a sense of panic in the space. I wondered if Ben fought sleep so hard because, one night nine months ago, he had gone to sleep and woken to find his life torn apart. I wondered if his desperation to stay awake was a kind of innate self-protection, to keep everyone where he could see them, alive and well. Ben's cries would trigger Faye's, and it was clear that the only thing they wanted in the entire world was Nikki's physical touch. She was the one they asked for. They never cried for their dad.

By the time Ben and Faye were asleep, I was a shell, hauling myself upstairs to Noah's room. Some nights he was already sleeping. Other times I could barely keep my eyes open long enough to read through a page. Just as the littler ones needed Nikki, Noah needed me. And like Nikki, I was both there and gone—existing in an in-between, just out of reach.

We assumed that, after the writ of habeas corpus and Chana's fury at Nikki's release, she would get the case to a grand jury pretty quickly. We had no idea when, though—the prosecution was under no obligation to let us know it was happening.

We'd mostly given up hope for the "fair and open" presentation that we'd been promised since the early days. *But the grand jury might put two and two together*, our committee reminded each other. *They could subpoena Nikki's or Sarah's testimony for more information*, we reasoned in group texts and over coffee meet-ups, the last gasps of hope that the grand jury could possibly end in an acquittal. *It's probably going to take a few weeks to get a decision*, we rationalized, speaking from our experience of the sluggish court system.

It took eleven days, including weekends.

Nikki didn't have a chance to testify. Her witnesses and evidence weren't heard. And the prosecution publicly confirmed Nikki's deepest fear, the refrain she had heard Chris repeat to her for years, as a warning: They didn't believe her.

The grand jury set four distinct charges:

1. Murder in the second degree
2. Manslaughter in the first degree
3. Manslaughter in the second degree
4. Criminal possession of a weapon in the second degree

Jurors could find her guilty on any of these—the highest charge, Murder in the second degree, carried the highest sentence, potentially 25 years to life. I passed on the devastating news to Nikki over the phone.

Within hours, maybe even minutes, of digesting this worst-case scenario, the charges were published in the *Poughkeepsie Journal* and emailed out to subscribers as a Top Story.

Some of the online remarks I read I agreed with, like "I hope this girl has a good attorney." And some expressed confusions that I shared. Like, "How could she be charged with both murder and manslaughter? Does the prosecutor think it was intentional or accidental?"

I choked back the comment I couldn't type in reply, the one no one was asking: "And how is she charged with possessing a gun that legally belonged to the man who threatened to kill her with it?"

The answer, I was told, was strategy. The more charges leveled against a defendant, the more likely it was that one would stick. Strategy trumps truth, every time.

This doesn't mean she's guilty, we assured the supporters who had been donating to our bail fund and receiving our update emails. *The grand jury didn't hear Nikki's side of the story*, we explained.

Because of the promises the prosecutors had made—saying that Nikki could have a fair shot at the grand jury *as long as we did X, Y, and Z*—we had all taken big risks, like being deposed in the DA's Office with no lawyer present.

Nothing we did ended up influencing the outcome. It now seemed that our Herculean efforts and vulnerable truth-telling were for nothing. Worse, we felt they had been weaponized. And Nikki's surrender felt like a trap.

Surrender, or "letting go," is against my nature. I came into this world tensing against life. According to my parents, my earliest days were labeled with the word *colic*, which basically meant I screamed incessantly, inconsolably, for hours at a time, my newborn body tight and stiff. From then on, I've physically held on and held in, as if my whole being was a clenched fist. As a little kid, I was known to hold my bladder until the point of pain, occasionally peeing my pants in first grade because I couldn't gauge when I needed to release. As a teenager, I'd often lie in bed at night, in my own vulnerable space between awake and asleep, and feel the tension I'd spent the day ignoring. Many nights, I'd fall asleep imagining scissors cutting me loose—snip, snip, down my torso—and visualize the subtle way my body would expand, open and relaxed, unbound.

I held on through high school with rigid goal setting, praised for my tenacity and ambition—traits that were rewarded. But as I moved into adulthood and sought out therapy and self-reflection, *surrender* became a learned portal to release that inner constriction, like the snip, snip of scissors.

Nikki's surrender had me thinking about my own understanding of the word, written in the center of my Venn diagram of personal growth—from Al-Anon group meetings to yoga class meditations to spiritual books I bought to change my life.

I didn't define it in the same way the court system did: a white-flag raising, a sign of defeat and submission. To me, surrender didn't mean liking or agreeing with what was going on; it was simply a radical acceptance of reality, exactly as it is, without the resistance that things could or should be different. It was an acceptance that *allowed* inviting in the fear and doubt and anxiety as a teacher and guide, a welcome part of the whole.

This had been a practice, an act of trust that I could safely operate in the world without grasping and tensing, waiting for a shoe to drop. But here?

Now? In this storm of relentless falling shoes? *Here*, through fight-or-flight adrenaline dumps, *here*, where I was entangled in a legal system that operates like one big chess match? Could I surrender to *this*?

No. Most times I couldn't. Most times it felt like everything around me was one giant confirmation that the world is an unsafe place, that every worst-case scenario would, in fact, come true, and I was absolutely right to tense and grasp and stay on my toes.

And yet sometimes, in moments, I could. Not in some great Zen achievement, but from basic necessity, as if the persistent feeling of being overwhelmed had a weight to it, grounding me to a reality that was not mine to fix. Surrender felt like sinking under the agitated surface and remembering:

I'm powerless.

It was the same powerlessness that had brought me to my knees (causing me to retch over a toilet the previous spring), and yet sometimes—at a red light, in the county jail's visiting room, lying in bed at night—the same word could feel like liberation. The act of true surrendering felt like an unclenching, a release of the idea that there was something to control or change.

I'm powerless.

Whether I was surrendering to a benevolent Higher Power in a group meeting, or a highly powerful court system that operated through control and coercion, the release was all the same.

sistering

One of the many great paradoxes I was experiencing was that my life was both unmanageable and in need of constant managing. How could I possibly let go while also needing to carry so much?

There were legal complexities to fundraising that required work—and all of our outreach and advocacy had to be done quietly, in coordination with other groups and advocates who operated these kinds of underground communication networks. Speaking publicly came with very real risks—gag orders, retaliatory rulings from the judge, unintended consequences from correctional officers who could make Nikki's life (more of a) hell. We saw this play out in other cases, and heeded the warnings of Nikki's legal team. Managing all of this was, in and of itself, a full-time job.

Luckily, I was surrounded by a group of women who didn't wait for me to ask for what I needed or to delegate—they jumped into action, right by my side. The scaffolding was built on day one—starting with the people who sent meals and gift cards, made calls to their networks, and gave money. But it wasn't until after Nikki's indictment—when the legal reality came into focus, and the horizon was suddenly, devastatingly, farther in the distance—that a real structure came into place. We were in this for the long haul.

Elizabeth coordinated Nikki's jail visits this time around, so I didn't have to manage the schedule—which required gauging Nikki's desire to see people, and coordinating who was going when. Her younger sister, Rebecca, organized a carefully scheduled "book train" to the jail—making sure that Nikki had enough stories and poems to escape into, but not so many that she'd get in trouble for breaking the rules. She could have only four books at a time in her cell, and quickly became the unit's "library," as she described it to me, passing around volumes of poetry and sharing fictional worlds.

My Aunt Debbie took on the task of printing photos and mailing them to Nikki. The county jail didn't allow Nikki to have actual photographs, but we could photocopy pictures onto paper. Which meant that every week my aunt would compile the images I sent, drive to her local Staples, and pay to print them out on white computer paper. My aunt would send her these ordinary moments—of Noah, Ben, and Faye smiling around the table of an Olive Garden, brand-new Build-A-Bears propped up next to them, taken the first time I was brave enough to bring them all out to the mall on my own; of Ben and Faye sitting in a big green dentist's chair during their first scheduled appointment with me as a guardian, during which I was repeatedly called "Mom" ("She is *not my mom*," Ben said, eyebrows scrunched, jaw tight); of them holding balloons outside the dentist's office, smiling as if Faye hadn't scream-cried her way through the visit while Ben yelled, "Don't hurt my sister!"

My aunt considered it a small job, an easy way to contribute. But it wasn't a small thing for Nikki to receive the large manila envelopes filled with photocopied evidence of her children out in the world, smiling and laughing on a day she'd never see. My aunt provided a portal into their lives being lived without her, and a way to stay connected to what they were doing and wearing, the toys they were playing with, the way their room looked. Nikki would tell me about sitting on her bed and studying each picture.

People signed up to send Nikki money every week. Guards would read commissary balances out loud for everyone to hear before each biweekly shop, so we made sure she had enough, but not so much that the other women around her would hound her for money. We learned the rules and worked as a group to plan and organize. I can't imagine that many incarcerated people have this level of support on the outside.

The caregiving largely fell on me, a function of single motherhood—like registering Ben for kindergarten, bringing them all to birthday parties and sports games, and looking after sick kids. But I did have a backup support system to catch the overflow of those needs: a dad and aunts who were willing to be available for any last-minute babysitting.

And some of it I still had to carry on my own—like the relationship with the Grovers, which was complex and difficult, at times confrontational. No one wanted the kids to lose more people in their lives, and so we all fumbled our way into an arrangement: the kids would visit the Grovers every Sunday. No one would talk about our personal opinions and feelings, and we'd be civil toward one another for the sake of Ben and Faye.

"Listen, I know you're going to be on your sister's side, just like I'd be on mine," his mom had said, catching me off-guard during a Sunday drop-off. Ben and Faye had run inside the house, and it was just the two of us standing next to my car, one mother to another. "And you know I'm going to be on my son's side, just like you'd be on your son's side." I nodded. I did know that.

When I saw the pain of Chris's parents up close, it was impossible to ignore. I also gave them the benefit of the doubt, knowing that Chris's family was likely sitting in meetings with Chana, hearing her theory that Nikki was a manipulative liar who faked abuse allegations and murdered their son in his sleep, when he was defenseless.

I felt sad for them, and I hated knowing that, in a matter of months, they'd have to face the evidence of abuse and have their own inner reckoning. And I was angry that Chana was peddling a false narrative that was only making it harder for our family to form a cohesive reality for the kids.

Yet I never had to carry the emotional toll on my own for long.

Our committee talked on a near-daily basis about legal issues, about the kids' trauma, and about *me*. They remained dedicated, generous, and reliable—a counter to all the real-life examples of why I should never trust anyone ever again.

I was carrying loads that I previously would have thought impossible. When I started to splinter under the weight of it all, the people around me, the *women* around me, stepped in.

"Of course you're struggling," they said. "You're holding up the sky. Let me stand on either side and take some of the burden."

I'd learned the carpentry term *sistering* from Glennon Doyle—the same author whose writing had bonded Elizabeth and Nikki. Maybe she'd shared it in a blog post, or maybe I saw it on Facebook, but the concept had stuck with me: When a joist, or a support beam, is weakened, damaged, or bowed from supporting a bigger structure, carpenters will reinforce it on either side, sometimes on both sides, with another board. And that reinforcement is called *sistering*.

In my enormous effort to sister Nikki and support my breaking family, I became a joist. And now I needed sistering, too. The wisest part of me knew I had to allow it, and to let these women hold me up, or else I'd buckle under the weight of it all.

CHAPTER 35

room 311

Finally the court did something right.

After twenty-nine long days, Dr. Crenshaw's petition was seen and approved—surprisingly speedy for our overtaxed court system, which I'd come to see as a clunky robotic machine with rusty, slow-moving gears. Visits would take place weekly.

The kids clapped and cheered when I told them the good news. Nikki was excited, too. In anticipation, she sent home a hand-drawn calendar for the month of July with a heart marking every Wednesday. She knew that the kids needed a concrete image to hold on to and a way to count down the days. We hung it on a cork board in their room, and Ben took a pink marker and colored over the hearts, expanding their size. Then he connected each heart with a line, a visible string.

On the first pink-hearted Wednesday, Ben and Faye changed out of their dirty preschool clothes into their favorite outfits, picked out the night before: a floral sleeveless dress for Faye, and a red shirt with a yellow lightning bolt for Ben.

"I! Am! So! Excited!" Faye squealed from the back seat. We were turning out of our neighborhood, heading for the hug they'd been craving for the thirty-two days since Nikki's surrender.

I looked at Ben in the rearview mirror, strapped in next to Faye. His legs kicked with nervous energy.

"How far away is it?" he asked.

"It's not too far, actually," I said, not sure whether he'd feel relieved that his mother was nearby or betrayed that she had existed just out of arm's reach all this time. There was no reaction from the back seat, just a settled silence. Whatever was going on in the kids' internal worlds was not mine to know.

My own mind was a mess. Would they be scared by the way she looked? By the musty smell coming off her oversized orange jumpsuit? Would seeing the officers at the jail trigger their traumatic memories from the "Bad Night"? Would they be able to say goodbye at the end?

"When we go in, we'll meet with Dr. Crenshaw in a big waiting room," I said. So much of what I knew about parenting young kids came from Nikki and what she'd learned in her training as an early childhood teacher. She'd explained that when a kid is about to do something new, especially if it's stressful, like a doctor's visit or the first day of school—or a jail visit with Mom—it's good to talk about it beforehand: what will happen, what won't happen, what the physical space will look like.

"This is the same place that I go to visit your mom, and there will be officers there to help us learn the rules and bring you to her. They might take your pictures, and they'll probably make sure that you don't have anything in your pockets that you're not supposed to have."

"Like toys?" Faye asked.

I smiled. "Yeah, like toys, or food, or anything, really. But I think Dr. Crenshaw will bring some art supplies." They both loved to draw and color. I looked in the rearview mirror, and their faces were neutral, both looking out the window.

"Is it the same police station as last time?" Ben asked, remembering the place where they were first separated from her.

"No, it's not. It's a different place. We'll stay together with Dr. Crenshaw until the officers say it's time, and then I'll say goodbye and you three will follow the officers to the room where your mom will be. Actually, I've never been back there," I added, lifting the tone in my voice as if they were about to do something really cool and special, their own adventure. "You'll have to tell me what it's like!"

They were quiet.

"Do you have any questions?"

"Can we sleep there?" Faye asked, hopeful.

"No, kids aren't allowed to stay there; it's just for grown-ups. It's not a place where people live; it's where they stay until they can come home."

"When are you picking us up?" Ben asked.

"I'll be there waiting for you at seven o'clock; it'll be almost bedtime," I answered. The sun was just starting to set. "From the time you're with Mom, you'll have an hour to visit. So that's like two episodes of *PJ Masks*," I said.

"I'm just happy I get to hug her," Ben said.

"Here we *aaaaare*," I sang as we pulled into the large, mostly empty lot. I parked under the big letters plastered on the side of the building: J-A-I-L. I held my breath.

Ben was just starting to read, and I knew he could sound out that word if he wanted. I had already prepared a response to the inevitable realization: *Jail is where they keep people when they're deciding whether someone did something wrong or not.* (Like many people, before Nikki's arrest, I may have used the words *jail* and *prison* interchangeably, not realizing that jail is where people are held before a trial—or to serve short sentences for lesser crimes—and prison is where people typically go after they're found guilty.)

This, of course, would open up the question I wasn't prepared to answer: *What did Mom do?* Ben knew that his dad was dead, but not that his mom had killed him.

We walked in silence through the glass front door, where Dr. Crenshaw was waiting for us with a big, friendly smile.

"Hi, Ben! Hi, Faye!" He'd clearly come straight from work, with a laminated badge hanging from his neck and a blue canvas bag at his side.

Faye waved and smiled. Ben clung to my side with a skeptical look on his face. "Remember your manners," I whispered to him, knowing that this wasn't a place that tolerated rude behavior.

We had to wait to be called, so I led Ben over to the small two-shelf bookcase to pick out a book.

When the kids were called, they approached the desk with Dr. Crenshaw. An officer waved the metal detector around Dr. Crenshaw's body, nodded, and then turned to Ben.

"Hold out your arms like *this*," the officer said with a smile, stretching his arms out and stepping his feet into a wide stance. Both Ben and Faye mirrored the pose. Then the officer waved the wand over Ben's arms, torso, and legs. *Shit, I didn't prepare them for this part*, I thought.

But Ben didn't flinch, and neither did Faye when it was her turn.

They were smiling, looking toward the heavy glass door, waiting for it to slide open. Faye looked at me and ran back for one last hug.

"Have so much fun, baby girl," I whispered into her curls, kissing her head. She skipped back to her brother's side as the door loudly clanked open, sliding into the wall. Faye paused and waved before disappearing. Ben didn't look back.

I sat for a minute, alone, pressing my feet against the floor. I took in the room from a child's perspective and wondered whether the guards would yell at them. I hoped this visit would more than balance out the pain they'd feel when they had to separate from Nikki again.

I knew that I'd be tempted to have a fun, silly song queued up for the ride home in the car, and to focus on the positives. I looked over to the other sliding metal door to the left, the one *I* entered to visit Nikki, and thought back to something she'd confided on a recent visit: When people in the past had reacted to her visible bruises with dismissive laughs and a *Whatcha do now, clumsy girl?* attitude, she'd felt the need to match the lighthearted mood. I decided that when I came back to get the kids, I wouldn't meet them with a goofy grin and hype-man energy; I'd meet them where they were, wherever that was.

I can no longer remember what I did with that first hour, or even whether I briefly returned home. Noah was at soccer practice with my Aunt Kathy.

Maybe I went food shopping at the nearby grocery store—which was what I ended up doing most Wednesday nights that summer. Maybe I sat in the parking lot and caught up on the texts and emails that had piled up over the late afternoon, or scrolled through the curated social media feeds of people who seemed freer and happier than I was.

All I know is that, at 7 p.m., I was sitting in the same blue seat as when they had gone in. I was alone in the room, no officer behind the desk. I heard a faint echo of voices in the hallway, and then louder laughs, until the kids appeared behind the glass door with smiles and happy eyes. They waved, and I waved back, matching their expressions.

Eventually the door crept open. Ben bolted through it and raced toward me, jumping in my arms. Faye was close behind.

"How was it? How was Mom?"

"Great!" they said in unison. Their bodies felt relaxed in my arms in a way I hadn't felt in a while.

"I'm so happy to hear it." I kissed both of their heads and turned to Dr. Crenshaw, who was trailing behind. He, too, was smiling. His eyes looked tired.

We made our way back outside, now under a bright crescent moon. The sky was clear. The kids ran ahead on the sidewalk toward the parked car, one of four in the lot. I walked slowly behind with Dr. Crenshaw, as he filled me in on the visit.

"So, the first thing they did was check her body for bruises," he said to me quietly. "They checked her neck, arms, Ben tried to lift up her shirt."

Wow. Part of me was startled by that image of the kids making sure their mom was safe and not being hurt, and at the same time, it made a lot of sense. If I had constantly seen bruises on her face in the past, so had the kids.

"Ben also had a lot of questions about her clothes," he continued. "At one point he said, 'Why are you wearing jail clothes?'" My eyes darted up toward those four letters on the building. "He didn't press it further, and Nikki took it in stride. She said something like, 'Yes, I have lots of orange shirts and pants upstairs.'"

"He didn't ask more about jail?"

"No, but there were enough clues that, if they were ready to see, I think they would have. I think they're both inching closer to understanding what the situation is, but at a pace they can handle."

I nodded, knowing I'd be the one filling in the blanks once they were ready.

"Faye initiated a play drama where she pretended to leave Nikki and told her to be sad and cry." I smiled, knowing all too well how Faye directed her play with the people around her.

"So Faye ran around to the other side of the table"—he motioned a half circle with his hands—"and then came back around to her mom's out-stretched arms. Nikki made a big fuss over how glad she was to have her back, how much she'd missed her. This act of turning the passive into the active with the two of them reenacting the sadness of being apart and the joyful, loving reunification is really at the core of play therapy. And the fact that Faye repeated this—that's another hallmark of play therapy, to gain mastery of a painful situation through numerous repetitions."

I wondered if adults did that, too. Were we all a bunch of hurting children acting out our pains in our actions, instead of through play? Were we repeating difficult experiences and patterns—situations we kept finding ourselves in—to gain mastery?

I opened the back door to strap them into their five-point harnesses. Ben had already buckled himself, five going on fifteen. Faye didn't fight me as I put her arms through and tightened the car seat. They both smiled wide satisfied grins. Dr. Crenshaw stood on the sidewalk, waiting to say goodbye.

"They have such a strong bond, Michelle," he said. "That love is going to get them through the rough days ahead."

God, I hoped he was right.

CHAPTER 36

the shape of a family

We spent that summer soaking in as many moments of joy as possible. I said yes a lot: Yes to ice cream after camp, to movie nights on a bed of pillows on the living room carpet. Yes to slip-and-slides in a friend's backyard, and afternoon dance parties around the kitchen. Yes to a trip to the Playland Amusement Park. Yes to Noah's repeated request to go to sleep-away camp, which I paid for with some of the tax rebate I'd received, thanks to my sudden status as a head of household with three kids.

Without the structure of school, I was forced to change the shape of my life over the long summer months, and my family did its best to fill in the gaps where my reach was thin. No one could step up all the time, but people did what they could. I couldn't and wouldn't have undertaken something as ambitious as the Playland trip on my own, but I had my mom's sisters and my female cousins along to help. Another cousin took Noah for a weekend guys' trip to the beach. I was grateful for the familial connection, our shared guilt and grief over all we'd lost together.

I still found a way to get to the jail every week, and usually twice. Nikki needed me now more than ever. Trial was scheduled for October, and although John had submitted a bail application, Chana submitted another opposition. Nikki was dangerous, she argued. Nikki deserved to stay locked up.

I was getting an education in the politics of the justice system. Prosecutors are elected and promoted based on their conviction record. The more "bad people" they lock up, the better they look at their job. It was a game of perception.

"It's in Chana's best interest for Nikki to stay in jail," John told me candidly over the phone. "Statistically, the longer someone is incarcerated before trial, the more likely they are to be convicted."

On our side, getting Nikki released on bail was critical for a slew of reasons, perception included. I could understand what John meant: Jurors aren't ordained with crystal-clear perspective, wiped free of unconscious bias. It's easier to identify someone as a criminal when they're playing the part, chained and shackled, treated like an animal.

And watching Nikki wither away in jail—malnourished and dehydrated, isolated, without any means to heal or process her trauma—was heartbreaking. The upper unit of the jail had no AC, no fans, and windows that only cracked open for minimal air flow. The smell in the visiting room alone was enough to suggest they'd all come from a sauna, wearing jumpsuits thick with sweat and body odor. At this point, she'd endured hundreds of strip searches by officers who had no regard to what traumas made her cower.

At my visit on a sweltering July day, Nikki looked like she was about to pass out. She was quickly disappearing toward ninety pounds, and the orange smock hung on her protruding collarbone like a hanger. I knew that officers were giving her daily Carnation Instant Breakfast drinks to put weight on her, and they threatened to put her back on twenty-four-hour constant watch if she continued to lose weight—as if she were choosing this.

"Any ice lately?" I asked. She had told me about the times an officer would walk around with a bucket of ice, and the women would stand at their cell doors, cups extended, begging for relief. Those were the *best days*, she said, the best she could possibly expect in the heat wave.

Nikki shook her head. No ice.

I'd been sitting so long in the visiting room, with its high-pumping air conditioner, that I was chilled to the bone. I rubbed the goose bumps on my bare arms, trying to warm myself up. Nikki, however, looked to be drinking in the cool air, a sense of relief on her face. The jail seemed to operate only in the uncomfortable extremes.

I'd recently come back from a weekend retreat at Omega, a brief period of respite in a place built for healing—the antithesis of this visiting room.

All the elements that help us feel more human had been removed from here: Soft lighting was replaced with harsh flickering fluorescent bulbs; connection, like hugs, was monitored and restricted. Looking around the room, I knew it had to be intentional. No one could accidentally strip away our innate humanity like this; it was by design.

"I said to one of the officers, 'You wouldn't let a dog sit in this kind of heat,'" Nikki told me, demonstrating the kind of sharp tongue that had "got her in trouble" with Chris, and that prosecutors were using to discredit her as a good, believable victim.

"And you know what she said?" Nikki continued, holding up her hands like scales. "'Here are the dogs'"—she lifted the scale in her left hand—"'and here are you guys in orange'"—she lowered her right hand.

Along with the heat, Nikki was subjected to lengthy psychological tests from two opposing forensic psychologists—one we were paying for, the other working for the prosecution. She had to retell her story and relive her traumas, all with the goal of being believed. After each session, she'd recount her impressions in the visiting room, where she'd worry out loud that she hadn't made any sense, and that they didn't believe her. She looked smaller and sicker in each successive visit, like a paper-thin version of her true self. And whether it's right or wrong, appearances matter in front of a jury.

Our need to get Nikki home was about more than her image—even more than her physical health. To uphold her civil liberties, her right to a fair trial, she needed adequate access to her lawyers. She needed to be able to participate in her defense, which was nearly impossible from Dutchess County Jail. Her attorneys tried to get there as often as they could, but it was nearly an hour drive for each of them. And the jail didn't make it easy—getting in to see an incarcerated person was a long production, even for professionals. The mail process was slow. And phone calls were monitored.

So until we could get her home, the air-conditioned Sister Visits were a legal necessity. Trial was scheduled to take place in about two months. John and Chana were submitting motions and planning pretrial hearings, and I continued to be a vessel for information.

During our visits, she'd ask me to log into her Facebook account to find specific photos that illustrated different incidents for the attorneys; comb back through her emails to find something she had written to a friend. I almost always left with a piece of scrap paper, given to Nikki by a sympathetic guard, on which she'd scribbled notes for me to pass on. It was clear that Nikki had left breadcrumbs through the years in case she ever needed to prove the abuse. It was up to me to retrace her steps, gathering the clues to help her attorneys understand.

"I'd do it myself, but I can't have a computer here," she'd say, frustrated with all the ways her ability to explain herself were stifled. She knew her story better than anyone—it made complete sense to her, because she had lived it—but she was too restricted to be able to fully help save her own life.

Out in the real world, I found ways to fill the long summer days, taking advantage of all the small freedoms that Nikki missed. One day, while Noah was at sleepaway camp, I found myself at a nearby playground with Ben and Faye. It was hard to be sad on a seesaw, or while being pushed high in the air toward a cloudless summer sky.

On the way out of the park, I took their hands, Faye's on one side, Ben's on the other. We were three off-kilter humans with varying degrees of broken hearts, walking toward a quaint village diner for some food. Ben looked down at our shadows silhouetted against the street we were crossing.

"This is exactly what a family looks like," he said.

I smiled because I knew what he meant. This wasn't the family we had chosen; some days it wasn't the family we wanted, but we had each other. One bigger shadow walking two smaller shadows safely to the next place. This is what a family looks like.

survival is resourceful

I was sitting in my car in late August. I had spent the day ricocheting from one task to the next, from back-to-school shopping to household errands to legal calls, and the final thing on my list was stopping by Sarah's office to pick up some paperwork Nikki had given her during a professional visit. I had started collecting all the pretrial motions and correspondence with the prosecution and judge—stacks of overlong paper covered in wordy legalese, which Nikki couldn't keep in her cell for too long for fear that they'd be seen by gossip-hungry correctional officers who liked to spread rumors.

"There's an envelope in there for your birthday," Sarah mentioned on my way out. I had just turned thirty-two. Nikki remembered everyone's birthday—friends', friends' kids', distant family's—and she'd remind me about them over the phone, a feat that amazed me. Her thoughtfulness carried over to the jail, and she spent her limited commissary money on cards and paper to mail out, to let people know that, despite everything going on in her life, she was thinking of them.

And now, there in the car, I was holding my own gift from Nikki. I carefully put my finger under the envelope's flap, on which she had written *happy birthday*, and pulled out a small flat package wrapped in green paper. A thin orange thread, the same color as her jail jumpsuit, was wrapped around the package and tied in a bow—clearly she had ripped it off her clothes to repurpose as a ribbon.

There was also a card, beautifully collaged with pictures of delicate wildflowers and two women's hands clasped lovingly together, ripped from used magazines. Six letters were cut out and glued on the bottom right of the card: s i s t e r. She wasn't allowed to have scissors, so I knew she had care-fully torn each piece by hand.

When I turned the thick card over, I saw that it had been made from tearing the lower fourth of a marble composition notebook cover, the kind we used to bring to elementary school. I could still make out what she had written in the space where it said, "NAME: Unit 11/Cell 17." She had been reduced to numbers.

I could see the binding of the notebook in the crease where the card opened, where she must have ripped out all the pages to write letters. On the opposite side of the card was a letter to me in script:

dear sister,

i wish so badly that i was there to celebrate you on your birthday. you are literally holding our world together right now, and you deserve more than a day to recognize how truly special you are. i have loved you always, but somehow i've grown to love you more with every year we spend together. you, my sister, are a gift. may this day be filled with so many hugs, kisses and laughs. know that you are so very loved, and i miss you every day.

sister.

My first instinct was to document this. I pulled out my phone and took pictures. *This* felt like evidence. Evidence of her character, evidence of her ingenuity, her resourcefulness.

I moved on to the small square gift, in wrapping paper that said *green heritage*, recycled from the packaging of an off-brand toilet paper company. I tugged at the orange thread and removed the tape, which was a VO5 sham-poo label that she must have peeled from a bottle bought on commissary.

Inside I saw four green cardboard rectangles with the familiar Irish Spring logo—the soap of our childhood. But when I turned them over, I saw that on the back side of the boxes, she had collaged affirmation cards from magazine pages—four separate messages, written sister to sister:

"BE HERE; EVERY MOMENT COUNTS" was glued on top of a collage of flowers. A reminder to be present, not to take these ordinary moments for granted; moments I knew she wished she could have back.

"P a u s e & ask yourself: What do I need right now?" seemingly ripped from a magazine like Oprah's *O*, encouraging self-care and stillness.

And the last two were messages to remember my power and sovereignty:

"I am one woman & I am enough!!"

"Wake up call: You're a mother f-cking superhero." (That one made me laugh.)

As if answering my lingering question of *How, Nikki?* I pulled out a small piece of lined paper, on which she had written the story of the cards:

> over the course of a week, i collected any "used" magazine an inmate was willing to part with (here, they are deemed useless once the color is rubbed off the pages). after commissary day, i was able to secure two discarded soap boxes and half a tube of state toothpaste from the garbage.

She'd made a little drawing of the hand-raising emoji with a handwritten #jailhousesupplyshop.

> state toothpaste is the key. this completely insufficient gel on your teeth is surprisingly effective glue.

She ended with the hashtag that she used with her sewing business, #mamade, and added #jailmade, knowing it would make me smile, which it did. She ended with:

made *just for you* with love, toothpaste and trash,

sister

I paused to take in what was in front of me, and let in a swirl of contradictory feelings—admiration for her resiliency, astonishment at her artistry, gratitude, sadness, appreciation, sadness, sadness, sadness. I also felt angry. Angry that it was taking so long for people to believe that she had been protecting herself. Angry that taxpayers were footing the bill for her to be locked up in a place where she had to resort to using toothpaste as glue. Angry that real people in my community were crafting an alternative narrative that suggested she was crazy, a narcissist, or as Chana had started to call her in briefs written to the judge, a "master manipulator." I knew how much good she could do if she were out here in the world—and it made me want to scream.

The kids continued to spend Wednesday evenings visiting Nikki, but by midsummer we started alternating which one of them went, so that they each had alone time with their mother to process, and soak in her undivided attention. After every session, Dr. Crenshaw emailed me detailed therapy notes, which I'd print and mail to Nikki. I made an extra copy for my own records; they helped me understand what was happening under my roof, and to recognize the repetitive play themes that I may have overlooked.

Ben and Faye still checked Nikki for injuries. They still reenacted play scenarios that involved abandonment, loss, and joyful reunion. And at the end of every session, I was there in the waiting room, whether the guards gave them one hour or three—I never knew what to expect.

Faye's Wednesday visits were always a little lighter than Ben's, who, according to the therapy notes, would spend much of the time "training" Nikki and Dr. Crenshaw to fight the perceived powers that kept his mom away. I could imagine the three of them punching and kicking the air around the room, preparing for a war that Ben created in his mind. He was usually depleted by the end of each visit, and the car rides home were quiet.

I also started to observe their play at home in the context that I'd learned from Dr. Crenshaw, as a way to process their experiences. I noticed that Faye had started using her dolls as a canvas, scribbling on them with markers.

One doll discovery stopped me in my tracks.

Faye's Build-A-Bear Poppy doll—one she'd made a few weeks after Nikki's arrest—was lying on the carpet next to her white toddler bed. I saw a dark circle drawn around the doll's left eye, and more black gashes on its arms and legs. A piece of Ben's craft duct tape covered Poppy's smile.

"Oh no, what happened to Poppy?" I asked Faye, carrying the doll into the living room, where she was building a structure out of colorful magnetic blocks.

"Poppy was being bad," Faye said casually, without looking up.

"Yeah, she was being bad so we had to teach her a lesson," Ben chimed in from the couch.

I got full-body chills. They didn't hear that kind of language from me.

But I did know—from Sarah and from Nikki's attorneys—that Nikki used to have her mouth duct-taped closed, her limbs bound and restrained as punishment for disrespecting Chris. Did they know? Had they seen?

Around the same time as I found Poppy, Dr. Crenshaw's play therapy notes started to include darker admissions—memories, often through drawings, were brought to the surface, indicating that both of the kids, but especially Ben, had seen things in the middle of the night that no child ever should. Unlike other drawings, which Ben spent time on and showed proudly, he did these particular drawings hastily, and covered parts with his hand. I don't know the specifics of what Ben disclosed in the therapeutic space of Room 311 or what exactly he and Faye had seen in the middle of the night, but I know that Dr. Crenshaw sent some of the drawings to respected colleagues in the field, who all concurred that the depictions were beyond the scope of normal childhood imagination, and indicated what one expert called "complete chaos."

Knowing the violence that happened at night, I could only imagine what they saw.

Nikki was beside herself when the reckoning came: Despite all her best efforts, she hadn't protected her kids from being affected by the violence. It was something she had to face head-on—not only with the kids in Room 311, but with her attorneys. They briefly considered having the kids testify, and Dr. Crenshaw wrote letters directly to the judge, which were passed onto the prosecution as well.

That's the only reason I stayed as long as I did—I thought I was the only one being hurt, I thought I was protecting them, she cried over the phone and in Sister Visits, unable to hide from harsh reality.

I, too, was floored. Not because the kids were exposed to violence—that seemed credible, even inevitable—but because I'd spent nearly a year with these children and had no indication of the dark memories they'd suppressed. It was a disconcerting reminder that the inner lives of the people around me, even the smallest people in my care, were never really mine to know, to fix.

"Can we play dragon egg?" Faye asked me one morning in late August, before the boys were up for the day.

"Sure!" I said. It wasn't the first time she wanted to play this game, which came with a consistent storyline: She was a baby dragon left alone in the woods, abandoned by the mama dragon, and I was a stranger who finds her and takes her home.

She instantly rolled off my bed onto the floor and got into position: legs tucked in, back rounded, head and arms pulled under her body.

I stood up and pretended to walk around the room like I was taking a nonchalant stroll. I knew my lines.

"Hmmm, it's a beautiful day in these woods, *doo-doo-doo-duh-doo*— wait! What's this?" I stopped next to the Faye/egg and leaned down with exaggerated interest.

"Wow! What kind of egg is this?" I said to the room. I put my hand on her back and gave her a little jostle, knowing it would make her giggle.

"Whoa! This egg just made a noise!" I put my ear up against her still back and listened. I breathed her in.

On cue, Faye unfurled one arm behind her like a wing cracking through an egg. Then the other arm, which flapped as she turned over as a smiling baby dragon.

"Oh, oh! It's a dragon!" I said with as much enthusiasm as I could express, as if she were the most incredible creature I'd ever laid eyes on. "I've always wanted a dragon!"

She flapped her arms like a dog wagging its tail. She smiled, jumping into my arms.

"I'm going to take you home and take care of you forever and ever and ever!" I said to the dragon, and the girl curled in my arms.

CHAPTER 38

you will be found

dear sister,

it smells like september.

*like gunpowder and jail and the last time i ever took my
kids to the park.*

A full trip around the sun, and Nikki wasn't even close to being free.

We all kept adapting. Unlike surrender, which felt like a choice, adaptation was something our bodies were doing for us, like our lungs breathing or our hearts beating—an act of survival.

"I miss Mommy," Faye said one morning. She didn't say it in a cry or whine; it was stated as a quiet fact. She wasn't even talking to me. I was in the kitchen chopping up orange and yellow peppers for a vegetarian chili, Nikki's recipe. Faye was talking to Ben, who was sitting next to her on the couch.

"Me too," Ben said. Every night he slept with Nikki's shirt over his face, holding a framed picture of her. Ben wrapped his arm around Faye, and her attention moved back to the TV. Nikki would never let them watch as much TV as I did, and I felt a pang of guilt. Her hands-on/screens-off mothering set a standard I was constantly falling short of.

Distracted by a swirl of critical thoughts, I didn't notice that Ben had left the room until he walked back in with a small pink backpack and the framed picture that normally sat next to his bed. I watched Faye open the bag and pull out the white shirt that Nikki had worn when she came home from jail, the same one Ben slept with over his face.

"Now whenever you're sad, you can get this backpack. Okay, Faye?" His face was serious, his tone soft.

"Okay, Ben, thank you," she said, hugging the bag to her chest.

The more I watched Ben and Faye instinctively form their own rituals and comforts around the loss, the easier it was to believe that our bodies know what to do to regulate themselves, that there's something inside us that wants us to be soothed, to connect, to belong. Something innate in us that wants to live.

Ben was having a tough time acclimating to kindergarten—I had to be on call in case he ended up in the school psychologist's office, throwing objects and refusing to go back to the classroom. When that happened, I'd have to pick him up for some one-on-one time. I typically hung around a coffee shop near Vassar College, an equal two-mile radius from both the jail and Ben's school, where I wrote emails, talking points, and case summaries to send. Sarah's office was around the corner, and some days I'd stop by to get more legal paperwork or, quite often, a stack of drawings or collages Nikki had made.

Some of the drawings were done with ballpoint pen, including a series of self-portraits done of her in a jail cell, her body in different positions—sitting with her knees pulled into her chest, her head in her hands; curled facedown on a mattress pad, her back rounded like a turtle shell; standing in front of a barred window, face up to the sky, hands over her heart. They all said the same words: *You will be found.*

One day in mid-September, the manila folder Sarah passed me contained something heavier than art.

It was a thirty-two-page forensic psychological evaluation, which was like a systematic review of Nikki's entire history: from multiple interviews with Nikki and the people around her (like me), and a review of all available records—from medical to court documents—all done through the lens of intimate partner violence. The forensic psychologist who had conducted it was an expert—"*the* expert to hire," we were told—and it cost us $10,000 just to retain her for the analysis and report. We didn't have that kind of money, but a prominent local family gifted it to us, saying, "We know you and your sister will do good things in the world," only asking to stay anonymous.

Now here was the report, which was also sent to the prosecutor and judge.

"Ms. Addimando is a 29-year-old Caucasian female who appeared younger than her stated age," the report began. I could picture Nikki sitting across from the woman, desperate to be believed.

> Her mood appeared depressed and she was often tearful, shaky, and anxious when discussing difficult traumatic material…Her insight into her psychological difficulties was good although it appeared she still seemed to engage in minimization and denial of some aspects of the abuse and its consequences.

This tracked with what I had come to realize about Nikki: She wasn't exaggerating for attention; in fact, she was minimizing the true horrors in her life—even to herself. She, too, was engaging in her own version of denial.

I went on to read the methodology of how Nikki was interviewed—16.5 hours in Dutchess County Jail over the course of three days, during which she was tested for personality and mood disorders using a variety of clinical models with names like the Danger Assessment Scale and the Abusive Behavior and Observation Scale.

The report was organized as a coherent narrative, starting with Nikki's childhood, then her education, and the years she lived with Chris—including a chronological list of medical documentation through the spring and summer before the September 2017 shooting. From my talks with Elizabeth and Sarah, I knew that this was when she had become more serious about leaving, packing a bag, strategizing and safety planning with her surrogate sisters. As she was trying to leave, the violence was getting worse—and according to the medical records in front of me, it was much worse than I had allowed myself to believe. I thought back to Sarah's solemn head shake when I asked if the "spoon" story was the worst I was going to hear.

May 12, 2017, four months before the shooting:

> Nicole presented to her midwife reporting that Chris had physically hurt her, including her vagina. She reported that Chris makes her have sex against her will and uses objects. She reported that Chris had a gun and inserted it into her vagina. She reported that Chris has threatened to kill her, her children, and her family.

If I had heard this before, I must have blocked it out: The barrel of a gun was put inside my sister's body?

Reading excerpts from the actual medical records was sobering, bringing me right up close to the reality of her injuries: "Her vulva was torn and had scars that were not present at her postpartum exam," the midwife had written. "There are previous tears and scarring. There was a bruise on her buttocks, bruising on both her breasts, and red rope like burns from being tied up on her breasts."

I thought back to May—a time I was seeing Nikki regularly after work, when she'd hang out with Noah until I could get home. There were rope burns under her clothes? How much pain was she hiding?

A month later, in June 2017, while I was trying to heal from the end of my marriage, Nikki went to the midwife again. Around this time, I was starting every morning with a yoga practice, repeating affirmations like *I am safe and lovable*, and I had downloaded a dating app to start inviting some fun back into my life. The report read:

> June 14, 2017: Nicole presented for a rape and sexual assault exam in obvious distress. She reported that Chris had inserted her with objects (wood and metal) and his gun.

I had known from Kara that homemade weapons had been recovered from Chris's car. She had sent me some pictures of daggers and swordlike creations.

She reported feeling ashamed and scared of Chris, and that the beatings increased if she said anything about breaking up...She reported that Chris will kill her if she leaves...She is having difficulty holding urine and is bleeding (more than a period)... Medical exam revealed vulva trauma. Her tissue was swollen and looked inside out.

"Inside out." That was how she had described it to me in the bathroom on that day. Had Nikki already gone to the doctor and heard the midwife use that language? Was that her way of testing me, of dipping her toe into the possibility of letting me in? Or had I already dismissed her with a quick "ew" when she reported it to the midwife? Also that day: "She believed that no one will help her leave...She is afraid that her parents will think she did something to encourage the attacks."

I don't know how I would have reacted if I had seen what the midwife documented:

The inside of her vaginal tissue was raw, red, damaged, and bleeding frank red blood. She had conjunctiva broken blood vessels. Her rectum was swollen shut, bruised, and bleeding.

The last midwife exam entry was on August 6, 2017:

States boyfriend Chris at gunpoint raped her after tying her and hitting. Used an object. Nicole could not tell me what it was, she was choked up...She stated that he used the object to penetrate her vaginally while he penetrated her rectum back and forth. I could not insert a swab as was so swollen shut.

I felt physically sick and looked away from the report, up at the coffee patrons typing and chatting around me. August sixth, I kept repeating the date in my head. This wasn't ancient history—it was a month before the shooting, three weeks before my birthday, the same time period as when

Nikki and the kids would watch Noah after school and do laundry at my place. It was a Sunday, I realized, flipping through my phone's calendar, desperate to ground that horrific experience in real life. Sundays she typically would have gone up to the Grovers'. I wondered if she had posted anything to her Instagram that day.

I didn't have to scroll far. There it was, August sixth. I couldn't believe what I was seeing.

It was the *invisible string* post, the one I'd seen in the early days after her arrest, the one that broke my heart thinking about the distance that string had to stretch.

Now, with the context of the midwife report, I saw it completely differently:

B: mommy, I didn't like not being with you today...

Ben had said that Nikki wasn't with him that Sunday—now I knew where she was, at the midwife.

...what would I do in my life without you?

I looked at the picture she posted, Nikki and Ben with their eyes closed, lying on a pillow, holding hands. But this time I realized that the right side of her face was pointing away from the camera, and Ben's blanket was pulled up past her chin, covering the lower part of her face. The only part of her body uncovered was one hand. *She was hiding the injuries*, I realized. It was right there in front of me, all this time.

As hard as it was to read, I found myself flipping through the thirty-two-page report again and again, rereading the astute insight into Nikki's story. It was all here, ready and able to be read out to a jury:

> Ms. Addimando assessed Mr. Grover's state of mind to be one that was capable of killing her. He had repeatedly demonstrated not only his ability, but his willingness, to inflict serious forms of violence and sexual torture against her, especially with weapons including a gun. The Child Protective Services report represented a significant turning point in that Chris finally knew that authorities would be looking at him and he said that to Nicole. For all

these years, he had been able to hide in plain sight while abusing Nicole with impunity. Now that cover was being threatened.

I could picture Nikki's attorneys reading out the report's conclusion to the jury, preceded by a dramatic "ladies and gentleman of the court":

When Mr. Grover brandished his gun, loaded his gun, spoke of killing her, refused to let her leave with the children, and then ultimately threatened to kill her and himself, she imminently feared for her life. Ms. Addimando reasonably believed that when the opportunity presented itself and she was able to get a hold of the gun, shooting him was necessary to defend herself from Mr. Grover's threats to commit a murder-suicide, leaving her children parentless. There is ample evidence in support of a finding of the seriousness and severity of chronic intimate partner violence in this relationship and a lethality assessment provided empirical support that this relationship was one of high risk for serious or deadly intimate partner violence.

I passed it on to the rest of the committee as good for the case, and celebrated the potential in the visiting room with Nikki. It was all here in black-and-white. People would see. They must.

CHAPTER 39

meet you at home

A fter a full year of fundraising, months of fighting the prosecution to
allow us to make a bail application, and nearly two months after the
judge set bail—$400,000 cash or $600,000 bond (meaning collateral)—
we finally came up with the money. We had just over $100,000 in donated
funds, and there was no way we'd get to $400,000 anytime soon. So we
opted for the $600,000 bond—and in lieu of property, of which our family
had none, six close family and friends promised their annual salaries to a
bondsman none of us fully trusted. It was risky and stressful, and took longer than we wanted—and just when we had the bond signed and delivered,
Chana found another wrench to throw into our plans: She requested a bail
source hearing. She argued, in a motion I read, that Nikki's family didn't
have the means to post such a high bail, and so the sources of the bail money
were not a close enough tie to Nikki to ensure that she didn't skip out on
court.

It was an old rule left over from the mob days, and especially hurt families
who didn't come from money.

As if Nikki voluntarily surrendering back to jail meant nothing, Chana
was now arguing that Nikki was a flight risk. *You have got to be kidding*,
we all said to each other, exhausted from the constant effort and consistent
disappointment.

And so, one day in that first week of November, I sat on my bed, texting
Elizabeth about an email we were sending to the donors whose money and
pay checks we were holding in limbo for potential bail. I was surrounded
by big plastic storage bins. A couple of them were filled with puffy jackets

and snow boots from the winter before and had stayed out for so long that they had turned into furniture, usually holding stacks of unopened mail or piles of laundry. On some level I had to accept that this was how we had to live, out of sheer necessity. I came to see the boxes and piles as a visual representation of this transitory, unsettled time. If anyone had seen the state of the apartment—especially around the change of season—they might have thought I was a hoarder. Except in this case, instead of compulsively holding on to my own stuff, I was housing and holding on to everyone else's stuff for them, consumed by the mess of it all.

Our email had to go out to thirty-five bail donors to let them know that, prior to a bail source hearing—another court date when we'd need bodies in purple to show up in the middle of a workday—Chana had requested that every single donor call her for an interview.

I wrote out a list of what people needed to know: Call this number between 9 a.m. and 4 p.m., identify yourself as a bail donor for Nikki Addimando, and briefly share how you're connected to Nikki or the family. I asked every person to stress that they'd given the money as a loan to me or Elizabeth—the two people to whom Nikki had the strongest ties—and that they understood that it was my responsibility to repay the loan. I put the burden squarely on my shoulders, so that Chana couldn't argue that the ties were too loose.

Still, the bail source hearing had yet to be scheduled. The time on the clock had stopped again. More scheduling. More waiting.

Once again, Chana was playing every card to keep Nikki in jail.

Why? I'd wonder constantly. Her vitriol felt personal, but based on what? Was this all just a bluff? An attempt to break Nikki's spirits to win a court case? Was this a case of an overinflated and bruised ego, after the habeas corpus release? Or did she actually truly think Nikki was dangerous, and deserved to stay away from her kids—who, as the recorded jail calls captured, cried for Nikki to come home. Did she believe that Nikki also deserved to be kept away from her own mom, who was swiftly dying? The cruelty was astounding.

* * *

I was really good at compartmentalizing—we all were, Nikki, Mom, Dad. We have internal drawers for where we store hard and uncomfortable things, and then we keep the drawer closed through all sorts of coping strategies: distracting, denying, ignoring, numbing. Being really, really busy. Compartmentalization also helped me *stay* busy. It's what allowed me to handle all I was handling. It wasn't magic or a miracle that I was standing on two feet, as some surmised—it was simply a well-honed, heirloom defense mechanism.

But, I also had a sense that we'd need to open those compartments and look inside. Because if we didn't, then the pressure would build and build until eventually the hinges would blow off.

And so a few days before Thanksgiving, I made the time to drive down to Westchester to my aunt's Bronxville condo draped in a canopy of colorful autumn leaves, and opened the compartment labeled MOM.

I didn't recognize the woman looking at me through the doorway of my aunt's bedroom, a big grin on her face, propped up in a rented hospital bed. She was fifty-nine years old, but looked much older. Her face was swelling from all the medication, filling in any fine wrinkles she'd had before, while the rest of her skin was becoming crepe-like, as if her body was deflating underneath. Her hair, once long, thick, and shiny—a prized part of her beauty—was growing back in white-gray patches after chemo, dull and downy, sticking straight in the air. It was like watching her life reverse—back to baby hair, full cheeks, and a dependent, delicate body that needed careful support.

The cancer had been cut out of her stomach, but she lay in the bed with one hand on her still-distended belly. I could see her thin skin blotched with deep maroon marks that looked painful.

She noticed me staring at her arms as I sat down next to her. "They don't hurt," my mom slurred out, shrugging her shoulders. Golf was playing on the TV in front of her. She'd never watched or played golf in her life.

"How are you feeling, Mom?"

"I can't complain," she shrugged again, smiling. "It could be worse. It's not the electric pain," she said. "At least I'm here and not in the hospital."

I looked around the room at the table full of pill bottles next to her bed, at the half-finished drinks to stay hydrated. I imagined some of those morphine pills and the marijuana vape pen at her side had something to do with her upbeat attitude, but it also seemed like she was stripped down to her most raw, optimistic self. She was always good at looking at the positives. That was her thing. She repeated the phrase *this too shall pass* like a mantra. So much that it had become ingrained in the very way I saw the world around me. *This won't last forever, I can tolerate this for right now, if I hang on it'll all get better.*

I tried to hold a conversation with her, but she dozed off every few minutes. I watched her chest rise and fall irregularly.

It was never more apparent how skilled this woman was at holding on, despite it all. How good she was at enduring. This was the lesson she'd taught us, above all others: how to get through anything, to keep pressing ahead, to persevere.

Yes, this may have contributed to both Nikki and me, in varying degrees, sticking it out in really bad situations—to keep going, going, going, instead of stopping and assessing why. *Eventually it will get better*, we both reasoned, waiting for it to pass.

But it was also undoubtedly why I had the stamina for the criminal legal system, which, I'd learned, was an endurance race. This was what all the women in our lives had trained for.

I sat and watched my mom asleep inside a body full of pain, thinking, *I wish you had also taught us when to stop enduring.* I wish that she had learned that lesson herself.

Mom existed in a space between life and death, similar to Nikki, except I knew Mom was heading in only one direction. And quickly.

The last time Nikki saw Mom, she had been standing in the frame of our dad's screened door, smiling and waving, as I drove Nikki back to jail to surrender. That was nearly five months earlier. Mom's immune system was too compromised by her chemo treatments to visit a crowded, unsanitary jail, and she had gotten too weak to write letters or even talk on the phone. It felt as if she was being pulled away from us like a receding tide, and we couldn't get Nikki unchained fast enough.

Nikki still wrote letters to her, though. I saw them piled up next to Mom's bed. Every single one ended with the same line: "I'll meet you at home mama."

back to december

On December 22, 2018, after nearly fifteen months behind bars, Nikki was finally released on a $600,000 bond that had taken a series of small miracles to secure. In light of Nikki being charged with murder, the owners of my rental apartment refused to let her stay with me. The charges against her had become her identity, and I tearfully scrambled for a backup plan, which ended up being my dad's one-bedroom apartment less than ten minutes away. It wasn't ideal, but a couch was better than a metal slab with a thin foam pad; an ankle monitor was better than a cage.

We gave Ben and Faye the only thing they wanted for Christmas: Mom.

The kids knew that Nikki couldn't stay with us—which I said was because we already had too many people living in my 1,400-square-foot apartment, not because their mom was charged with murder. And they knew she couldn't leave Dad's place—clear as the blinking red light on her ankle monitor. It was one of the first things that Nikki showed the kids when they reunited, which we said was a condition of her visit. No one pressed us for deeper answers; life was already so unpredictable and nonsensical that I imagine a bulky black electronic device strapped to her leg was just another oddity of life.

During the school week, they slept at home—my home, *our* home. On the weekends, I dropped them off at my dad's and they slept with Nikki on a blow-up mattress in the middle of the living room. They were happy just to have her physical presence—wrapping their bodies around her on the couch while they watched a movie, feeling suspended in her arms as Nikki spun them around the living room, laughing out loud.

Although I was initially upset at my landlords, the living situation may have been for the best. It helped us keep a steady routine, reinforcing that, despite all that was changing, the four of us—me, Noah, Ben, and Faye—had a home base, a tangled temporary nest to last through every season, outside and separate from their mom's cage. Nikki was still confined, restricted. But in our home, we were free in a way that we'd taken for granted. Yes, it was messy and chaotic, woven together with pieces from our past, and new people and places that supported us. Yes, we ultimately lacked solid ground and security, and I struggled to confidently keep us all safe while petrified that another big life storm would sweep us away.

But we could run outside in the grass, take long walks to regulate our nervous systems, cheer and clap at their schools' winter concerts, and chat about our days in the car. I don't know about the kids, but I couldn't unsee the difference; I couldn't unfeel that sense of freedom. I carried that gratitude in my pocket, like a leavening agent, helping to lift us all through the transition.

Then it was New Year's Eve, which was also Ben's birthday. He woke up next to his mom on the blow-up bed in my dad's small living room. The Christmas tree was still up. There was no rush to dismantle the holiday joy. The room was decorated with streamers and balloons, including an oversized golden "6." Nikki and I had quietly decorated while Ben slept on his "alone time" sleepover, after I brought over a stack of wrapped gifts. Nikki wasn't free to shop in stores; she could leave the house only when the probation department said so. If she were to go so far as to walk outside the door to get fresh air without written permission, they could revoke her bond, remand her back to jail, and I and a handful of friends and family would be contractually obligated to pay back $600,000 to our lenders of bail. So I did the shopping.

Later that night, we gathered around Ben to sing—Nikki and I, Noah and Faye, and my dad. Ben smiled before he blew out his candles, saying, "I already have my wish."

"Okay, folks, I'm going now," my dad announced, pulling his coat on.

"Pal, Happy Birthday." He kissed Ben's head as he passed. He wanted to get down to see Mom before people started drinking and driving. He wanted to be with the love of his life and give her a New Year's kiss.

My dad carried an overnight bag out of the house with him. He planned to sleep on my aunt's couch. Noah and I planned to sleep in his bed, and we would all have a rare "sister sleepover," with Ben, Faye, and Nikki sleeping in the living room.

All three kids swore they would stay up until midnight. But by 11 p.m., it was just me and Nikki awake in a quiet apartment.

While Nikki shuffled around stacks of legal documents that she had hidden in the closet, I sat down with my brand-new 2019 calendar and started to fill in the month with which days and times I needed to bring Nikki to court, or to John's office to prep for trial. As I filled in the dates the kids were going back to school and all the upcoming child-related obligations, I let out a long deep exhale.

"I'm sorry," Nikki said quietly. "This is so much for you."

"It's a lot for both of us, much more for you," I said. "Honestly this"—I gestured to the planner—"is nothing compared to what you're dealing with."

My phone rang; Mom was FaceTiming. It was twenty minutes to midnight and we had promised to all be together on the phone if we couldn't be together in person.

"Hi, my babies!" Mom slurred with a big, goofy smile. "It makes my heart happy to see you two together." All she'd ever wanted was for us to be close friends. Forget that our bond was now forged by compounding tragedies—we truly were closer than ever. There was no hiding, no competition. We'd been stripped to our truest selves, right down to the spirit.

I watched my dad and mom on the screen together, sitting on her hospital bed in my aunt's room. Framed pictures of the kids sat on a shelf behind them, where she could look over and see their faces. Nikki and I were reflected back in the small box at the top corner of the screen. I could hold the tears back from rolling down my face, but my red swollen eyes gave away my sadness. Nikki was finally here, and Mom was still just out of reach. It was all so wrong. So unfair.

"I'll see you soon, Mom, don't worry," Nikki gave a weak promise. They both held on to the hope of "soon." Soon Mom would feel strong enough to sit in a car. Soon Nikki would be acquitted and could come to Mom's doctor's appointments. Soon, soon, soon.

As the minutes crept to midnight, Dad leaned into the screen and said, "When all of this is over, I'm taking you all on a cruise."

I watched Dad smile nervously. I watched Mom's face barely react. He saw Mom's expression in the screen, too, and stopped smiling.

She knew she didn't have another year. She knew this was the end.

Dad looked away, off to the side of the room. No one said anything. Tears streamed down my face.

mommy's dying

Less than twenty days later, on my way home from dropping the kids off at preschool, a text from my Aunt Debbie interrupted a normal Wednesday morning: "Come to the hospital, doctors say your mom only has a few hours left."

I pulled over on the side of the highway just before getting on the Mid-Hudson Bridge. It was peak commute time and cars whipped past. I felt myself float out of my seat as my fingers automatically texted out requests and plans for school pickup without me. I glided down to the train, where I parked, bought a ticket, and boarded.

A text came in from Nikki: "Michelle. Michelle mommy's dying."

Elizabeth was already driving Nikki down to the hospital—the judge and probation department approved what they called "a compassion visit." It happened quickly—proof that the court system can move with speed when it wants to.

"We're hitting all the green lights," she wrote.

Mom was in a hospital room waiting to be moved to the hospice floor, to her death bed. She'd never be leaving this building again. She'd felt her last fresh air on earth.

I was acutely aware of that as I stood in the small shared room, cramped tight with my dad, two aunts, and cousin. Nikki was curled up in bed with my mom when I got there, wrapped in Mom's arms, deep purple marks spreading across her papery skin, IV tubes snaked around them. I was told that my mom had lit up when Nikki walked in, confused, saying, *How are you here?*

It was clear that my mom thought Nikki was free. No one corrected her.

What I witnessed in that hospital room was exquisitely painful. Mom was in agony, her heart was beating out of her chest, we could feel it. She writhed. She looked terrified. I paced back and forth in the hallway, while Nikki stayed next to Mom, holding her hand. I demanded to know when someone would help my mom—it was inhumane to allow such catastrophic human suffering.

Soon, soon, I was told. Her private room would be ready and they'd relax her into a coma; then we would wait for the end.

We were told she had only hours to live, but once Mom was medicated and settled in her new room, she stabilized. We stayed until we had to get the very last train out of Manhattan—we hung up photos of the kids, in case she opened her eyes again; we said our goodbyes through sobbing tears.

A few times Mom grunted. "She's trying to say something," a hospice nurse said casually, on her way out the door. I felt gutted. She had things she needed to say, but was trapped in her coma, being buried alive with important words inside.

Dad stayed behind for the night, and Nikki and I reluctantly walked to the train station together, a sister ride we took in complete silence.

My mom hung on for another day. And then two days. Three. Four.

The judge continued to extend Nikki's compassion visits, underestimating our mom's ability to endure a slow, drawn-out death.

And we needed that time, sitting around Mom's bed as an original family of four, taking turns telling funny *remember when* stories, and stealing intimate and emotional alone time with her—whispering, sitting, holding her still body, knowing she'd never open her eyes again.

When it was Nikki's turn, she played the Carrie Underwood song "Temporary Home"—maybe as a message that they'd still meet each other at home, just not this one. I played Snatam Kaur's "Long Time Sun" and other sacred music, hoping to guide her on to the next realm. And when it was my dad's turn, I heard the haunting love songs from *Somewhere in Time*, the movie they'd watched together throughout my life, curled up on the couch. I watched from the doorway as he leaned over Mom's bed, tearful yet stoic, stroking her forehead.

Despite the gnawing pain, I also felt a reverence, a gratitude, while pacing the hospice hallway, only a short walk from the maternity ward. It felt like the veil between worlds was thinner, and all that existed in that space was our love for each other.

By the third night, I knew it would be the last. Before leaving, I sat alone on the edge of her hospital bed, next to her small body curled up like a fetus. One hand was resting on a small stuffed turtle, the other on a monkey wearing a hospital gown that said, HANG IN THERE. "We like to give her something soft to hold on to," the nurse said. Mom's fingernails were painted a pretty mauve color—they'd been done by Nikki as one last act of care.

I didn't know if she could hear me, but I felt a pressure to say something. Would these be the last words my mom ever heard me speak? How could I possibly say everything that needed to be said? On the train ride down that morning, I had scrawled notes in a journal, trying to prepare myself for what I wanted to say.

I took the notebook out of my bag and started with Nikki, because I knew she was Mom's biggest worry.

"Nikki has a big purpose in this world, Mom," I began, the words catching in my throat. "Everything in her life has led her to this point, and she's going to help a lot of women. She's going to help change laws. She's going to break patterns that have trapped the women in our family for generations."

She didn't respond, but I could see her eyes moving behind her closed eyelids. I kept talking.

"The role you played is exactly the role you were supposed to. You did such a good job, Mom. There are no mistakes; everything you did was for a reason. And I'm going to stay here, playing my role—raising Noah, Ben, and Faye—and they're going to be okay because I had you to learn from. It's my job to be the mother now. And I will continue to care for Nikki, although I'm sure her spiritual strength and courage will carry her. She got that from you, Mom."

Could she sense the tears on my face? Did she want to reach out and hold me, trapped inside her body? What were the words she wasn't able to say back to me? I continued, "I want you to know how loved you are. Everyone from my friends growing up to the people you've worked with over the years—anyone who knew you—remembers your kindness and compassion. You were good to people, Mom, and that's how people will remember you." I needed her to know that she wasn't reduced to her blind spots. I needed her to know that she was forgiven.

"Thank you for devoting your life to us. Thank you for taking care of me, for loving me, for giving me such a special connection and love to miss. You did a good job. I couldn't have gained all of this strength without you." I could feel Mom straddling worlds. And deep down, under the words meant to release her, to free her, I knew I still needed her, and I knew she still needed us. "Nikki was given permission to come back tomorrow morning, but if you need to let go before that, you can."

I closed the notebook. I touched her familiar hands. She made small noises. "You don't have to say anything, Mom," I whispered. "I know you love me. I'll tell Noah you love him. You don't have anything left to do or say. I can take it from here."

How do you know when you've said all you can say? The train schedule was immovable, and I had no choice but to go. I stood up and gathered my things, whispering one last *I love you* before walking out the door, leaving her body behind.

At 5 a.m. I woke up to a group text from my aunt: "She's gone." Both of her sisters had stayed the night, keeping a vigil on either side of her bed.

I sat up expecting to feel wrecked with grief, but instead, I felt proud of her. *She did it*, I thought. Under the light of the year's first full moon, she let go. I could only hope that she released that big cry on the way out.

PART IV

courage

"Nothing changes if we are silent."

—Nikki Addimando

discovery

It was a quiet Tuesday in the middle of February, without any legal appointments or a probation-approved reason to drive Nikki anywhere. The phone wasn't ringing. There was no fresh fire to put out. The kids were at school. Dad was at work. All the upheaval around Mom's death and funeral had passed; she had been cremated and her remains were in a box on a table across the hall from where Nikki and I sat in my dad's apartment.

Nikki pulled out the large brown accordion file system, marked LEGAL CONFIDENTIAL, which she had been keeping in a closet blocked by Faye's large plastic My Little Pony castle. Even though I knew that no one was monitoring our conversation on a tapped phone line or recording our "Sister Visit" with an overhead camera, as we unpacked the folders, it was hard to shake the feeling that someone was listening.

There were seemingly hundreds of pages of new evidence that Nikki had recently read for the first time during this new legal phase called "Discovery." This is when both sides become privy to the bulk of the evidence produced prior to trial in order to assess each other's case, make requests to have certain parts suppressed or redacted, and inform the inevitable plea negotiation period. Despite calls for reform, in early 2019, it was standard practice for this to happen within days of trial beginning—in Nikki's case, trial was expected to begin in less than a month.

Nikki stood up and walked over to the large block of windows that took up most of the wall at the front of the apartment, above the wooden toddler table we had recently moved into the room. Multicolored balloons were scattered around the hardwood floor, left over from three back-to-back birthdays since Christmas. Faye was now four, Ben was now six, and my Noah was—double-digits!—ten. We celebrated with banners and streamers, mustering up excitement for their relentless growth while part of me wished we could stay frozen in time.

"Dad wants me to keep the blinds closed," Nikki said. His place was at ground level. Newspaper reporters had brought cameras to every pretrial hearing and her face had been displayed under the headlines. There was a biting sense of vengeance in some of the social media comments from people on Team Chris. My dad wanted to keep Nikki hidden and safe.

"But I need the light," she said, pulling the blinds up to the top, spilling long strips of afternoon sun onto the hardwood floor, brightening the stacks of manila folders filled with sticky-tabbed papers, labeled with words like: *Elizabeth text messages, Michelle deposition, Therapy notes, Pornhub.*

I helped organize piles on the family couch, a couch that was now doubling as Nikki's bed. A soft brown blanket was folded and draped over the arm, with a fluffy white pillow on top—luxuries, after sleeping on a thin mattress pad for the past year.

This kind of freedom to work on her defense also felt like a luxury. She had done some preparation with the attorneys in their office, but a lot of it—seemingly most of it—she did right here, at night while the rest of us slept. She needed uninterrupted time to sort through the stacks of reports—bank records, web searches, forensic documentation—and make timelines and cohesive arguments to present to her attorneys. Not because her attorneys were incapable, but because they were inundated by the sheer volume of discovery handed over, and the short time frame they had to review it all. It was too much. If Nikki didn't help, key details could easily be missed.

Most of what was in front of me had already been discovered: first by the attorneys and then Nikki, and so bits of information had already trickled down to me as news was breaking and emotions were high. And the big "A-HA, WE GOT 'EM!" headline from our attorneys, among *all* the transcripts and reports handed over, was the grand jury testimony. The attorneys told me about what they'd read in the transcripts with a kind of flabbergasted astonishment, as if they were just now seeing the prosecution in a more sinister light.

"They lied!" John said over the phone one day.

The gist was that Chana had a police detective tell the jury about the crime scene, and during questioning, she asked him if the gun was wiped down. The detective replied, under oath, "They told us that the gun was wiped down," and "they told us that there appeared to be residue left over from it being wiped off."

"Wiping the gun is an admission of guilt to a jury," John interjected, because why would someone wipe down the gun if they weren't trying to hide? He also pointed out that the detective didn't clarify who "they" were who told him—the definition of hearsay.

It didn't stop there. Chana then asked the detective if there was anything around that could have wiped the gun, and the detective responded that there was a box of baby wipes nearby.

And all the while, Chana knew, or certainly should have known, that there was no proof that the gun had been wiped. No test had been made for solvents. Moreover, fingerprint evidence on the gun indicated that it had *not* been wiped. John told me that only Chris's prints were found on the slide, the part of the gun that loads a live chamber. "Only one person got that gun ready to kill and it wasn't Nikki," John said, boosting my hope that he'd be able to connect the dots and lay out some zingers for the trial jury. The previous jury, the grand jury, heard only one side—which didn't include anything about Nikki's documented abuse. All they had was the prosecution's narrative of Nikki shooting Chris in the head and then using a baby wipe to clear the evidence, despite that being based on a lie.

"Wait until you see this," Nikki said, sorting through the piles and organizing as she went. I could hear a quiet exhaustion in Nikki's voice. I felt it, too. Like part of my body was slipping into Power Saver Mode, overloaded with information and uncertainty.

"Here…" Nikki reached across the floor and handed me a folder labeled CHRIS SEARCH HISTORY in Sharpie, provided by the official New York State Crime Lab. It was thick, with multiple paper-clipped stacks of Excel spreadsheets with the words *Search History* and *Web History* organized in columns of data: search words, headlines, URLs, dates and times. Nikki had already highlighted all the pornography—words like *forced, tied and abused, painful, punished teens,* and *broken dolls* repeated, thousands of items spanning hundreds of pages and three months of time. My face contorted into disgust as I flipped past search after search of videos titled things like *Shut Up and Take It* and *Thats What Girls Are For.*

This wasn't *Fifty Shades of Grey* submission-domination role play; it was brutal violence against women. The words I scanned included *whores abused, berated and humiliated, bitch got what she deserved.* The connective tissue between every video and web search was misogyny, an unapologetic hatred of women, a *stay in your place or get punished* vibe. The word I saw highlighted more than any other in the search results was *forced. Forced* as in *raped.*

Thousands of searches were listed, nearly fifty in every thirty-minute increment, entered at all hours of the day and night. Many were sandwiched in between ordinary web searching, like checking his bank account and searching for gymnastics warm-up routines—sometimes showing only seconds in between on the time stamps.

"I had no idea," Nikki said. "I mean I knew what he was doing to me, and I knew that was bad, but I had no idea how obsessed he was with watching this stuff." She gestured at the printed pile. "He was so much worse than I even knew."

The thumbnail images that accompanied the search histories were so disturbing that I had to make myself not look away.

"What the actual fuck?" I said. These were graphic images of women, and also girls, pinned down. If you could see the woman's face—meaning she wasn't held down by the back of her neck, or covered by multiple men lying on top of her—she was usually crying or screaming, mascara smeared from tears, eyebrows scrunched in pain and disgust. One video titled *Tiny Teen* looked like a prepubescent abduction; another video showed someone tied down and limp. These images looked like they had been shot on cell phones propped up in the corner of a living room, or on the dash of a car, or in a bathroom. They looked like crimes.

"Who is checking on these women? How is this legal?" I said, waving the papers in my hand.

"I guess people assume it's consensual," Nikki said flatly. I wondered how many times that had been drilled into her by not only Chris, but by the system's response to her reporting what he had done to her.

"Nothing about this looks consensual," I said. What was most upsetting to me was that Chris wasn't an outlier on the fringe of the dark web. It was clear these videos of men inflicting actual pain and torture on women was a thriving and mainstream genre of porn. *This is the smoking gun*, I thought. *These search results say everything.*

Just as I was about to close the file, a different word jumped off the page: *suicide.* It was in the last seven searches on Chris's phone, done between 11:26 and 11:28 p.m. the night he died: *part of brain to shoot in suicide.*

I thought back to how Nikki had described the events of that night—not just to me, but to police on the side of the road, and to multiple legal teams and during her psychological evaluations. Nikki always, every single time, said that Chris threatened to kill her *and then kill himself.*

Chris had intended to commit murder-suicide. It was a pattern shown by abusive men whose wives or girlfriends try to leave them—all it takes is a quick Google search of domestic violence homicides in the news. Sometimes entire families, including the kids, are killed. Stories like this are in the newspaper every single day: The United States averages eleven murder-suicides daily.[1] I'd read about five local women in the Hudson Valley killed by a current or former partner within the past six months alone, and of those five, three of the men killed themselves, too.

"Look back in July," Nikki said, pointing to the stack of papers in my hand. "I saw that he searched for suicide back then, too." She looked as aghast as I felt.

I found the pages from the summer of 2017, and sure enough, he was searching about suicide. This was around the same time that Nikki's medical records included words like *anal prolapse, frank red blood,* and *cannot examine, tissue too swollen.*

I wasn't a lawyer, but I imagined I could make a compelling argument with only the papers on that living room floor. There was clear evidence that what happened in September 2017 wasn't a random event: It was the culmination of a long pattern of increasing homicidal violence, escalating sharply when Nikki and people in the community began trying to get her out. This three-month span of web results corroborated it all. I imagined an expert could take the stand and make the argument that these search results demonstrated a compulsive obsession with violent sex, illustrating how sex addiction manifests. I imagined I could show that Chris was a troubled young man with his own hidden secrets that were threatened to be revealed; a man who had already been planning to die that night.

Turning to Nikki, I said, "And Chana has all this information." It was a fact I couldn't quite believe. When I read through the emails that Chana had sent to Nikki's attorneys, and the motions she had submitted to the judge, she had argued that there was no way to tie Nikki's abuse to Chris. He didn't show his face in any of the still shots that Sarah and the police officer had documented in 2015. There was no way to prove that it was *Chris* who hurt Nikki, Chana maintained; it could have been anyone.

"This seems like all the proof you need," I said, handing her back the folder.

"You'd think so," Nikki said, her voice low, weighed down by a resignation that I knew had been instilled in her by her attorneys—and by everyone and anyone who had any experience with the system.

CHAPTER 43

pleas

The trial was scheduled to begin in March, three months after Nikki had been released on bail. As the start date loomed closer, Nikki's attorney, John, began broaching the idea of a plea deal. Usually fatherly and caring, his advice had begun to have more of a bite, like a splash of cold water to the face. *Trials aren't about the truth. This is a murder trial first and foremost, not a domestic violence trial.* And *if Nikki ignores the plea deals*—as she was doing, because there were no single-digit plea offers on the table—*she'll have to face what's known as the trial tax.* The trial tax is the concept that if you choose to put the court through a very time-consuming and costly trial, then you can expect to face higher sentences if convicted. Maybe that's why over 90 percent of felony cases are settled before they make it to a jury.[2]

I had no idea. I truly did not know that constitutional rights—like the right to a trial jury of your peers; like the right to the counsel of your choice, or a speedy trial; like the right to be presumed innocent before being found guilty—were an illusion. *The facts of a case matter less than what the jury believes about the story.*

John wasn't confident that a jury could overcome the "bad facts"—the parts of Nikki's story that would be hard to explain to a jury. There was the fact that Nikki had suffered at the hands not just of Chris, but of multiple abusers throughout the course of her life (*they'll paint you as a slut*), and that her memory was fuzzy or disjointed when it came to discussing these past abusers (*they say you're lying*). There was the question of how Chris ended up in a nonthreatening position on the couch (*they're insisting that he was asleep*), and perhaps most hurtful, the Dutchess County DAs had given the Putnam

County DAs a recording from back in 2010, during the investigation that Dave was leading into Chris's abuse. They had my mom's voice talking to a police detective, saying that Nikki was a drama queen (*even her own mother doesn't believe her*). There was other unfortunate evidence that was easily distorted without context—including a few angry text messages she had sent Chris in the span of nine years, on par with how pretty much every couple I know fights (*a real victim doesn't fight back*). There were "controlling" behaviors around the kids' safety—like insisting that Faye stays rear-facing in the car, and doesn't visit her in-laws when she has a fever (*she wore the pants in the relationship*)—and texts and comments she had made in jest (like one particularly damning text where she jokingly wrote a friend: "I haven't found a way to kill him and get away with it, so I'm still here," with an "eek" emoji). The judge agreed to redact the rest of the text conversation, like when Nikki wrote out all the reasons she couldn't leave Chris yet and how she intended to do so once the kids were in school. Because there was so much evidence—thousands of pages of documentation, an overwhelming amount of written words—it was also easy to pluck out sentences, black out the context, and collage together a new story, one that put Nikki behind bars for the rest of her life.

There were explanations for all their concerns. I'd had numerous conversations with Sarah and other domestic violence experts. I knew that it was common for children with unprocessed sexual abuse to grow up to be revictimized—as was clearly stated in Nikki's forensic psychology report.[3] I knew that trauma memory often wasn't linear, and that abusers don't need to have a weapon in their hand to have control over a victim. The one about my mom was tough to explain—I didn't even have a fully formed reason, except that my mom had been in a stage of life where it was easier to assume Nikki was a "drama queen" than in need of real help, and that she had a tendency to fawn around men, especially men in positions of power. She didn't know she was being recorded, and she certainly never imagined it would one day be used as a threat to convict her daughter. Yet because Mom wasn't alive to be put on the stand to verify her words, they likely wouldn't be admissible.

Unfortunately, a lot of Nikki's evidence was at risk of being suppressed for the same reason: Chris wasn't alive to authenticate and confirm.

With jury selection only a few days away, the legal team reluctantly yet persistently prepared for trial. That meant Nikki had to go down to John and Ben's office for hours of preparation. Typically, I just dropped her off or picked her up, usually between trips to the mall to shop for her trial clothes. Her attorneys had given very clear directions about what she should and shouldn't wear: Nothing masculine, like pant suits or professional-looking attire. Nothing low cut or flashy. No heels, even on a sensible boot. No bright colors. No dark colors. They wanted her to look small, pretty, and young, in soft neutrals. I spent hours sweeping through clothing stores, looking for beige sweaters and white cardigans, something that a jury would make a snap judgment about, that conveyed believability and likability.

But today, John and Ben had asked me to join at the end of one of Nikki's sessions. I wondered if they had changed their minds about putting me on the stand. For the past few months, they'd told me that my testimony wouldn't be useful because I hadn't known about the abuse, although there was a possibility that they might need me to rebut something. That didn't stop my mind from pulling me onto the witness stand, usually while I was in the shower. My body would be shampooing my hair and my head would be in the courtroom, talking into a microphone, making my answers ever sharper and more concise, focusing on the details that I wanted the jury to know.

I had the luxury of being in control of those anxiety-producing mental role plays, while Nikki was forced to indulge in that kind of practice with her attorneys. I don't know exactly what went on in the office for the three or four hours she spent there, typically three times a week, but I saw how quiet she was when I picked her up. She told me it was less "rehearsing" for trial, and more her attorneys catastrophizing and Nikki shutting down. Some days they'd have to go through piles of evidence, including images of her naked body that she had to watch others review. One day, they gave her a Benadryl to calm her anxiety, and filmed her attempting to answer a line of questioning with a tablet in her face so that she could watch her performance. All I saw was the aftermath: Nikki sitting in the passenger seat and staring straight ahead, as if she'd been hollowed out.

And that's how she looked when I walked into the room that day, interrupting the end of a seemingly tense session. John paced on the far side of a conference table covered with papers and lined note pads, as if they'd been cramming for a test. Take-out containers were pushed to one side. John's face was stony and serious, and he moved like a man who wanted to loosen his necktie and pour himself a stiff drink.

I took a seat next to a very small and still Nikki, and smiled at her second attorney, Ben, who sat across from me. He was older, with white hair and a calming energy that balanced out John's palpitating stress. Jimmy, the investigator, another older bespectacled white man, smiled and waved from the corner of the room, as if he were out of the conversation and only auditing the goings-on (while charging me $85 an hour to do so).

John slid a white lined legal pad over to me with three pen-drawn columns: GOOD, OKAY, BAD. He told me to listen as Nikki answered questions, and to mark down which column her answer went in.

I don't remember what John asked in his first question to Nikki, voiced as if by the prosecution, but I remember his tone was harsh, as if he were trying to toughen Nikki up to withstand Chana's wrath. It seemed like a stress test, to see how Nikki would hold up under pressure.

I looked over at Nikki as she sputtered out fragments of sentences, as if the words became choked in her throat on their way out. I didn't check off a single column on the list. Instead, I sat, pen perched in my hand, watching Nikki, wondering what the hell we were doing here. What was I watching? Nikki being verbally and emotionally abused—retraumatized—in the name of practice? Nikki had a vacant look in her eyes. Her lips were pale. I wondered if she might pass out.

The difference between Nikki intelligently making arguments to me while putting together the pieces of "discovery" in folders on our dad's apartment floor, or the way she was at home with the kids—spinning them around the living room while Ben played the guitar, doing "spa day" masks and makeup with Faye in Dad's bathroom, the walls echoing with their laughter—and what I was seeing now was stark. I was looking at someone who was petrified. I thought back to Sarah's description of Nikki as being "selectively mute." I saw it now. It was as if someone had lowered the dimmer on her inner light. I was meeting a version of Nikki that I hadn't seen before.

This version seemed to scare the hell out of her attorneys. They needed her to get on the stand and be believable. They needed her to get words out.

I knew that they truly believed that Nikki was a victim not only of abuse, but of torture. There was a soft pity on their faces, and I could only imagine how much responsibility they felt to salvage this young mom's life.

But I still wasn't sure that the lawyers themselves understood it. To one another, they referred to Dave as an "affair," no matter how many times the context was explained: This man in a position of power gave Nikki a roof over her head and the promise of safety; she was young, vulnerable, and incapable of consenting.

"We're going to have to eat that fact," John said. They made it clear that, when it came to trial, if you're in the position of having to *explain*, then you've already lost. People make up their minds quickly, and this idea of a babysitter fucking a family's married dad was a well-worn trope that would be hard to overcome.

Nikki's attorneys said that Chana wanted to expose Nikki's "uncharged crimes," by which they meant the prosecution would imply that Nikki had falsely accused men of rape—and this would decimate her character on the stand. But what about *Chris's* uncharged crimes? The ones that were uploaded, broadcast, tracked, and documented? I felt like I was living in an upside-down world.

"I hear what Chana will say about Nikki, but what will you say about Chris?"

"Oh, we'll make him out to be a monster," John said, as if to comfort me. But something about categorizing Chris as a monster didn't sit right with me. It was too easy. Chris wasn't a mythological creature, something subhuman and "Other"; Chris was an ordinary man. A well-liked man. A functioning member of society—and in my most compassionate moments, I could even see him as a victim of that society, taught that men deserve sex and women should be punished for not giving it to them. He had to exist in a world where he was turned on by rape and violence, as evidenced by all he consumed on the Internet—something that could end his career and publicly shame him. I saw nuance and complexity—which, I'd quickly be corrected, were not things that the court understood. The system is black or white, right or wrong, victim or defendant. Chris, in turn, would have to be reduced to that, too.

I could feel the attorneys pulling away from the porn aspect, relying on the bruising, burns, and lacerations in the forensic nurse and midwife exam. Sarah had said that, when choosing which Pornhub screenshots to submit as evidence, John and Ben chose some of the milder options, saying, *We don't want to shock the jury.*

When we got around to talking about the porn, I said, "This wasn't like—*normal* porn," looking for them to affirm my own reaction to all I saw in that file folder.

Ben looked back at Jimmy, and the two caught each other's eyes. "Eh, it's not that abnormal," Ben said. I felt frozen in fury at this locker room elbow jab across the room.

On the one hand, Ben was absolutely right—#forcedsex is a highly trafficked sex term. Degradation and aggression are an accepted part of the porn industry—choking, gagging, slapping, it's standard all-American porn.

But I was disgusted. I wish I had said *something*, anything, to rebut that comment. I wish I had brought up how the sheer frequency of his searches indicated a pornography addiction, or gave voice to the fact that the cornerstone of BDSM kink is *consent*, which Nikki did not give.

But I didn't. I swallowed my words and felt my stomach sink, listening to John repeat the same words he always said: "Trials. Aren't. About. The. Truth."

They had made it clear: Even though they believed Nikki, they didn't believe she had a good chance of winning the case. Over the past couple of weeks, I had watched these well-respected, composed professionals become completely frazzled. Their faces were constantly tense, eyebrows pulled together in alarm. A lifetime of conditioning suggested that I should defer to the older professional white men in the room, to believe that they must know more than me. But their blind spots and ingrained misogyny were showing. Their generalized acceptance of the sexually violent pornography, and their excusing most of Chana's abusive power moves—were dumbfounding. We had done everything we could to connect them with experts who could explain the nuances and consequences of Nikki's exploitation and abuse. If they didn't get it now, what hope was there for us with a jury?

Just as I sank into a subdued resignation about the unmovable realities of patriarchy and rape culture, the conversation shifted to plea deals. As if by design.

I looked down at the piece of paper, three empty columns. I looked over at Nikki. Her eyes stared blankly at the table. I understood: I was here because they wanted me on their team. They wanted Nikki to fail the performance test. They wanted me to convince her to take a plea.

Then John took a seat and leaned toward Nikki across the table, looking right in her eyes.

"Listen, no one is going to be more upset than me if you get convicted." It took everything in me to not roll my eyes. *No one* is going to be more upset than you? Are you sure?

It wasn't the first time I heard John say this, so I knew how the sentence would end. He was going to say—"Every day I'm going to have to look in the mirror and agonize over what I could have done differently," subtly making Nikki responsible for his pain, inserting his own well-being into this impossible choice that Nikki was being forced to make.

Even though I was trained to be polite and defer to elder men, I couldn't help myself, a laser-red rage seemed to cut a hole through my numbness and I cut him off mid-sentence, my heart pounding in my ears—

"You're going to tell yourself that you tried your best and you respected your client's wishes?" I said. John smiled and pointed at me.

"Ah, no! No, that's what I *should say*," he said, as if I were wiser than he was, and then he finished the sentence as I knew he would.

I didn't say another word. What was the point?

Nikki and I stood up and drifted out to the car. Neither of us spoke on the forty-five-minute drive back to the kids.

wolves

They won't believe you.

This was the warning from her attorneys, who were making a case for a guilty plea. This was the promise from an ambitious prosecutor, threatening to confirm that no one, including a jury, would believe her. They were the words Chris had said—swearing that it would be his word against hers; and it was, even in death.

As we waited for the trial to begin, I obsessed over how many times she had been told her story didn't matter. The truth didn't matter. A string of *They won't believe you*'s leading all the way back to that five-year-old girl who'd been abused by Butch. I couldn't get him out of my mind. Nikki had been younger than Ben when she went on that sleepover. I now had a front row seat to how these traumatic events were shaping his little life. And unlike Nikki—whose experience was never validated or acknowledged—we did everything we could to do the opposite with Ben and Faye. I figured that if there was any silver lining, and some days I wasn't sure that there actually was one, it was that Ben and Faye's trauma could be held in the light, where it had a better chance of being processed, maybe even healed.

Nikki never stood a chance. So many days, my mind would pull me back in time, and I'd wonder: How much had Butch changed the course of Nikki's life? What did the other untraveled paths look like? How much pain and suffering could have been prevented if only Nikki had got the help she needed as a kid—better yet, if Butch had never violated her in the first place.

One day during our pretrial preparation at Dad's dining room table, a question rose insistently to the surface—the kind of question that I would normally have suppressed to avoid making Nikki uncomfortable. But this time I spoke out loud:

"Hey, Nik?" I asked from my chair across the table.

She looked up, probably expecting me to ask another question about a search history or some detail from a report. I almost bailed. It would have been so easy to keep not asking.

"Something I think about a lot is how you didn't feel safe to tell Mom or Dad that Butch had hurt you," I said, rushing ahead before I could retreat. "I have a hard time wrapping my head around it, knowing how the kids run to me the minute they scrape a knee or feel something weird going on in their bodies. Like—the instinct is to go to your parents for comfort, right? Butch must have scared you so much to not tell Mom what happened, to believe that you had to keep that secret."

It's statistically very likely for child victims of sexual abuse to hide it—out of confusion and shame and fear. But I guess I was hoping Nikki had a straightforward reason for why she never went to Mom for help. Maybe I should know in order to prevent the same thing from happening to Noah or Ben or Faye.

Nikki looked confused. "But, Michelle, I did tell her." She said it as if she had told me a hundred times before, as if this were a well-known piece of the story that I should know.

My jaw fell open. "What do you mean?"

Nikki put down the phone in her hand and straightened herself up.

"It's one of the clearest memories I have from that time," she began. "I don't really remember a lot of talks that Mom and I had, but I remember this one very, very clearly. We were walking in the backyard, back from the swing set—do you remember the swing set?"

Of course I did. It was where I had broken my elbow in first grade. Most of my memories from that time are fuzzy, but I can still put myself right back on the ground under the swing set, looking out at my sister's toddler-size feet running toward the house to get help.

Nikki described how she walked with Mom along the row of lilac bushes, past the aboveground pool, then a big, tall tree in the middle of the yard to which our dog's lead was attached. I could imagine her small sneakers walking next to my mom's, the two of them hand in hand.

"I remember the smell of lilac, the peeling paint on the garage to the left. I don't remember exactly what I said, only that it was really hard for me to say whatever it was. But I said *something*, I'm sure of it," she said in a distant tone, as if she had left her body and was far in the past.

"I know because afterward she led me to the steps of the back porch, just me and her. And her only response was to tell me the story of 'The Boy Who Cried Wolf.'"

My mouth opened wider. I tried to imagine Faye coming to me with a scary and hard truth that she'd worked up the courage to share, and choosing the right response. It wasn't as if Nikki had said that Mom was distracted or emotionally activated—Nikki waited until it was just the two of them, walking in the peaceful backyard in broad daylight. Why would Mom choose *that* story at *that* time?

Oh, Mom, what did you do? I thought. *You were that first voice that disbelieved Nikki? You were the source of this strangling belief that's growing like an uncontrollable weed, wrapped around Nikki's freedom and safety?*

"Oh my God," I said, slowly shaking my head. It was darkly ironic, beyond anything I could have scripted. It would almost be comical if it weren't so utterly tragic.

"Yeah. Yep. She basically said to be careful because someday no one would believe me. Then she went into the house and I stayed outside watching a daddy longlegs climb the white lattice along the porch, thinking about what she had said. I think that's one of my deepest memories of Mom giving me life advice. It really stuck with me."

I must have thought about that moment a hundred thousand times from that point on. I have never stopped thinking about it. How much had that story and its message seeped into Nikki's very foundation, affecting the way she saw herself and the world? How did my mom's view—that label of "lies for attention"—affect how other people saw Nikki?

I wanted to know why my mom told her that story. I wanted her to have a chance to stand up for herself and explain why she responded as she had. I couldn't believe this was an answer I'd never get from her.

Yet when I was quiet and not running through my own inner judgment of all my mom had done right and wrong, I already had my answer: My mom didn't know why she responded that way, why she ignored what was in front of her. She wasn't conscious of all the ways trauma had rewired her own alarm systems to overlook whatever Nikki had told her, and all the ways society had programmed her to instill that lesson in her baby girl: *Stay quiet and don't make accusations, because you'll be labeled a liar.* I knew, in my very bones, that the story was told as an act of protection. Protecting Nikki from our culture, but also protecting herself.

What other secrets did my mom keep? Had she ever told her own mom that she was "date raped" at fourteen by her friend's older brother? Or that her boyfriend Nicky hit, burned, and choked her? How would my grandma have responded?

It was easy to heap all the blame onto my mom. She was retelling one of our culture's most popular teaching stories, likely parroting back the lines that had been fed to her.

But what if we have all gotten the story wrong—

Maybe the little boy wasn't lying—maybe he saw the wolves, but they were wearing sheep's clothing.

Maybe the little boy got the whole flock killed because he'd learned that it's not safe to speak out, and so he never asked for help.

Maybe, *just maybe*, it was never a child's job to be responsible to watch for grown, dangerous wolves.

the truth is worth fighting for

Forty-eight hours before the trial was to begin, Chana proposed a plea deal lower than anything suggested before. It was passed along to Nikki with a qualifying note: "This is a good deal, you should take it."

A plea negotiation is a quiet process, and it gives the system what it wants: guilt and punishment. How much of each is up for debate. The number of years of their life a person will serve is written on scraps of folded paper and slid from one side of a negotiating table to the other. It would be easier, preferable, for all concerned if Nikki were to say "I'm guilty" and offer up the time specified to spend in prison.

"John got a text from Chana at 6 a.m. Apparently if I agree to plead guilty to three-to-nine years on a Man 2," meaning manslaughter in the second degree, "she'd get her boss and the family on board." Chana wasn't making a formal deal on the record, but seemed confident that she could convince her boss, the elected DA Robert Tendy, and the Grovers.

We were sitting at Dad's dining room table. I was drinking a mug of coffee when I had enough adrenaline to keep me going for days. Nikki was eating a bowl of thick soup that smelled of curry and warm spices. She was typically sick to her stomach, unable to keep much of anything down—except this soup, made with love by our friend Marnie, an intuitive healer who had a small practice in town. She and others in the local mom community dropped food on Nikki's doorstep, not wanting to intrude.

We all wanted to fill her up, in any way we could. Close friends dropped by with their new babies—babies whose births Nikki had missed. High school classmates dropped off a big stack of clothes for Nikki to have for trial. People brought whatever they had—essential oil rollers, a singing bowl, fuzzy socks, a massage table, and an offer for free acupuncture sessions. Their support lifted Nikki, and me beside her, keeping our heads above water. But the storm clouds were moving quickly toward us, and Nikki was looking to me to help steer the way.

"What do I do, Michelle? Just tell me what to do."

John was being more insistent now in his recommendation. It was irresponsible, selfish, unwise to turn down this deal. Nikki had said she'd consider a single-digit plea deal, but now that it was here, it was a complicated choice.

I shook my head. I couldn't give her definitive answers; but I could research the hell out of it, call on other experts in the field who'd reached out in support, and help her weigh the pros and cons.

Three to nine years. The lower number in an indeterminate sentence is when you're eligible for a parole hearing, and the higher number is the maximum amount of time you could serve. So in three years, Nikki would have a chance to go to a parole board and ask to be released. The board could say yes or no, and if no, then Nikki would wait for another parole hearing date in a couple of years, on and on until nine years was up. With a plea of three to nine years, factoring in the time she already served, she would be eligible for her first parole in about twenty months.

That was an enticing proposition. It might have been enough to get Nikki to say yes—to resolve the situation privately, keep her humiliation hidden, no need to drag the case out in the newspaper for the kids to one day find and read. There would be no additional trial fees—a whole new crop of future invoices for the attorneys' and experts' time in the courtroom. So far we'd raised just over $50,000 from nearly 1,000 different people, nearly all of which was going to the pretrial costs of experts, reports and analysis, and even mandatory transcript fees that cost hundreds alone. If Nikki took a plea, we'd stop hemorrhaging money out to people who may or may not have been able to help, but charged hundreds of dollars an hour to try. It could all be over, a sweet release from litigation—and anything additional that people gave could go right to Nikki, to restart her life.

I didn't lay the financial argument out to Nikki—I knew that she'd be unfairly influenced if she thought it would help the people she cared about the most, and who had already given more than she felt comfortable with.

But I did bring up the fact that, from my deep-dive research into plea deals, it's incredibly rare to be released by a parole board the first time—or ever. Parole reform is an entire branch of advocacy, and the information out there is loud and clear. What's more, I'd learned that criminalized survivors of domestic violence are *specifically* known for being denied, because, among other reasons, the parole board will often misconstrue someone identifying as a victim with that person not having remorse or taking responsibility. "The abuse excuse," as I'd heard it. It was so prevalent and egregious that recently, within the previous year, a group of lawyers and advocates banded together through the nonprofit Sanctuary for Families in NYC, and formed the Initiative for Incarcerated Survivors of Gender Violence, specifically with the goal of reforming the parole system for survivors.[4] Through their press releases, I'd learned that this was an ongoing and persistent problem—which didn't make Nikki's chances of being granted parole in twenty months seem likely. Reform takes time. Sometimes lifetimes.

Still—I reached out for answers, including the people who sat on boards and worked these cases. Authors who wrote about the issue, well-researched journalists, big-name advocates who have been fighting the fight for decades—I sent the emails, made the calls, out of some desperate hope that someone would have the answer for her.

No one in my extensive outreach could give me a straight answer, just like I couldn't give one to Nikki. The terrible unfair truth was that—after a lifetime of living as a victim, without autonomy, feeling trapped without choices—she was expected to make the hardest choice of her life. (The choice to pull the trigger wasn't hard because it wasn't a choice, she had told me; it was an automatic survival instinct.) Despite the lack of clear direction, there was a consistent lack of confidence in the parole system, and the general consensus that, once the system has a grip on you, it doesn't want to let you go. So in taking the deal, assume that you're taking nine years.

Twenty months and nine years are not the same.

"Nine years is so long, Michelle, it's too long. Ben and Faye will be teenagers. Noah? He'll be an adult. I'll miss it all. I'll lose everything."

I nodded.

Every time Nikki got close to convincing herself that a plea was the smarter decision, I'd see a rebuttal come from somewhere deep inside her. In talking our way through each scenario, looking at it from all angles, it became very clear that Nikki already knew what she needed to do.

"I feel like they want me to shut up and go away," she'd say. A condition of the plea was that Nikki had to forfeit her right to an appeal, meaning that no higher court could examine the prosecutorial strategies (like lying to the grand jury by saying the gun had been wiped) and biased judge's rulings (like removing Nikki's chosen counsel). She'd be stuck with that prison sentence and no testimony, no explanation on the record; only guilt and full responsibility.

So it would have been easier and more economical if Nikki were to say, "I'm guilty," giving the prosecutors what they wanted, which is a high conviction record, and it giving Nikki a lesser sentence than the lifetime she could face behind bars. A plea deal was the safest choice for everyone. Except Nikki, who would have to go to prison and face more unknown atrocities.

Another complicating factor was that there was currently a bill on the New York governor's desk called the Domestic Violence Survivors Justice Act (known as the DVSJA), expected to be signed into law any day. And when it was, then judges would finally have the discretion to consider whether a person was a victim of domestic violence at the time that they committed a crime, and whether the abuse was a significant contributing factor to their actions. If so, judges would have a new more humane sentencing structure with lower limits, as well as noncarceral options. Even *with* a guilty verdict of Nikki's highest charges, under the DVSJA, Judge McLoughlin could sentence Nikki to a flat five years.

Five years was better than nine years.

But if Nikki accepted the current offer of an indeterminate range between a minimum of three and a maximum of nine years, then when the law got passed, she'd be ineligible. To be considered for a lower sentencing structure under the DVSJA, she would need a minimum sentence of eight years. Anything less than that wasn't considered "unduly harsh," despite the argument that spending one minute in jail for surviving was too much.

It was a gamble. An impossible decision. But when every argument and counterpoint was boiled down, Nikki always came to the same conclusion.

"I think the truth is worth fighting for. I don't want to be shipped away to prison without telling my kids that I did every last thing I could to come home," she said one day, sitting between me on one side, and my mom's ashes on the other. There was an assurance to her body posture, a clarity in the decision. It seemed like a matter of principle, of integrity, and I admired her for it.

"Plus, I don't know, I feel like I'm *supposed* to speak out. Nothing will change if I stay silent."

I couldn't argue with her because, fundamentally, I felt the same way. So much of this felt like it was being scripted in real time, as if all of us—including and especially Nikki—were playing a role for a larger reason, bigger than our individual selves. And there was something about Nikki in particular—the way that people were drawn to her case from all over, pulled in by their own experiences with past and present abusers, amassing a growing number of supporters; and the fact that this case was happening at a particular time in history, coming off a year where a "nice guy" doctor with USA Gymnastics was under fire for sexual abuse, and in a cultural moment where the #BelieveWomen hashtag was trending around Christine Blasey Ford's testimony to the Senate Judiciary Committee. I felt like we were in the right place at the right time for Nikki to finally speak her truth, proving once and for all that she was not crying wolf.

If Nikki was committed to doing the hard work of facing her fears and walking into the fire of a public trial, then the least I could do was stand by her and support her. If she felt that speaking out publicly would be the highest good, I believed it. People in the community, other victims, were watching Nikki's case closely. She wanted to be brave for all the other women living in fear, in pain—she wanted to be brave for her kids.

And yet. Sometimes I'd feel a wave of panic: What if freedom wasn't at the end of this road, but martyrdom instead?

What if she had never been a shepherd—or a sheep, or a wolf—but was instead a scapegoat, destined to be led into the proverbial woods with society's guilt and the sins of men heaped on her back, sacrificed to absolve the system for not acting sooner and failing to protect us all?

Those are crazy thoughts, I'd tell myself, yanking myself back into my body. I had to believe that this would all work in our favor, as if the ending was already written out.

CHAPTER 46

The People v. Nicole Addimando

Monday, March 18, 2019, 10 a.m.: opening arguments begin.

Eight women and four men were selected by what Nikki described as a head-spinning game where Nikki and the prosecutor chose and vetoed different jurors based on their jobs, family life, and statements they made during jury selection. Anyone who had any experience with domestic violence was wiped from the jury pool, under the reasoning of "bias." But if someone hadn't walked in Nikki's shoes, how could they possibly be considered her "peers"?

"They're a real motley crew bunch," a friend of mine, Heather, texted me from the courthouse hallway. I was desperate to know who these strangers were—ordinary people holding not only Nikki's fate, but my own. But I couldn't go into the courtroom during trial, along with the sixty other potential witnesses, in case I had to take the stand. Instead, I dropped Nikki off each morning—watching her drag herself out of my car, and dodge news cameras as she scurried inside. Then at the end of the day, I'd pick up her crumpled body, knowing her dignity, privacy, and very sense of self had likely been torn apart in the courtroom.

In between, I lived those days inhabiting two worlds—on the outside, everything appeared normal. I brought the kids to school as usual, still smiled in the grocery store at check out, answered *good* when someone casually asked me how I was. But I wasn't good. I was mentally inside Judge McLoughlin's courtroom on the fourth floor, and emotionally reeling from the high exposure of the small-town media frenzy in headlines labeled ADDIMANDO MURDER TRIAL.

I had a ritual, which I enacted every day of the three-week trial:

First, I'd return to my quiet home and light the three candles I had set on my kitchen counter like a makeshift altar. One candle was white, labeled SPIRIT. I'd light that candle and pray to whatever invisible forces I could imagine, silently calling out for help from the lineage of ancestors who'd all played a small part in leading us to where Nikki now stood in a courtroom in Poughkeepsie.

I'd light the second candle, a pink one for HOPE—the same candle that Elizabeth lit each morning, as if maybe our collective prayers, our synchronized yearning, would shift the winds of fate in our direction.

And lastly, I'd light a blue candle for JUSTICE. I was careful not to pray for a specific outcome, and tried to rise above my desperation—as if I could trick a higher power into believing I wanted whatever was for the highest good, when in reality, I wanted my sister to be safe. I wanted the system to tell her three words, breaking the spell that had trapped generations of women: *I believe you.*

Then I'd scroll through my phone and look for any bits of news that the *Poughkeepsie Journal* had posted on their site, or on the journalist's personal Facebook page, where she'd give hour-by-hour updates—and then read through hundreds of comments and reactions.

Nikki's case had a grip on the community—at least the portion that listened to morning radio on their commute, or subscribed to the local paper, or spent time scrolling through their social media feeds. For months, but especially during the weeks of trial, I'd read passionate defenses ("Nikki was a beautiful and kind mother, and every time I saw her she had bruises on her"), flippant assumptions ("let her rot"), accusations ("all you supporters didn't help her when you saw her injured, some friends you were")—all while knowing that I couldn't publicly type out a response, not yet at least.

Even for those who didn't know Nikki or Chris, I saw a split response: There was a knee-jerk, "so he slapped her around a little, she didn't have a right to kill him" reaction, and a black-and-white "killing someone is wrong no matter why" mentality. Others, while only knowing the barest details of the case, saw that there was more to this story: "He must have been beating her up, there's no other explanation, I survived domestic violence and I'm lucky to be alive." The polarity of the reactions suggested that there was no space for nuance in the legal system—or in some people's minds.

Most people posted simple symbols of support: Those who supported Nikki commented with a purple heart, and people who supported Chris commented with black and red hearts. Sometimes the hearts would be accompanied by a phrase like #IStandWithNikki or #MTGStrong, referencing the gym where Chris had worked, whose members insisted that he was an innocent victim and Nikki was a lying villain.

Purple, the color of domestic violence awareness, became a signal that I was seen and understood, and I looked for the color everywhere I went, as if it was a sign that the world had my back.

The Nicole Addimando Community Defense Committee only became more organized and intentional as the trial went on, making court calendars and organizing support gatherings for the hundreds of people around us who were paying attention. Thanks to the organizing of our committee and our growing email list, we filled at least half of the courtroom with people wearing purple clothes for every single session.

And so on trial days, after praying and scanning the news, I'd head out to the City of Poughkeepsie around 11 a.m., find parking, and wait for the courthouse's morning session to end and a crowd of people to pour out of the door—a sea of purple and red, with formal business suits mixed in. I didn't have to be there, but I *had to be there*. I needed to be as close to Nikki as I could get, and I needed to hear the reactions firsthand on how things were going, as if their answers were tea leaves to predict all of our futures.

I wasn't in the courtroom to hear Chana call Nikki's experiences a "rehearsed story of abuse and bizarre narration of events." I didn't hear her claim that the CPS visit wasn't an inciting incident for Chris's homicidal reaction—but instead, a trigger that Nikki's "house of cards was about to fall"—a sign that CPS would soon uncover Nikki's false allegations and cause her to lose her kids. I read that in the paper, struggling to find the logic in Chana's story.

I didn't watch Chana repeatedly put up a picture of Chris in a pink tutu at a gymnastics meet, as if *this goofball was too silly to be an abuser*. ("It's like playing an episode of *The Cosby Show*, and saying Bill Cosby couldn't be a rapist," Nikki told me one day after court.)

I also didn't have to see my sister's genitals blown up on a giant TV screen, like the worst nightmare I could have designed for her. She had spent a lifetime hiding her body and having it ripped open against her will. Here she was again—with everything she had struggled to keep hidden—exposed and magnified, in full color, in front of everyone she knew. The idea that she had *planned* this, had *wanted* this, was beyond the scope of reality.

But I had many friends who were there. And the people who sat in that courtroom and heard the venom in Chana's voice as she attacked Nikki's character and spun lies—they never fully recovered. I watched them cry, shake uncontrollably, and pace along the Poughkeepsie sidewalks with a vacant look in their eyes. Nikki wasn't the only one being victimized and traumatized during trial; so was everyone who had to witness it.

Most of Nikki's supporters, which included a dedicated group of people who went to the trial nearly every day, would eat lunch at a diner across the street, Alex's Restaurant. I'd meet them there to hear snippets of quotes, fears, and predictions.

Some days I'd be met with a *we just won* excitement, like when, on day one, Nikki's attorneys said that only Chris's DNA was on the slide of the gun. Or when, on day two, the county medical examiner took the stand and said there was no proof that Chris was asleep when Nikki shot him—despite Chana repeating it on loop, as if saying something again and again would eventually make it true.

Other days, quite a lot of the days, I'd see an *oh fuck* expression. Every professional that testified for Nikki—including the midwife who documented her injuries, and the forensic psychologist who interviewed Nikki—was discredited by Chana on the stand, distracting the jury from hearing what they had to say. Many who gave depositions, like Sarah, were deemed too much of a risk during cross-examination and never testified. And the prosecution's expert, a man who appeared to be a professional witness rather than a practicing clinical psychologist, said a version of: *Nikki invited the abuse, she liked the abuse.* He said that Chris "didn't fit the profile of an abuser."

The forensically documented burns on her labia from the hot spoon? Chana suggested they were bug bites or a bad wax job.

"Chana's doing this really brilliant thing—*evil-brilliant*," my friend Heather told me and a group of women wearing purple, sitting at Alex's Restaurant. "She asks a question about Chris, and then goes back to Dave, asks another question about Chris, then goes back to the maintenance worker. She's making it seem like 2009, 2011, and 2017 were all happening simultaneously, and for someone who doesn't know the timeline as well as I do, I can imagine it's really confusing."

"It's like John and Ben's strategy is to give as little information as possible, not to overwhelm them," she continued. "They say things and let the information hang, without providing context or connecting dots. Like all of Chris's searches"—which we had all thought would be a slam-dunk day for Nikki's defense. "Her attorneys didn't connect the searches to what he then did to Nikki. It's like they think the jury will be smart enough to put it together on their own."

To be fair, anyone on the witness stand—whether it was a cell phone technology expert, or Nikki herself—was restricted to a very narrow ask-and-answer formula, where the witness was not able to talk freely, only answer whatever the question was, however the judge allowed it to be phrased.

There was also a tremendous amount of evidence successfully suppressed or excluded, like the name of Chris's porn account, which included his last name, the bio on the page that fit his description, and all the misogynistic and violent captions that he wrote. The jury couldn't see medical records, which named Chris. And—after what was described to me as a "forty-five-minute sidebar" conversation between the prosecution, defense, and judge—only a very small handful of Chris's searches were allowed to be read to the jury.

"And Chana's strategy," Heather continued, "is to overwhelm the jury with information, repeat baseless lies as fact, and confuse the hell out of everyone."

Heads nodded around the table.

But Chana's alternative theories made no sense. Nikki concocted a fake story of abuse for attention and then...didn't tell people? She meticulously planned a murder and then went to the police for help? Why? There was zero evidence of an affair: Not one romantic text message came up; her own search history wasn't riddled with violence and pornography and suicide. There was no financial gain, since she wouldn't have seen a penny of life insurance; they didn't own property or make much money at all. Her only secrets were the ones she kept for the men who kept hurting her body. Her secret was that she was in pain. Her secret was that she'd been totally and wholly alone, and she'd always been afraid that she wouldn't be believed.

The jury can't actually be buying this, we collectively hoped.

At the end of March, Nikki was scheduled to testify.

I spent the entire day with my heart in my throat, feeling like I couldn't take a full breath, or clear my fuzzy, unfocused mind. I circled the courthouse that morning, looking up at the top row of windows, knowing that right then, in that space, Nikki was doing the hardest thing she'd ever been asked to do.

Would she shut down, like she did in John's office? Would her already taxed body be able to sustain this kind of pressure?

A text pinged on my phone: "She's amazing."

Another flashed up: "Oh my God, the court is taking a short break but Nikki is doing INCREDIBLE. I don't know how she's doing this."

I heard from her attorneys midway through the day—they couldn't contain how proud they were of Nikki's performance. "She didn't falter, she didn't get tripped up, she answered every question clearly, consistently, and credibly," John told me on the phone.

Another person I knew called me shortly after, saying that a local judge was in the audience for Nikki's testimony and said, "She was one of the most credible witnesses I've ever seen."

When I picked her up from court that day, Nikki carried herself with a different air. She looked exhausted, but there was life in her eyes. She was able to speak. All she wanted was a good meal and a night with her babies.

"It feels sort of like being in labor," Nikki said on the ride home, "like I'm pushing this testimony out of me. Is that weird?"

I smiled, shook my head. "Not weird. It's pretty miraculous, actually."

That night the sky turned purple. I wasn't the only one who saw it—my news feed became dappled with hopeful purple sky pictures, all dedicated to Nikki.

That had to *mean* something, right?

verdict

M y purple flower died," Nikki said. It was now April twelfth, a month after the trial had begun. We were standing by the windowsill in Dad's apartment, looking down at the row of potted plants that friends had dropped off for her over the last three weeks.

She pointed at a single hyacinth flower, tall and sturdy, planted in a mason jar. The purple was fading to brown, crumbling at its ends. Thick green leaves folded around it like a hug.

"Do you think it's a sign?" she asked. She was dressed in a white sweater, the front of her hair neatly pulled back into a clip. She wore a gold locket around her neck with Ben and Faye's picture inside, and had our mom's pocketbook over her shoulder.

Closing arguments had been on Monday, and today was Friday. The jury had been deliberating for the past three days, so clearly there were some disagreements. That worried me. I had hoped they would have seen it clearly and make a quick and unanimous decision to do the right thing.

During each day of jury deliberation, I had sat in the courtroom between school drop-off and pickup. Finally allowed into the room, I had made it my job to be in those seats and wait for a decision. I had a note typed up in my phone, ready to be copied and pasted to our full list of supporters, asking them to come to the courthouse to hear the verdict. I had watched the jury file in at the beginning of each session, be given the same oral instructions on how to apply the law, and leave without any papers in their hands. They weren't permitted to make any notes. If they had a question, they had to write it on a piece of paper, and it would be passed to the judge. Then the judge would call the jury back into the room, answer the question orally, and the jury would file back out.

Today was day four of jury deliberations, and Nikki was due in court soon. Whether the jury came to a decision or not, Nikki had to be nearby. Waiting.

She had still been in pajamas when I came back after Noah and Ben's school drop-offs. Faye, however, was home for the morning, so she and Nikki had soaked up extra mommy-daughter time. My dad had taken the day off from work, ready to be wherever he was needed. Today he was tasked with spending the day with Faye, and maybe picking up the other kids from school if I was stuck at the courthouse.

Fancy Nancy was on the TV when I arrived, and the two of them were curled up on the blowup mattress where they had slept the night before, entangled in each other's limbs. As the trial ended, the kids started spending more nights with Nikki, all of us sensing that any day could be the last. We didn't talk about it with the kids, but I wouldn't have been surprised if they could feel our anticipatory anxiety.

I wasn't eager to separate the two of them and bring Nikki back to the courthouse for yet another day of jury deliberation, but that was my job. If Nikki was late to court, even at this stage, her bail could be revoked and she'd be immediately remanded back to jail—and the $100,000 cash we were holding for bail loaners, together with the $500,000 in collateral, would all belong to the court.

And so I did what I'd been doing for the past five weeks of trial: Gently push her to pick an outfit and gather her things, with a slight panic in my chest and throat, while the rest of my body ached to keep her here, safe, where she belonged.

As I stood there in front of her dying purple flower, an unpleasant thought crept into my mind. The day before, when I performed my daily candle-lighting ritual, the blue justice candle votive had filled with smoke. It happened suddenly before my eyes, and when I aired it out, I saw that the glass was coated with a thick black film. Was *that* a sign?

"What if they just let me come home?" She whispered it like a little sister with an exciting idea. Her eyes still carried a gleam of hope.

I don't know how she did it. Somehow—under the crushing weight of knowing that this could be the end of her normal life as a mother—she was still able to stand her bones up and follow me out the door, away from her four-year-old girl, who had already grown for half of her life without Nikki home and free.

Nikki hugged Faye goodbye. She kissed her cheeks and pulled her body away from Faye's. I didn't hear her say she'd be back soon, only the deepest truth she could say: *I love you.* Her voice cracked. Faye's small hands unclasped Nikki's neck. I turned to leave, tears balancing on my eyelids. I pulled out my phone to check the time, blinking the tears down my cheeks. *Ten minutes.* It would be tight, but we could make it.

Nikki's attorneys had rented a space across from the courthouse to regroup in between sessions. I scanned the sidewalk for news cameras; they were up toward the corner, so I pulled over at just the right angle so that Nikki could hop out and scurry to the door without being spotted. I parked in the familiar lot and looked out across the road at the DMV, sitting there like a big gray box. My hands were shaking. My stomach felt empty and hollow.

Something would happen today and I couldn't control it. *Allow it*, I begged my nervous system. I sent out a silent prayer: *While I still hold to the belief that my sister does not deserve one more minute of criminalization and punishment, I'm trusting that there is a higher good. And I will continue to play my role to serve that good.*

Bargains masquerading as acceptance.

I let out a long exhale and stepped out into the chilly Poughkeepsie air, walking across the street, and up to the courtroom.

The newspaper reporter was sitting in the front row, laptop open. No one else was in the room. There were eleven empty wooden pews to choose from. The court reporter sat in the front of the room, to the left of the judge's empty seat, and uniformed officers leaned against the walls, smiling and chatting like colleagues. Chana paced in and out of the room, and each time I followed her with my eyes, willing her to look at me, to *see me*. She never did.

I chose a seat in the middle of the room, behind the defense's table.

An hour later, Nikki texted from across the street, sitting with her attorneys: "What's going on over there..." The waiting was brutal. It was still just me and the reporter in the audience. "Chana is here in a purple dress," I responded with an eye-roll emoji.

Slowly the room started to fill up: gymnastics families whose faces I recognized from the social media comment sections, claiming that they went to court every single day and could see that Nikki was a liar; two older women from Elizabeth's church who, also, went to trial every day and saw Nikki as a victim.

Some more familiar faces entered the room, but it stayed deafeningly quiet. If the judge wasn't present, we could talk quietly among ourselves, but no one did. I pulled out a copy of *The Alchemist*, a gift from a friend earlier that week. My eyes scanned the words but couldn't take them in.

Then I heard a rustling. Lawyers came in and out the door on the side of the room. Tense whispers passed back and forth. John mouthed to me from across the room: *Verdict...jury...now.*

I pulled my phone out of my bag and opened my notes app, fingers shaking, to copy and paste the message I had prepared in advance to warn people who weren't here with us that the verdict was about to be read.

> The verdict is in. If you can, come to the courthouse ASAP. 10 Market St. Poughkeepsie. This is a MASS TEXT so please do not reply here! If you have a question, text me directly and I'll try to respond. Otherwise, I'll see you here. [*Purple heart emoji. Prayer hands emoji.*]

Within minutes, Chris's entire family walked through in a line and filed past me to the left side of the room. *They must have been waiting in the DA's Office*, I realized. We didn't make eye contact.

Nikki walked in, surrounded by her somber-faced attorneys. My eyes followed her as she passed, knowing that she'd never look up—petrified of seeing someone she used to know and love wearing red and black, rooting for her conviction.

The heavy wooden door opened, and one of her former gymnastics coaches walked in wearing a purple shirt. She sat on the right side of the room, *our* side. It opened again: Dad, who slid in next to me. I let out a deep sigh, thinking, *Here we go.* Another purple shirt, then another. A couple of well-dressed strangers took their seats at the front—people from the District Attorney's and Public Defender's Offices down the road. On and on, until it was a full house, all of us sitting in the pew-like rows, a roomful of people wishing fiercely for two different outcomes, telling ourselves two different stories.

I looked up at the clock, it was nearly three o'clock, time to pick up Ben. I'd been waiting for more than five hours. I nudged my dad, telepathically communicating, while gesturing toward the clock. He had agreed to get Ben for me; I needed to stay, I needed to see this. Dad exhaled sharply through his nose with a look that said, *I can't believe I have to miss this.* He looked back at Nikki, his baby, who was about to hear her fate, and they locked eyes. I saw his mouth say *Ben* and he pointed up to the clock. I watched a nearby officer's body tense, ready to intervene, but my dad slipped out the door before he could be chastised.

Within minutes, we were all rising. The jury filed in, and I looked each of them in the face, willing them to make eye contact. I wanted them to see how desperate I was for their mercy. I wanted to glean what might happen. One juror was crying. *What does that mean?* I wondered.

I clutched my copy of *The Alchemist* to my chest and repeated a line I had just read: *When you really want something the whole of the universe conspires in your favor.*

When I really want something the whole of the universe conspires in my favor.

. . . the whole of the universe conspires in her favor.

I silently repeated it in my head, desperate to alchemize our trauma into a positive outcome. I sat back down and pulled my purple scarf up over my mouth, feeling the fabric moving in and out with my breath.

The judge read through his prepared instructions and asked the jury if they had come to a conclusion.

"Yes," said the forewoman, a middle-aged blonde with a soft voice.

"And how do you find the defendant?"

The pause seemed to stretch seconds, minutes, a lifetime.

"Guilty."

The word cut through the quiet room.

Then one by one, each juror said the same word: *Guilty. Guilty. Guilty.*

I stopped hearing sounds.

I felt pure, unfiltered powerlessness. Nothing I could do would change the words that had been spoken. A conviction of murder in the second degree alone, without the gun charge, carried a *minimum* of 15 years to life in prison, but the judge could choose any number between 15 and 25. With "life" on the back end of the sentence, the parole board could potentially keep her locked up until she died.

The jurors filed out between me and my sister. They all looked to the ground. Between their bodies, I watched Nikki stand up from her wooden seat, put her hand behind her neck, and unlatch her locket. She gave her handbag, Mom's handbag, to her attorney. A female officer pulled Nikki's hands behind her back and handcuffed her before yanking her away from the table.

I watched it all, still sitting down, scarf still wrapped around my mouth. I felt a tug at my left arm. A friend of ours had collapsed to her knees and was shaking me, screaming, "What's happening?"

Sobs echoed around me. I didn't know where the sound was coming from, but I knew it wasn't me; I couldn't make sound. Nikki had been afraid that, if this moment were to come, she'd hear half the room cheering, celebrating her living death. But no one did. I watched the Grovers stand up and walk past me, heads down. They weren't smiling.

I somehow walked from the courtroom, down the flight of stairs, and sat on a bench in a hallway. Elizabeth sat next to me. Other committee members gathered—three women, five women, seven women. My aunts came over. A few other women who had come to court every day. We congregated around our shared pain, and whimpered and wailed as footsteps marched past us on the cold marble floor. I kept my eyes down on the floor.

"I don't understand, they just take her?"

"How can they just take her?"

I sat on a bench and waited for direction.

"It's not over," someone's voice said. I didn't look up to see who it was.

It felt over to me.

Elizabeth led a prayer, in a small, sad voice. "Mother God, be with us. Just hold us in your arms and care for us, we're tired and we're scared. Please just help us feel the light shining even though it feels so dark right now, I know it's out there."

Nikki's attorneys walked over, and someone handed me Nikki's handbag and locket. I wasn't sure my wobbly legs would hold me up, but I stood anyway. I half listened to the attorneys talk about post-trial motions and preserving the record for an appeal, but everyone sounded like they were talking underwater.

Wendy—who'd showed up at the jail that first night, and who kept showing up every day since—offered her home for us to convene at, saying we could stay as long as we wanted to grieve and steady ourselves, to be together. We followed one another down the stairs, past the metal detector, and out to the familiar corner of Market Street.

It was eerily quiet. There was no crowd, no media frenzy, just one camera. We stood in a group, waiting for Elizabeth to be done talking to the reporter, an interview that would be printed online in a matter of minutes: "I just wanted to say that we are heartbroken and devastated, and that we are thinking of Nikki's two children, Ben and Faye, who will go to sleep tonight without their mom. And that we understand that this is why women don't come forward."

As she was talking, Caitlin hurried up the street, running up to us in front of the courthouse. As she neared the group, she collapsed in a loud, primal cry. It was clear from our faces: The worst had happened.

I pulled up to Wendy's house, a cozy ranch on a cul-de-sac off a road I'd passed by for decades without ever driving down it. She had brought dining room chairs into the living room, making a semicircle in front of the couch, where I sat between Elizabeth and Dr. Crenshaw. Rachel and Laura cried. My aunts sat behind them, trying to offer comfort. Caitlin came with her partner and new twin babies. Sarah and Wendy dropped to the floor in front of the coffee table, their heads in their hands. Together we sat in numb shock, like extinguished candles.

My phone rang. A name I hadn't seen in four months flashed up: *Nikki DCJ*.

"It's her," I said, shooting up to stand. Wendy ushered me into her bedroom and closed the door to give me privacy.

She was wailing as soon as I picked up. "I can't do this," she managed to squeak out. "I put up with the abuse for so long," she sobbed. "So that I wouldn't be away from Ben and Faye. I can't live without them."

We both cried until the two-minute call was up. I promised to go see her that night.

Back in the living room, I turned to Dr. Crenshaw. "What do we tell the kids?"

"The truth," he said.

Dr. Crenshaw followed my car home from Wendy's.

Ben knew as soon as he saw us. Nikki had prepared him the best she could—at this point, he had asked so many pointed questions that we had to give him the most age-appropriate truth possible. Yes, his mom had killed his dad because she was scared, and she was protecting herself. (Ben never asked why his dad had hurt his mom.) And he knew that a judge was going to decide whether she had to go back to jail for longer, or if she could come home now. He also knew that his grandparents, who he continued to see most Sundays, were sad and mad that his dad had died, and didn't ask the judge to help his mom. It was much too much for any child, at any age, to hold. And yet, we had no choice. The only other option was to hide and dodge and cover up—which, in the long run, never worked.

As soon as I walked up the stairs and turned the corner into the living room with Dr. Crenshaw trailing behind me, Ben let out a howl from the pit of his stomach. He balled his fists up. He ran and attacked the two of us, kicking and flailing, throwing anything he could get his hands on. Finally he picked up a pillow from the couch and threw it like a Frisbee toward my makeshift altar, hitting one glass votive—the pink HOPE candle—which shattered on the linoleum floor.

The sound seemed to pierce Ben's fury, breaking him open into deep, primal-sounding sobs. We all sat and watched in reverent silence. Noah took Faye into her room to distract her from the chaos. He, too, knew what this meant without us saying a word, and he didn't have the luxury to react.

Dr. Crenshaw called the county's mental health crisis team, which sent a trained professional out to our house to help. But by the time they got there, maybe twenty minutes later, Ben had agreed to take a run with me—knowing it would help his body feel better. We didn't talk about his mom, I just jogged at his side, sometimes sprinting to catch up, appreciating the chance to run out my own grief and the fear coursing through me. If I were as honest as Ben, I would have roared out my pain and smashed glass against the tile floor, too.

I felt broken, but the birds were still chirping. The world was going on as if nothing had happened.

There's an ache that comes from knowing someone you love is suffering. Everyone in my house, and in extending circles around me, was hurting in unique and varied ways. But we had each other. Nikki was alone.

That night, after the kids were settled and asleep and the wreckage had been tidied up, I went to see her.

She wasn't classified, again, and so I went to a booth visit, again. It was like starting all over, and there in the jail visiting room, realizing we were back to *this*—to commissary funding, jail visiting, Nikki in orange—my body had a full ugly-cry meltdown.

For the second time in two years, Nikki was taken away and her stuff was suddenly left behind. And once again, it was up to me and my dad to sort and box it all. My dad kept himself busy to avoid feeling the grief. We didn't talk about all that Nikki had suffered, and he had been spared from seeing a lot of it up close because he was on the witness list, too, and so he hadn't gone to the trial. Instead we packed and labeled. I made a small pile of clothes and shoes to keep accessible in case she came home sooner than later, so we wouldn't have to dig through boxes in my garage. I wasn't ready to give up yet, even if the reality was that I could be packing up these boxes for *life*.

I gathered her artwork, which she had made as a coping tool during the stressful days of trial prep. My favorite of the paintings was of a group of women in shades of purple, blue, and pink, circled together, dancing under a bright moon. She had told me that she made it with a quote in mind, one from the writer SARK that Sarah had sent her while she was in DCJ the first time: "The circles of women around us weave invisible nets of love that carry us when we're weak, and sing with us when we are strong." And also, I thought, when we've been defeated.

One of the paintings had been done by Ben, borrowing his mom's art techniques. He'd painted a blue heart on top of a background of shaded purples, all ripped and glued back together; the heart was stitched with red thread. He titled it "Together Again." I felt a pang in my chest, around my own torn-up heart. I packed the picture away with the rest.

The last thing that I packed was the pocketbook her attorneys had handed me after the verdict—the bag that used to belong to our mom, and I knew Nikki had brought it to court each day, clutching it like a security blanket. I opened it up and saw it was clean, uncluttered, unlike my mess of a handbag. She had a few stones inside—two given by a friend who figured any bit of magic and positive energy could help; one given to her by

Ben: a clear stone with a small angel figurine inside. He wanted Nikki to have something from him when they were apart, and had picked it out of a basket labeled GUARDIAN ANGELS at the checkout counter of a gift store in Poughkeepsie. Nikki kept that stone in her pocket every day of the trial. It didn't protect her.

I also saw a small purple pouch I had bought her one day while shopping aimlessly for trial clothes. It was a pretty lavender color with small, embroidered bees, a nod to our mom's nickname, *Bee*. Nikki carried essential oil rollers inside, which she used to calm her nerves. Not drugs, nothing to self-harm—*essential oils*.

I unzipped the pouch to look inside, and folded behind the oils was a small white napkin, probably from a lunch break between trial sessions. I could see blue ink bleeding through, and unfolded it to see what it said. There in big beautiful calligraphy letters was the word HOPE, surrounded by stars, small dots of light to keep her safe.

I felt crushed, as if that word sucked the last bit of good feeling out of my body. What was hope amid *all of this*?

I kept her belongings carefully stored away. The pocketbook went up on a shelf, her makeup bag and wallet still inside. I took her locket and stones and put them in my apartment, next to the candle we had burned at my mom's funeral and a picture of me and my mom hugging. I also had small objects for Noah: a heart-shaped rock he'd found, back when he collected outside treasures and gave them to me as gifts, and a picture of him smiling under a bright sun. I'd have called it an altar if I believed in prayer anymore.

PART V

unbroken

"For a seed to achieve its greatest expression, it must come completely undone. The shell cracks, its insides come out and everything changes. To someone who doesn't understand growth, it would look like complete destruction."

—Cynthia Occelli

CHAPTER 48

wild purple flowers

I n our tight-knit community, Nikki's verdict became one of those *where were you when you heard...* moments. People I'd run into would talk about their memories. It was discussed on Facebook, in private group comment sections and in scathing public posts. One question echoed among them: If Nikki, with all the evidence and witnesses relevant to her case, wasn't believed as someone who suffered abuse and whose life had been threatened, what did that mean for other victims? One local psychologist reported that she had been hearing more hopelessness from her clients, citing Nikki's verdict as the reason.

The letdown felt bigger than the ending to just one person's story.

People around us reached out to offer me what they could, and I let them. Marnie, the woman who had brought soup to Nikki, came forward to offer healing therapies at the practice she ran in her house. I accepted.

"I feel like I'm one step away from tumbling into despair," I told her during a session, a few weeks after the trial. All the data was there for me to accept that life is meaningless, all our efforts were for nothing, and any version of prayer or hope was futile.

"Just remember," she said, "when a seed is planted in the dark soil, it doesn't know the light is coming. But I promise you it is. Just hang on a little longer."

Against my better judgment, I decided to believe her and wait for the light. And without fail, every single time, the light did come—first in small flickers, then a growing flame, always in the form of people.

* * *

While we waited for the judge to set a sentencing date that would dictate, with horrible finality, the extent of Nikki's prison term, the Domestic Violence Survivors Justice Act was signed into law by New York's governor, Andrew Cuomo, as part of his 2019 Women's Initiative one month after Nikki's guilty verdict. The timing was uncanny. I felt a glimmer of hope.

From May through August 2019, our committee jumped into near-constant action—drafting letters and scheduling meetings with the organizations and individuals who had either written or voted for the legislation, letting them know that Nikki's case could potentially test the law's strength, either giving it validity or rendering their efforts useless. Nikki's attorneys asked for a DVSJA eligibility hearing—or as it was known in penal code language, a 60.12 hearing—where supporting evidence can be submitted to corroborate abuse.

Sentencing was delayed. Our work was not yet over.

Elizabeth and I continued to visit the jail together, updating Nikki on these legal developments.

Elizabeth, who had spent nearly two years witnessing horrific injuries and had gone to sleep every night worried that her friend would be dead by morning—who did absolutely everything in her power to help Nikki, and spent countless hours reliving it for attorneys, prosecutors, investigators, and finally the jury—felt like her own truths had been erased along with Nikki's like a twisted Etch A Sketch. *Shake shake blank.* I saw a unique trauma being carried by her and everyone else who'd tried to help and couldn't.

"Have you heard of the purple fire flowers?" she asked one day in June. We were sitting in the visiting room, discussing our plan to hold a candlelight vigil outside the jail. We wanted to locate the window of Nikki's cell so that she could see us gathered outside. We knew the guards would likely shut us down quickly once we'd begun.

"They're these rose-purple flowers that grow only after a fire has scorched the earth," she said. "They're actually called Baker's globe mallow, and the heat from a forest fire releases the flowers' dormant seeds, and so after the destruction, purple blooms."

It reminded me of the poem Nikki had recently sent home from jail, written spontaneously in the lingering void after the trial—after having her life autopsied in front of her.

> there's something wild growing inside me—
> thriving still despite it all.
> for years it hid in the shadow of Fear.
> a vine, climbing the dark corners of my home.
> its prickly stalk grew around my lungs.
> strangled the words out of my throat.
> well, they cut it down when they tried to
> break me, but they didn't realize
> how deep my roots go.
> they spread my seeds when they forced me open,
> and now we are growing wild, purple flowers.

I thought of Marnie's promise that there were seeds buried under my feet.

And over the next month, through our scorched hope and collective crumbled grief, we started to rise.

The following month, our committee turned our pain into action by holding a vigil outside Nikki's jail window. More than a hundred people showed up in shades of purple—with their spouses and colleagues and children, cramming together on the sidewalk with signs: THIS IS NOT JUSTICE. FREE NIKKI. FREE THEM ALL. Elizabeth made a playlist with inspirational and moving songs, and we played music, took turns reading poetry, and gave speeches into microphones—loud enough for the entire street to hear. We braced ourselves, waiting for the Powers That Be to shut us down (despite the fact that we had a permit and had taken every precaution possible), but no one stopped us.

Amid our singing, crying, hugging, and holding, a big box of candles was passed around, and two committee members traveled through the group with lighters, making our inner flame visible in our hands.

I watched the light spread among us, one flame becoming ten, then fifty, then a hundred, as our voices blended together, singing "This Little Light of Mine" like a promise—as if generations of light were inside and around me, vowing to *let it shine, let it shine, let it shine.* For Nikki. For the kids. For me. For us.

We all sang toward Nikki's window, holding up our candles. And as the sun went down behind the big brick building, Nikki's shadowed silhouette became more defined. We could see that she was holding up her hand back to us.

We were the seeds spreading through the cracks of the system, standing tall in vibrant purple, rooted together.

"I think I dreamed that once," Nikki said later over the phone. "That felt like a miracle."

dear sister

Envelopes stamped DUTCHESS COUNTY JAIL started coming more often through that summer. It was as if Nikki needed to get her thoughts out, to be heard after being so firmly dismissed, denied, erased.

Not only were the letters more frequent, but they looked different. Her writing was smaller, all lowercase, and rendered in tight cursive loops.

Sometimes it took me days to open the envelopes decorated with the words *dear sister* across the back, knowing that I would be opening up her pain. I kept her letters glued shut until I had the strength to feel it.

> dear sister,
>
> if i did not have the right to defend myself, was i supposed to die? and if i died, wouldn't they say it was my fault for not leaving? that is what they decided. they said i was not justified. so tell me, someone please tell me, what was i supposed to do—kill or be killed?

The letters continued through the summer, when we had another agonizing heat wave.

> dear sister, it's july now, the flies stick to my face and arms. i really can't tell if the tickle on my forehead is sweat dripping

down from my hairline, or flies landing on my skin. both are persistent. there are so many different kinds—black, white, green, yellow. the green ones hop. the little white ones have scalloped wings that appear to have been dipped in opal dust. they may be the prettiest thing here.

And they continued all the way through the season, when I found myself sitting on the bistro chair outside my front door, taking deep belly breaths and listening to the birds and crickets and croaking frogs. It was late August 2019, and I was newly thirty-three years old.

I didn't want summer to end. I never did, but this year, in particular, I *needed* the warmth, the sun. Every part of me was clinging to the longer days and brighter light, the slower pace, the comforting blanket of August heat.

School would be starting in a matter of days. Ben was going into first grade, and Noah was starting fifth grade—his last year before middle school, the time I had assured him that all of this would be over. It wasn't over, not even close. The DVSJA hearing was scheduled during the first days of the new semester—quite possibly the least convenient time for me and the other moms who supported Nikki. In my more cynical moments, I wondered if that was intentional.

The longer I sat and breathed, the easier it was to remember that I'd been through this again and again for a lifetime now. Summer had always come back, every single time. The sun had never left me. I'd survived the cold darkness before. I could do it again.

Another school year, another high-exposure court experience, another unspecified period of waiting. Deep breath. *I've got this.*

dear sister, i bring a slip of paper that says body receipt to court each day.

Her letters continued through the DVSJA eligibility hearing in September, for which she had to be transported back and forth from jail in her orange jumpsuit, shackled at the ankles and wrists, and endure another public three-day ordeal to ascertain her eligibility for the new law, which was basically a condensed trial. I was in the audience all three days.

The defense called new witnesses and submitted more evidence, except this time there wasn't a jury: The decision was completely up to the trial judge, who, five months earlier, had watched the jury give their guilty verdict. Now he sat and listened, face in hand, as a different domestic violence expert, a woman named Kellyann who had decades of experience in the field, explained that there was no such thing as a "profile of an abuser"—debunking the prosecution's claim that Chris was too nice of a guy to be violent toward Nikki.

"I think the stereotype or myth or misconception is somehow that everybody would know, that if the person was abusive, we would all know it, and my experience has been time and time again that the reason abusers are very effective at what they do is because they operate one way in the public and another way at home," Kellyann said on the stand during direct questioning, wearing a bright pink blazer and heels. She spoke with a cutting clarity.

"And understanding that is very difficult for people to come to terms with because it's not an anger management issue. If it was an anger management issue, abusers wouldn't be able to control themselves anywhere. Domestic violence isn't caused by alcohol or drugs. Certainly it can exasperate or, you know, escalate the violence. And it's not a mental health issue. There is no way that the brain could be programmed to only harm certain specific people in your life. It's about power and control. And so you behave one way in the outside world, and you go home and terrorize the people you claim to love."

A young reporter from the *Poughkeepsie Journal* sat next to me in the wooden pew, a small notebook in her lap. She wasn't writing any of this down.

"It can also be hard for even close friends and family to come to terms with that," Kellyann continued. "You can have the little league coach who everybody's experienced as...a really great pep talker with their youth for the last five years and then go home and terrorize their partner and/or the children...Time and time again, we can see it play out that individuals will always say, 'It doesn't make sense to me, that was a nice person'; and it's hard for victims to find universal support in what's happened to them. It's a very effective tactic for abusers.

"When we hear the word *isolation*, we often think isolation is a physical isolation: You can't leave the house, you can't have friends, you can't have family. That's certainly very true, but isolation is also being very effective at operating one way in the public and operating another way in your home, because you isolate the victim from the perspective that 'If you tell any-body, no one will believe you, because that's not how they see me every single day.'"

I thought of the people on the left side of the room, and Chris's friends who wrote "Chris would *never*" rants in online comment sections—I wanted to scream, "Are you people listening to this woman?" There was a relief in hearing Kellyann say these words out loud—*finally*.

On cross-examination, Chana's second-seat ADA, a short man named Larry Glasser, who looked like he was wearing a hand-me-down suit in need of a hem, waddled up to the podium. He didn't ask Kellyann many domestic violence questions, only this, in a high, nasal voice:

"If someone's in a horribly abusive relationship and they get abused, let's be stereotypical for a moment—every time their boyfriend or husband comes home from work, if the house is a mess, he abuses her. Then in that situation, as a survival mechanism, the victim would learn to have the house clean by the time he gets home because that might prevent or minimize the abuse?"

I looked around the room, to anyone who would catch my eye, communi-cating, *Holy shit, what did this man just say?*

Kellyann calmly responded: "I would argue that it's not about the house being clean, but victims do amend their behaviors in an attempt to see if they can prevent the abuse or tactics of control being used against them."

"Yeah, okay, fair enough," he continued. "I want to be clear, by no means am I blaming the victim, for example, not having a clean house, but as you said, a victim would learn over time to amend their behavior perhaps in the hope or the belief that some of the abusive behavior would stop; is that fair to say?"

Kellyann held her ground. "Or—victims attempt to amend their behavior, and it still doesn't stop, so no matter what they do, it doesn't matter."

Then the prosecutor brought the theoretical question closer to the case at hand. "Okay. So if, for example, a victim was horribly assaulted and abused, maybe burned with a metal object for being sarcastic towards her abuser, and every time she was sarcastic, horrible, violent abuse would occur and she would be victimized. Over time, in a domestic relationship like that, you might expect that the victim would stop being sarcastic or try not to be as sarcastic to her abuser, correct?"

He was trying to say that if Chris had burned Nikki with a spoon for "talking back" to him, then why would there be evidence in Nikki's texts that she continued to say mean things, like calling him an asshole? Why didn't she just fall into line and prevent the abuse from happening?

"Not necessarily," she responded. "It feels like an assumption on your part about the sarcasm, as opposed to victims still operate in relationships where they can be frustrated and say things, like we all do, in healthy relationships. Maybe the consequences are different in an unhealthy or abusive relationship, but the victim isn't going to be a robot. They still have the time that they want to talk back or, as you said, be sarcastic, but victims often try to defend themselves too. We have victims all the time that say they hit back because they are attempting to defend themselves."

Glasser wouldn't give it up. He started to whine, dragging out his words, as if Kellyann wasn't bright enough to understand him. "But if a victim was to claim, for example, that her abuser demanded respect from them and respect was very important in the abuser's mindset, as one of these survival mechanisms, the victim may try and amend her behavior to not disrespect the person, right? Wouldn't that be a logical thing for someone to try and employ as a survival skill?"

Mouth agape, I sat watching the two of them lob their arguments back and forth like a tennis ball. Eyes back to Kellyann, who spoke in an even tone, unruffled.

"There is not real logic in an abusive relationship," Kellyann said slowly, like a mic drop. "There are times certainly that victims will try to amend their behavior, but the idea that they would just toe the line every single time—they are human beings."

I wanted to cheer. I only wished the jury had been there.

On a different day of the hearing, the judge, for the first time, heard Nikki's therapist, Sarah, finally give her testimony, dropping what seemed like unarguable truths, like seeing Chris texting Nikki death threats in real time as she sat in session with her.

Sarah gave all of the reasons that Nikki didn't think she could leave—because she loved him; because she didn't want to split up the family; because all she wanted, above all else, was for life to go back to normal and for the abuse to stop; because she was terrified of the fury it would unleash in him; and because she feared that no one would believe her. There was a palpable irony in the exchange—Sarah saying that Nikki didn't press charges because she thought she'd be disbelieved, while the jury and prosecution actively did not believe her, proving Nikki's point.

I heard things in that courtroom that felt like open-and-shut, slam-dunk proof that not only was Nikki abused, but she was clearly abused by Chris. Like when another former therapist, who had referred Nikki to Sarah for more intensive treatment, testified to watching a hidden-camera video Nikki had found of Chris, identifiable on camera, raping Nikki while Nikki audibly said "no."

The explanation that Chana and her co-counsel Larry put forward was that Nikki had tricked all of the witnesses. She had lied to all of the mental health professionals and forensic nurses, and outwitted everyone with her carefully plotted mind games. Nikki was a "mastermind," as Chana suggested, duping people into believing her made-up stories. She was nothing but a little girl crying wolf, and *all these people* were dumb enough to believe her.

But the number of people who believed her was growing by the day. When I was sitting in that courtroom, a crowd of people stood outside—stretched out along the Poughkeepsie sidewalk, walking in a long loop around the courthouse, all wearing different shades of purple, and holding signs to the cars and cameras passing by: I STAND WITH NIKKI. Kids were pushed in strollers, husbands held their wives' hands, young students and gymnasts walked in groups.

A few domestic violence organizations came, including one, Hope's Door, that brought signs to educate whoever was paying attention:

20,000 PHONE CALLS ARE MADE TO DOMESTIC VIOLENCE HOTLINES EACH DAY IN THE U.S.

1 IN 4 WOMEN WILL EXPERIENCE INTIMATE PARTNER VIOLENCE IN HER LIFETIME

WOMEN AGES 16–24 EXPERIENCE THE HIGHEST RATE OF INTIMATE PARTNER VIOLENCE, NEAR 3X THE NATIONAL AVERAGE

Most signs were handmade, like my friend's, in which she wrote a quote from the groundbreaking book *No Visible Bruises* by Rachel Louise Snyder, answering one of the most common questions we heard about Nikki (and all domestic violence survivors): Why didn't she leave?

"[NIKKI ADDIMANDO] STAYED FOR HER KIDS AND FOR HERSELF. SHE STAYED FOR PRIDE AND SHE STAYED FOR LOVE AND SHE STAYED FOR FEAR AND SHE STAYED FOR CULTURAL AND SOCIAL FORCES FAR BEYOND HER CONTROL. AND HER STAYING TO ANYONE TRAINED ENOUGH TO SEE THE CONTEXT, LOOKED A LOT LESS LIKE STAYING AND A LOT MORE LIKE SOMEONE TIPTOEING HER WAY TO FREEDOM."

Snyder wasn't writing about Nikki specifically, but she might as well have been. The common phrase I heard in the domestic violence community was: "Leaving is a process, not an event." Nikki had been in process. And like so many other lethal domestic violence cases, it's common for someone to die in that process. Usually the victim.

Snyder's book about the realities of domestic violence included so much that I'd only just learned through Nikki's case—such as how domestic violence escalates and what a lethality assessment really means; how DV cases slip through the cracks of the county system funded by state and federal grants, and the epidemic-level statistics of women being murdered by their current or former intimate partners.

No Visible Bruises had been published weeks after Nikki's conviction, around the same time that the DVSJA law passed. It gave us hope that public awareness was shifting along with our own, and we constantly referenced or recommended the book in our We Stand With Nikki circle. Nikki's attorney, Ben, carried the book under his arm to and from the DVSJA eligibility hearings, and I watched him flip through the pages whenever court wasn't in session. He was trying, he was learning. I appreciated that.

My friend's sign ended with the sentence: #DVSJA WAS PASSED FOR SURVIVORS LIKE NIKKI.

That was our angle, our "hook" to get more news organizations and advocates paying attention. Nikki's case was poised to be the first test of the law, meaning that however the DVSJA was or wasn't applied would have very real consequences for other victims in New York. It would set a legal precedent that other judges in other counties could and would reference when making their own decisions.

Throughout that September, Nikki's case was talked about on Albany radio shows and within legislative circles, and it spread through the nonprofit advocacy network, growing our network by the hundreds. It got the attention of influential activists like Gloria Steinem and V (formerly Eve Ensler), who signed on to endorse the application, along with 40 other organizations and individuals—including some of the organizations that had initially stayed quiet. I didn't care how long it had taken people to show up, I was just grateful they were here now.

The case caught the eye of an independent documentary crew that was wrapping up a film about criminalized survival, focusing on the woman, Kim DaDou Brown, who had created and fought for the DVSJA over the span of a decade. The co-directors were hoping to get footage of the law working for Nikki, a happy-ending bookend to Kim's story of survival and advocacy.

And while we still weren't saying much on the record, we started to let some journalists in, including an investigative journalist, Justine van der Leun, who had earned our trust because of her laser-sharp observations and previous knowledge about what she called "the abuse to prison pipeline." There was a deep relief in having smart, unbiased people not only share our perspective, but also have a megaphone in hand. It felt like reassurance that even after a series of losses—even after an entire jury decided she was guilty—we weren't crazy for believing in Nikki's innocence.

People were paying attention. After a supporter sent Snyder a picture of the protest sign that quoted her book via Twitter, along with information about Nikki, Snyder then pitched the story to *The New Yorker* and secured our first major national news coverage a few months later. In the long-form article, Snyder wrote that Nikki's abuse was "among the most extreme I have ever come across in a decade of reporting on domestic violence."

It felt like something was in motion. Was Nikki's case only now starting to catch flight, like a phoenix; or maybe more aptly, like a rolling hill of fire flowers bursting through the ash? It felt like growth, like a *movement*. It felt like being in the right place at the right time, knowing I was sitting on the right side of history. And sometimes that feeling was bigger and truer than all of the hard feelings that came and went through those three days of the DVSJA hearings.

collateral damage

The hearing went as well as it could have, but it kicked up a steady stream of adrenaline and stress. At home, Ben cried every night for Nikki—a resurgence of grief. Maybe because, as a brand-new first grader, he felt that his mom should be packing his lunchbox, meeting his teachers, knowing his friends. She was near enough to hear about his days at school, but locked away and prevented from actually experiencing them. Maybe he wanted to be like all the other kids in his class, with moms, not *aunts*, waiting in the pickup line with a smile.

Or maybe it was because the cooling September air reminded his body of the night he lost both of his parents, and so his nightly cries wrapped around the word *mom*—the only one who was still alive, the only one who could still come back.

One night, he cried in a repetitive loop until the word *mom* sounded to me like a meditative *Om*, a chant to something bigger, higher, more powerful. His pain was unfixable. The only appropriate reaction was to show it reverence—a quiet recognition without empty platitudes or distractions. I stayed with him, played soft music on my phone, and checked in to see if he needed water, or a hug, or to talk. He refused them all.

The truest reason he was crying was because he needed to be soothed by Nikki, who used to rock his body to sleep, swaying him back and forth in the dark, until he finally relaxed. Ben had been a stubborn sleeper from the minute he showed up on earth, and Nikki a patient rocker. Noah was the same way. I, too, had spent an unquantifiable amount of time swaying, bouncing, and pacing around his nursery, energetically willing his eyes to flutter closed, living for the wave of calm that radiated off his body when my job was done.

I didn't mind stepping in and doing the same for Ben and Faye. In fact, I usually enjoyed it—coregulation works both ways. But sometimes I didn't have it in me. That night I was bone tired, with school bags to pack, folders to empty, and a load of laundry that needed to be dried so that Noah wouldn't be wearing wet jeans to school in the morning.

Suddenly the music that was playing paused, and my phone started to ring. The name *Nikki DCJ* showed up on my brightened screen. She had a knack for calling when her kids really needed her, like a mom who wakes up to the sound of a soft whimper across the hall.

"It's Mommy," I said in a whisper. Ben caught his breath and sat straight up. He wiped his nose on his bright yellow Pokémon pajama sleeve and took the phone. Usually, he talked to her on speakerphone, but sometimes, like tonight, he needed her voice pressed close to his ear, only for him.

I backed out of the room, giving them their space.

I went back to check on him a short time later—knowing that Nikki would have only fifteen minutes before the phone cut out, and he might need me to soften the pain from another goodbye. But the room was quiet. He was asleep.

I picked up my phone from his pillow. There was a running clock on the screen, counting up their time together, twelve minutes and five seconds.

"Nik?" I whispered into the phone on my way out the door.

"I'm here," she said, defeated. She was here on the phone, here in the jail, here in her body. *I'm here.*

"He's asleep," I said, delivering the news that she, even from twelve miles away, had been able to put her baby to bed.

A few days later I received a letter from Nikki in the mail, which she had written after we had hung up the phone that night.

dear sister,

tonight ben asked me how long i will love him, and i told him forever. he asked if i will ever give up on him and i told him that is the one thing i can promise—that i will never, ever give up. i'll keep fighting as long as it takes until i come home again. his voice got small and he said...even if it takes the rest of your life?

I took that in. Ben didn't know that his mother had been convicted of a crime that, under a normal sentence structure in New York, carried a sentence that ended in *life*. What must that have been like for Nikki, knowing it very well could take that long?

choking back tears, i whispered, yes.
    then he asked me to stay on the phone until he fell asleep, and i stood in the corner with my forehead pressed against the peeling paint, cupping the phone to my mouth while i hummed all the songs i used to sing to my baby. and when you came back for the phone, you whispered, "he's asleep" and that's when i realized i'd been rocking and swaying in that familiar way, but my arms were empty, and i was holding a cracked phone attached to the wall.
    we hung up and i cried from a reserve of grief i thought had already been depleted.

Despite my insurmountable grief, I kept visiting Nikki at the jail.

One day, while I was waiting in the long line, a gray-haired man struck up a conversation.

"Are you visiting your brother?" he asked. In the split second after the question hung in the air, my brain dissected his words. I instinctively jumped to distrust and defensiveness.

"My sister, actually," my mouth said, while my brain was still deciding what this guy's angle was.

A wave of recognition came over his face. I realized that he had known exactly who I was, by the way he asked the next question: "Oh, I think I know who you mean. Is she"—here he leaned in—"*notorious?*" He was whispering, like it was a dirty word.

"Notorious? I mean, I don't know? She was in the newspaper..." As soon as I said the words, my brain criticized me for saying too much.

"Is what she says true? Was she really being hurt by him?"

It was suddenly quiet in the hallway. I could feel people listening.

"Yes," I said simply, turning away from him and facing forward. The line slowly started to move.

"Do you think she'll have a boyfriend when she gets out?"

I froze. *Why the hell would he ask that?* I already knew the answer. It was the reason my body had been suspicious of him from the minute he approached me—there was something predatory about him I could *feel*.

I turned around and looked him square in the eyes: "I think she's done with men."

I didn't speak to him again.

Later, in the visiting room, I told Nikki about the encounter, pointing the man out two tables over. He was visiting a young girl in her early twenties, someone who lived in Nikki's unit.

"That's her sugar daddy," Nikki said, raising her eyebrows. "He puts money on her books and sends her packages, and when she leaves, he says that she can stay with him." The girl didn't have anyone else to go home to, and Nikki was scared that she'd relapse into drug addiction as soon as she left.

"What is he expecting in return?" I asked, already knowing the answer.

"So, what else is going on with this presentencing report?" she asked, changing the subject. While we were waiting for a decision about whether she could be sentenced under the new domestic violence justice law, the court system prepared for regular sentencing. Which involved the county's probation department writing an official presentencing report, or PSR, which includes a recommendation for the court. It's standard procedure, and we were told, it holds significant weight in the judge's decision.

What is *not* standard procedure is what happened: Someone who worked in the probation department reached out to one of our committee members on social media. They said that the probation department had changed the PSR after it was written, stripping out anything about Nikki's abuse and manipulating the text to argue that Nikki was a cold-blooded murderer—which, we were told, was not what the PSR had originally said.

Why? To cover up the cracks in the local system that allowed Chris's known abuse to go unchecked for so long? If Nikki was really a victim, then the system would need to explain itself—a system that was all interconnected, from law enforcement to the district attorney to the probation department.

Like every other glaring injustice, our committee processed this news with a mixture of shock and fury. But we had a contact in the probation department (a woman) reaching out to us, and we hoped she'd help us expose whatever corruption was at play.

I updated Nikki on the latest development: "So, Ben called the woman and asked if she'd make a statement on the record about her report being changed, and she refused. She's back-peddling now. I don't think she's willing to risk her job for this."

It wasn't the first or the last time we'd see someone in the community be quietly supportive and publicly neutral, out of fear for their job or reputation. We'd experienced it with politicians, lawmakers, reporters, PR professionals, former district attorneys, and now, the probation employees. I had dwindling patience for what, to me, looked like a lack of integrity. If your support wasn't loud and visible, it wasn't real. And refusing to expose actual corruption in the system, because your livelihood depended on it—I understood it, but I didn't respect it.

"This is crooked, Michelle," Nikki said, shaking her head, which was the only appropriate response.

These were the kinds of details that I hoped to see reported in the local papers or national news networks, but if people aren't willing to talk on the record, then it all becomes speculation. I promised Nikki that we'd keep pushing on the PSR, and that one of her attorneys would write to the judge and put the issue on the record. (The judge would ignore it, and the newspaper would never report it.)

Every Wednesday night, without fail and knowing Nikki felt dead without her children, I met Dr. Crenshaw at the jail with either Ben or Faye to bring my sister back to life.

Faye, in particular, went to extraordinary lengths to make those visits joyful, despite the bleak surroundings and unpredictable environment. Would they spend a long time, sometimes an entire hour, sitting in Room 311 waiting for the guards to bring Nikki down? Would they be given an hour together and then abruptly kicked out, or allowed to stay for a leisurely two, even three hours? Would the guards smile and use nice words, or yell and snap out of the blue?

Faye always planned for the best. She put thought into which Disney princess dress she would wear—the light-up Elsa costume? Or Belle's yellow gown? Whatever she wore, it was her fanciest, most favorite, Mom's-gonna-love-this outfit—down to the hair accessories and shoes. She also carefully chose which stuffed animal she'd bring on her visit days—sometimes she brought two. Then she'd bring the stuffed animals home and sleep next to them at night, keeping them close—like a physical bridge between her worlds.

On this Wednesday, at the end of 2019, Faye chose to wear her *Fancy Nancy* costume, a reminder of the last TV show she and Nikki had watched together, on the morning of the guilty verdict.

It had been a tough week; Faye had thought it was her turn the previous Wednesday, and dragged that disappointment through the following days. She was a little weepier than normal, quick to fall apart over tiny mistakes, carrying a need I couldn't meet. But we got through. During the times she felt extra sad, which was often in the car, we listened to CDs that Nikki had recorded of herself reading children's books through a volunteer program at the jail. Benevolent women would come in and record incarcerated parents reading children's books, and then send a CD and the book home with the family.

Finally it was Wednesday, and she marched into the jail singing and giggling, curls bouncing. I watched even the most hardened guards melt, just a little, when she turned a corner. She was vivid color in a black-and-white world, the embodiment of resilience and promise.

Today, however, she carried some of her week-long sadness along with the spunk. But she had a smile as she walked toward the sliding glass door, and a smile as she came skipping out, two hours later, with Dr. Crenshaw. She lifted up the sleeve on her costume to show that Nikki had made a "tattoo" with Crayola markers on her narrow forearm. It said *hope* in a beautiful pink cursive.

"Today we went to the pet shop again," Dr. Crenshaw said as we walked out of the building and into the moonlight. I knew that, while Ben often spent the session physically training Nikki and Dr. Crenshaw—sometimes to be a soldier in an unspecified war, and sometimes to be a world-famous Pokémon catcher—Faye usually directed a scenario in which she, Nikki, and Dr. Crenshaw would "drive" to a pet shop, located under the conference table, where imaginary animals such as polar bears or lions were kept in cages. They'd choose an animal and bring it home.

I knew that, lately, the baby animal then grew up overnight. "It appears that she is steeling herself for growing up without her mother and/or trying to minimize her need for her mother," Dr. Crenshaw had written in a recent summary.

"It was a little different, though," he said today. "This time the pet turned invisible—we could hear it, but not see it."

That night, Faye couldn't fall asleep.

"Why does Mama have to stay there?" she said into her pillow, wet from tears. "Why can't she come home?"

I remembered Dr. Crenshaw's advice that kids will ask for the truth when they're ready to hear it. I wasn't sure I was ready to say it.

"It's terrible that you have to be away from your mom, and we're doing all we can to get her home."

"But *why*? What happened to make her have to stay there?"

There it was. A question I couldn't dodge. I asked if she knew why, but she said no. I scrambled for words. What I came up with was some version of: "Your mom was scared that your dad would hurt her, and she protected herself. But that made your dad die. And she has to stay there while they decide if she did something wrong."

Her face was neutral, but I could tell she was listening intently. "Your mom didn't want your dad to die, and she wants to come home to you and Ben very much, and I think it's wrong that you can't be together right now."

I expected there to be more questions, but Faye got very quiet and replied, "I don't like going to sleep because I have nightmares." She'd told me this before, many times, although she'd never wanted to tell me what the nightmare was. But this time she continued: "I have a dream about Mommy, and Mommy has blood on her." I wondered if it was a memory of the "Bad Night," or something she may have "peeked" and seen in the middle of a different night, like Ben had confessed.

I told her that must be very scary, and together we imagined a more pleasant image of her and her mom that she could dream about, and she fell asleep shortly after that.

I walked out of the room feeling a little lighter, knowing I'd survived a conversation I'd been dreading for years.

A few days later, a letter showed up:

dear sister,

my baby girl took my cheeks in her hands and studied my face. i searched her eyes and asked, "what are you looking at baby?"

in her pure, honest voice she answered,

"you, mama. sometimes when we're not together, it's hard to
remember your face."

i pressed my lips together and swallowed the lump in my
throat, thinking, oh honey, sometimes when we're not together,
it's hard to breathe.

I thought of the invisible pet—was she worried that she'd disappear from her mom's memory, just like she was forgetting?

I added it to the box of letters I kept in my bedroom, another envelope filled with heavy words.

And then I went back out to the family—music played too loud, two different televisions going, everyone needing snacks and water—and found big and small ways to reinforce to Faye that she's seen, she's important, and she's unforgettable.

There was one kid in the house who wasn't forgetting so easily.

"Remember when you said the kids would be gone by the time I was in middle school?" Noah asked one night, when I'd finally made my way to the "easy" child, the child who ignored his own needs to be less of a burden to me. He had gotten himself ready for bed and was under the covers.

It was the beginning of 2020, and he was in the last half of his last year in elementary school. It was becoming increasingly clear that this "temporary" living situation wouldn't be over soon. My sweet Noah had endured so much: He'd dropped most of his after-school activities, like soccer and piano, because there wasn't enough time in our crammed schedule; his dad had been arrested in front of him for doing heroin in the bathroom of a local diner during their scheduled visitation time; and he still hadn't really processed the full weight of losing his grandma a year earlier. Noah kept his feelings close to him—literally holding his arms in a big X when I tried to talk about anything that made him feel vulnerable.

And then sometimes, when it was on his own terms, he demonstrated a startling emotional articulation that would stop me in my tracks.

"Mom," he said, "I know that when you decided to have Ben and Faye live here, you made the right choice as a sister, and as an aunt, and, like, as a human. I get it. But—" He hesitated. "You didn't make the right choice as my mother. I've really needed you, and I feel like I lost you like I lost everyone else. I feel like I'm left in the dust."

His words had the sting of a sucker punch. I tried to keep it together, not to fall to my knees and burst into tears—mostly because I wanted him to open up and share those important feelings. As hard as it was to hear, I knew that he wasn't wrong.

The truth is that, in mothering my sister's children, I'd sacrificed my own mothering of Noah. And now, in his last months of fifth grade, careering toward the preteen years, I could see him slipping away, right in front of me.

How much was I expected to keep giving? How much cost was too much?

CHAPTER 51

alive but still not free

February 5, 2020

Twenty-eight months after the "Bad Night."

Ten months after Nikki had been taken away with the word *guilty*.

Five agonizing months after the DVSJA hearing.

A text interrupted a quiet movie afternoon with Faye, who was home from her last year of preschool. She was turning five years old that week—marking a turning point where I'd had Faye for more birthdays than her parents ever did. Kindergarten was on the horizon. And Noah was turning eleven in two days, a sudden preteen. I had parties to plan, gifts to wrap, cakes to buy. But for now I was sitting on the couch, my arms wrapped around her, when my phone lit up. I glanced over and saw the name *John*, Nikki's attorney, and the first word of his sentence: *Unfortunately*.

I felt a hot wave spread from my head down to my hands down to my feet, engulfed, as I reached over to read the full text.

It was the worst possible scenario: Nikki's eligibility to be sentenced under the DVSJA law had been denied; the judge decided that Nikki did not qualify as a victim of abuse. In a forty-five-page decision, the judge had one message: *I don't believe her.*

I looked at the words typed out on my phone, and felt the couch drop out from under me. *How could this happen? How—after all we did, the publicity, the vigils and court gatherings, the advocacy and professional recommendations—how—after looking at all of the facts—how could he choose not to use the law?* And yet, here we were. Denied.

John asked me to go to the jail and tell Nikki before she read about it in the paper. My heart sank. *How is this possibly my job?* I thought. Why is it falling to me to have to look my sister in the eye and say, *They don't believe you. Even though you told the truth.*

I could have said no, but I didn't. It was easy enough for me to get to the jail—my aunt could come watch Faye, and I had enough time before school pickup for the boys. It was probably best for the news to come from me, rather than from an officer or another inmate who read the paper.

It was an excruciating experience—one so tender that I think I'll keep that moment just for us.

A week later, I walked across Market Street, with Elizabeth by my side, followed by the filmmakers who were documenting an unfortunate dilution of the law in real time, shifting the trajectory of their movie to a tragedy. The woman at the focus of the documentary was with them. Kim had spent nearly three decades either paying for the crime of survival, or fighting for legislation so that no other survivor had to do the same. She had an indomitable spirit, and felt an instant kinship with Nikki, whose story was eerily and maddeningly similar to her own. After all those years, and all that fighting and progress and victory—the judge didn't use the law. I had apologized when I met her; she gave me a big hug, swearing this wasn't even close to the end.

Now, together, we were walking toward what sure felt like an ending.

It was lightly raining, warm for early February. The sidewalks were packed with people by the time we walked up, more than I'd ever seen show up. There were the faces who had sat through dozens of court dates, along with media camera operators, and people I'd never met—nonprofit employees from nearby organizations, public defenders from surrounding counties, people who worked in the legislature, and the court system, and the governor's office. College students were bussed in, and several court-watching advocates had taken the train up from New York City.

We knew people wanted to bring signs again, and so our committee, along with Nikki, decided to enlarge and print some of the evidence already in the public record—like excerpts from Nikki's medical records and photos of her face bruised, her wrists showing deep red marks from being bound, highlighting the kind of violent injuries the judge had deemed "not domestic violence." We blew up records showing Nikki named "Chris" to medical professionals years prior, despite the prosecutor saying that there was no evidence as to who was hurting her. Others had brought their own signs, like one that read, IT'S NOT A CRIME TO SURVIVE A CRIME, and another that said, DO WOMEN HAVE TO DIE TO BE BELIEVED?

I walked through the crowd to the front door of the courthouse, with nearly everyone wearing or carrying something purple. I had on a purple hat, and I made eye contact with these people I'd grown to love. I was sure that they had no idea how much their presence, their steady commitment to showing up for the hard parts, meant to me. *Thank you* didn't cut it.

The electric energy of protest closed behind the heavy glass doors. I was back here, in this historic building, waiting in a line to walk through the metal detectors while uniformed officers stood and watched.

People in purple gathered on the first floor, in a side hallway with benches. People with the Grovers and the gymnastics gym went up to the second floor and congregated there. An officer took us up in batches to the fourth floor, starting with family. Anyone who didn't make it into the courtroom would stand outside in protest, waiting for the news of what the judge would do and say.

I took the elevator up to the fourth floor and walked into a packed room buzzing with quiet conversations. The jury box was filled—mostly by media people, sitting with laptops open, cameras in hand. But I was surprised to see a row of City of Poughkeepsie sergeants in white button-down shirts, signifying their high rank, and they were talking to Town of Poughkeepsie officers with blue uniforms and shiny badges. Why were there police from two separate jurisdictions here? Was this standard protocol for a felony sentencing?

As if reading my thoughts, Kellyann, the domestic violence expert who testified during the DVSJA hearing, leaned over and whispered, "What, did Nikki kill a cop?"

"This isn't normal?" I whispered back.

"I've never, in all my years going to trials of women murdered by abusers," she continued, "seen this much police presence at sentencing. Ever."

Why? I wondered.

Just then, Kristine Whelan walked into the room. The original Dutchess County DA who I'd once hoped would do the right thing and drop the case entirely. I had never met her—she never reached out for a conversation, or acknowledged our family in any way. But I knew who she was. I watched her cross the room and stand next to Chana, rubbing her back like a good friend. Then she turned and sat directly in front of me, close enough that I could have tapped her on the shoulder and asked her how she lived with herself. I believed that, if she had taken the concerns about Nikki seriously and pursued an evidence-based prosecution of Chris using the file that the police officer gave to the DA's Office back in 2015 (a file that mysteriously disappeared), then Chris wouldn't be dead. Kristine also could have chosen to drop the charges against Nikki and released her back to her kids immediately, knowing all she knew from Sarah. Instead she'd shrunk back and stayed quiet—perhaps because, I realized, if Nikki wasn't guilty, then Kristine would have had to take some blame.

Finally it started. The audience quieted, all eyes to the front of the room, to the man in a black robe and white collar, sitting high above the rest of us, the words IN GOD WE TRUST over his head. Nikki was led in, dwarfed behind her attorneys and a line of uniformed officers that surrounded her like bodyguards. Her hands were cuffed in front of her, and her eyes looked down to the floor as she walked.

For the rest of the proceeding, I had to watch my sister clad in an orange jumpsuit, her body visibly shaking, with the back of Kristine's shiny brown bob in my line of sight.

The room was packed. There was a hushed anticipation in the air, as if this was the hottest show in town. The voyeurism was hard to stomach.

Then the performance began. The prosecutors stated their names for the record, followed by the defense attorneys.

First Chris's mom, Gail, gave a victim impact statement. She talked directly to Nikki. I looked back and forth between Gail, a woman whose pain and grief I had seen up close, and Nikki, whose shoulders violently shook with tears as Gail spoke about all the ways their lives had been destroyed.

Gail ended with, "Our last wish for you is that you get to see Ben and Faye again when Chris does, and that's from his dad, brother, and I."

The coldness in her words was chilling. All this time, I'd convinced myself that their love for the kids must be bigger than their hatred for Nikki. Now I wasn't so sure.

Then the judge turned to Chana, who launched into the narrative she had spun that had secured the conviction: the one in which Nikki's lived experiences were changed, her survival strategies were labeled "manipulative" and "calculated," and the least generous assumption was made about Nikki's character—Nikki was a liar. I sat and listened to Chana say, "This truly was an abusive relationship. Only the Defendant was the abuser and Chris Grover suffered the ultimate domestic violence. He was intentionally murdered."

I audibly scoffed. A correctional officer shot me a warning look.

"Comments have been made by some that this verdict would somehow impact domestic violence victims from coming forward," Chana said, referencing the dozens of domestic violence agencies that had sent warning letters to the judge about the impact of a victim like Nikki, with such an unprecedented amount of documented evidence, being publicly disbelieved.

"Well, Judge, shame on those who would make such a statement and shame on them for instilling fear for any *real victim* to come forward. The system did not fail. There is an incredible domestic violence support system here in Dutchess County. Your law enforcement, District Attorney's Office, and victim advocates are second to none." I watched Kristine's head nod yes. I saw the police officers lining the room smile.

Suddenly I realized: *This* was why there was an unprecedented police presence in the room, and why most of the DA's Office had filed in to watch the show. Nikki's case implicated them, and her guilt absolved them.

"They are here to protect victims, to fight for them, to hold those who hurt the victims of domestic violence accountable," Chana went on, like a politician hustling for votes. "But also know that they, *we*, are here to protect against false allegations."

False allegations? Nikki never made allegations; other people around her, who'd witnessed the abuse, did it for her. A police officer saw a crime being committed and tried to get the District Attorney's Office to do something. That police officer could have chosen to arrest Chris anyway, but he didn't. The DA's Office could have chosen to go ahead with an evidence-based prosecution without Nikki's cooperation, knowing there was a legal firearm, two young children, and a situation of escalating violence being broadcast out to the Internet. But they didn't.

What would Nikki have possibly gained from pretending that Chris was abusing her, and then carefully hiding it from everyone except a couple of trusted confidantes? It defied logic. I wanted to scream.

When Chana's performance was over, John took the floor, giving a brief reiteration of the case and ending with, "If it wasn't abuse that Ms. Addimando suffered, I don't know that there is any other motive that can realistically explain why she engaged in the conduct that she did on September twenty-seventh, 2017." He sounded weak and convoluted next to Chana's fiery conviction.

Chana asked the judge for the maximum sentence of 25 years to life. The best that Nikki's attorneys could ask for was the minimum: 15 years to life. Either way, Nikki was about to get a life sentence.

Judge McLoughlin turned his attention to Nikki, who was standing directly in my line of sight, her back trembling under her orange jumpsuit. She was flanked by her legal team and surrounded by uniformed officers who looked ready to tackle her if she ran. She looked like a child standing amid a group of grown-ups. I could tell by the way her shoulders shook that she was crying. A balled-up wad of tissues was in one hand, and she periodically wiped her face. I heard cameras start clicking as the judge asked if Nikki wanted to make a statement, and she agreed.

I had no idea what she was about to say; all I knew is that she had stressed over what her "last words" would be. I knew that the attorneys had read her statement and, although they had given her the green light, had wanted her to accept responsibility and express remorse above all else.

When she started to speak, her voice sounded high, unrecognizable, broken up through her cries:

"I am so sorry for the pain, the deep devastating loss that so many people feel as a result of my action," she started, reading from a piece of paper that shook in her hand. "I'm sorry for the broken hearts and families that will never feel whole again. I'll live with this, what I did and didn't do, for the rest of my life, and I wish more than anything this ended another way."

Her voice took on a slight crescendo, sounding louder and stronger. "If it had, I wouldn't be in this courtroom, but I wouldn't be alive either, and I wanted to live." The room was dead quiet, as if we were collectively holding our breath, hanging on her words.

"I wanted this all to stop," she cried. "I was afraid to stay, afraid to leave, afraid that nobody would believe me, afraid of losing everything. This is why women don't leave. I know killing is not a solution and staying hurts, but leaving doesn't mean living. So often we end up dead or where I'm standing—alive but still not free."

I was supposed to be the writer, but I never could have written a sentencing speech so concise, so powerful. I felt a wave of something I so often felt while witnessing Nikki's resilience and power: awe.

She put down the paper and looked up at the judge. No one clapped. No one said a word. We all waited.

"Thank you, Ms. Addimando," the judge said flatly, as if he were bored.

"All right," he exhaled, getting back to the matter at hand. He went on to say that he'd considered the Presentence Report, prepared by the "competent probation department" (*despite Nikki's attorney putting the probation employee's comments on the record, and the judge ignoring that the report was changed*), the victim's family's statements (*what about Nikki's?*), the letters submitted by Chris's gymnastics students and friends (*what about the dozens of service providers' letters and witnesses to the abuse?*), and the trial record, testimony, and exhibits and submissions (*what about the parts of the record that were suppressed?*).

"To the victim's family, the Grover family, I just want to acknowledge your stoic, respectful presence as a grieving family. This entire process appropriately is about the Defendant's rights and making sure that justice is done and she gets her due process, but now finally it's about the victim. So, the comments that I've heard and the letters I'd read, and this includes the Defendant saying he was a great father, a fantastic coach. The letters I have read describe him as a kind spirit, patient. Students said he would make them laugh. There was a quote in one of the letters from one of the students from Mr. Grover [that] says, 'I do not believe in good-byes, I believe in see you laters.' So, you, the Grover family, has endured his loss, a trial where he has been accused of horrific acts, testimony about his death, testimony about his autopsy. I have to believe he's looking down and very proud in the respectful, humble manner in which you've conducted yourself in this process, and I would echo the sentiment that you are truly a testament to his memory. No sentence that I would decide would address your grief. I don't pretend it will."

My mouth hung open. He was a kind spirit? Proudly looking down?

Then the judge gave a lengthy summation of the trial, in which he argued that Nikki's baby slipper business and the freedom to see a therapist and have friends like Elizabeth meant that she wasn't truly helpless, as a true victim would be. He argued that, while it's clear she was abused, she only told people that other people hurt her and not Chris. "The jury didn't hear that you had learned helplessness. You had friends, advocates, advice, and options."

What the judge was not addressing is that you can have all of the support, love, and advice you need, but if there is an abusive person determined to stop you from leaving, then you could die.

He wasn't addressing the fact that she had very good reason to think that the courts would never recognize the severity and help keep her safe.

"I have to consider the Defendant's background, and I have very, very carefully," he continued, talking with a measured ease.

"I received many, many letters that were very positive about the Defendant referring to her as a positive person, a giving person, a kindhearted person. You have lived an otherwise law-abiding life. There is no criminal history. By all accounts you are a caring mother to your children. You've had jobs. You've worked. You're a productive person.

"You've also had difficulties in your life. I think it should be clear on this record that it is not a secret that you were abused when you were young, when you were five. I have a picture of you as a five-year-old[,] abused and unprotected by anybody else. It's heartbreaking to think a child would endure that and have no one to watch out for her. It has to have had a profound effect on your life."

I looked over at my dad. A pained expression was on his face.

"I think it's fair to say that you've had a complicated relationship with your mother, and it's clear that you've been abused by other men, and even though the abuse here that you allege is in this Court's opinion undetermined, clearly someone who would make the choices that you did is a broken person."

There was the motive, I realized. When the judge couldn't think of a good reason why Nikki would intentionally kill Chris—not for money, not for another lover—he concluded that she was a *broken person.*

It didn't matter who had broken her.

He kept going:

"No one really knows what goes on in the privacy of a relationship. Maybe he was engaging in intimate acts that you were very uncomfortable with and didn't want to engage in. Maybe you were worried people would find out that you reluctantly consented and would hurt you in some further proceeding. It is not clear."

I had to physically restrain myself from standing up out of my seat. Did everyone else just hear what I did: *reluctantly consented*?

"So, there will be two sentences meted out today. There is the sentence that I will choose under the law, and there is the life sentence that you have given yourself, because you'll have to explain these events to the two surviving victims, your two children. No punishment I can apply could be more severe than explaining to those children, as you must someday, what happened and why.

"The law allows a range of fifteen to life up to twenty-five to life. I must respect the jury's verdict while considering all the aspects of the case and your background.

"You've taken Christopher Grover's future, his future as a son, a father, a brother, and a friend, and you will forfeit a large amount of your future, so there are no victors here, but your family can visit you. The Grover family has to go to the gravesite. When you boil it all down, it comes to this, you didn't have to kill him."

You didn't have to kill him. As if a gunshot to the head is the only way to destroy a life. As if Nikki hadn't been killed a thousand different ways from the time she was a little girl. As if ending Chris's life and being rerouted into jail wasn't a death in its own right. She was being condemned to a living death, and all of us around her would be in perpetual mourning, potentially for the rest of her life.

Clearly the only way she would have been believed was if she had been a good victim and died.

The judge paused at the end of his speech and looked Nikki right in the eyes as he quickly doled out his sentence.

"You are to serve a term of nineteen years to life, credit for time served. As regards Criminal Possession of a Weapon in the Second Degree, the sentence is fifteen years plus five years post-release supervision. Those sentences are to be run concurrent by operation of law. There's a three-hundred-dollar surcharge, fifty-dollar DNA fee, twenty-five-dollar crime victim fee. Please listen to your appellate rights."

Court was adjourned. The judge quickly stood up and left the room, his long black robe sweeping behind him.

Rage was ringing in my ears, clearing the frequency in the room to a crystal-clear truth: Nikki could be in prison for the rest of her life. And there was nothing I could do about it.

CHAPTER 52

no end

This is where the story usually ends for survivors of violence ensnared in the criminal legal system: with a sentence, a period, a full stop. Whether it's done quietly through taking a plea, or publicly through the courts; being vocal in the media or playing it safe; having an abundance of witnesses and evidence, or none at all: Prison is often at the end of the road.

I had wanted to believe it would be different for Nikki. But even with private attorneys, community support, six-figure fundraising, and a dedicated and active network of advocates—even with the brand-new DVSJA law and a team of professionals who endorsed Nikki's freedom—the system can so easily claim the life of a mother, strip her down to an inmate number, and cage her for potentially the rest of her life. Like it's nothing.

People tend to think that when someone is sent to prison, we've attained some kind of conclusive justice.

Except it isn't over for us; it will never really be over. We're still here, navigating the discomfort of a correctional facility, longing to bring her home, knowing that none of us can really start healing until she is. We have no choice but to keep living in survival mode, triggered by an endless string of anniversaries and missed milestones. Nikki continues to hear Chana's voice in her head, retelling her life in a way that didn't happen. The kids still cry for her. We never really feel whole.

after

We knew that Nikki's case would be appealed—most criminal cases appeal their conviction, meaning attorneys file a motion saying certain constitutional rights were violated, and a higher court reviews it. They can only review what's on the actual record, and luckily Nikki's trial attorneys had the foresight to put a lot on the record through objections and motions. We were told that Nikki had some solid constitutional rights violations—from Chana misleading the grand jury, to the devastating removal of Kara, to the fact that the judge misapplied the DVSJA law. We were also told that less than 1 percent of cases get reversed, and appeals can take years to be seen, and just as long to be decided. There was no timeline, no expectation for a quick reversal.

Nineteen years to life was our collective sentence.

Yet somehow, as the fog lifted after sentencing, I felt a little lighter, more spacious. Not because I was happy. The worst had happened, and I'd do anything to turn back time. But the certainty of her sentence provided a solid ground, somewhere to start planting a new foundation. For my own sanity, I had to accept that this could be the end. I was raising Ben and Faye. I would support my incarcerated sister and spend countless days in a correctional facility. This was the life I was given.

Nikki never, not once, accepted it. She held on to hope, telling me, "If I stop imagining a reality where I'm free, I'll die." She said that every time the phone rang in her unit, she hoped it was someone telling her that she could go home. That sounded like torture to me. But to her, it was how she survived.

* * *

Luckily we had a bridge between what *was* and what *could be*—someone to inspire both of us to hang on. His name was Garrard Beeney, an attorney who was connected to us through the domestic violence nonprofit Sanctuary for Families, for which he sat on the board. We hadn't known who the right attorney would be to handle an appeal, which is a very specific type of law, and we were desperately searching and stressing. So when Garrard showed up—highly recommended, and pro bono—he felt like a divine gift. Unlike many lawyers I'd consulted, Garrard saw the injustice through the lens of domestic violence, and had a spirit of advocacy—he wanted to right wrongs one person at a time, he told us, and correct the injustice of the law being weaponized to create more harm. He was both intellectually sharp and deeply empathetic—a true unicorn among the dozens of attorneys I had met. And he and his well-resourced law firm, Sullivan & Cromwell LLP, offered to file and argue the appeal free of charge, giving us a respite from the financial stress of legal bills.

We also had a committee that, after the verdict, became even more organized with new members, now twelve deeply connected and unstoppable women. We were a force, meeting weekly on Zoom, with meeting agendas. The continued fight for Nikki's freedom—spreading the word on social media, fundraising for a possible second trial, and organizing multiple events each year—required hundreds of unpaid hours, sometimes at the expense of their own family and work obligations. Every single one of us on the committee felt pulled to help, and we leaned on each other through the trauma of it all. We loved each other through action—taking care of not just Nikki's needs in prison, or my needs as a single mom of three, but each other. Our little group felt like lightning in a bottle, electric, magic.

More eyes found my sister's story—which rocketed after sentencing, when our committee's social media team (two of my closest friends and I) finally started publishing the words and pictures we'd been keeping private. The judge said *what*? Her sentence was *how long*? What does *reluctant consent* mean? Posts went viral, amassing millions of views. Someone, a complete stranger, decided to start a #FreeNikki Change.org campaign that caught fire—eventually garnering more than six hundred thousand signatures, and directing tens of thousands of people to our We Stand With Nikki pages.

It was against this background of noisy advocacy and outrage that, in the summer of 2020, Nikki's appeal was filed with the Supreme Court of New York State's Appellate Division. There was no way to know how long it would take to be seen and decided, but we knew it was our last hope.

Life continued. Within weeks of Nikki's move to prison, a global pandemic broke out—putting incarcerated people at an especially high risk of dying. An entire book could be written about our experience loving a person trapped in a prison during the pandemic—visits were closed for months at a time, the rules were inconsistent, the danger seemed ever present. At one point, Nikki was quarantined in a steaming hot cell for twenty-three hours a day, and every time we talked on the phone, it felt like I was getting a call directly from Hell.

Yet even with COVID restrictions and a forty-five-minute drive to the prison, Bedford Hills Correctional Facility was a major improvement over Dutchess County Jail. We could send her thirty pounds of food per month, including fresh fruits and vegetables, which she'd keep in an unrefrigerated bucket. She now had a prison-issued tablet, which used an outside vendor to provide email services. Instead of writing and mailing letters, we could now email each other using virtual stamps—$15 for 100. Each email cost one stamp, a picture two, and every thirty-second video clip cost four stamps. I paid around $50 a month to Securus Technologies, just to talk to her on the phone. Her monthly food packages cost around $300 a month, because everything costs more through a prison vendor, especially during COVID.

When the prison was open, we'd visit with mandatory masks and hand sanitizer. COVID had shut down the playground and children's center, but officers would give the kids coloring pages and a few crayons in plastic wrap, and Nikki would play spelling and math games, teaching them in whatever ways she could. When we were allowed, we'd play cards or board games. When we weren't, we'd play six-feet-apart games like "Miss Mary Mack" and "Bubblegum, Bubblegum in a Dish," miming the actions across the table.

Both Ben and Faye, on separate visits, ripped out a wiggly tooth at the visiting room table so that their mom wouldn't miss the milestone.

She'd missed so many milestones.

Five first days of school, four soccer seasons, every school concert and dance recital. They'd changed six shoe sizes, learned to read and swim, and Ben was now riding a two-wheeler bike. Faye was long potty trained, no longer hollering "I'm done!" from the bathroom and looking for someone to wipe her. Noah's voice was starting to deepen. A large swath of their fleeting childhood had already slipped through our fingers like sand, gone and irretrievable—no matter what the appellate court decided.

The pandemic had slowed an already glacial court process to a near halt, and it wasn't until the following April—two years after Nikki's conviction, nearly four years after her arrest—that oral arguments for her appeal were made virtually and live-streamed through the court's website. All of us on the outside watched over the computer with bated breath. Would the judges decide that Nikki should have a second trial? Would we need to go through this *all over again*? Would the judges decide that Nikki should be resentenced under the law, and send the case back to Judge McLoughlin for a new sentence? Those seemed like the likeliest outcomes—other than being denied altogether—and our committee prepared for all scenarios.

Every single day Nikki called asking if I had heard from Garrard. "Can I come home now?" she'd say.

Despondency had settled in my bones, a familiar whisper of *nothing matters*. Because for every person who found our committee's We Stand With Nikki pages and wrote something like, "I believe her," there were two people who wrote "I am like Nikki"—either they'd escaped, or more chillingly, they hadn't. Sometimes "I am like Nikki" meant charged with killing someone who'd been trying to kill them. We Zoomed with other defense committees, shared info, and followed and amplified other active cases—happening everywhere from Alabama to California to right in New York City. And together we watched the prosecution and the system replicate the same result again and again: Women were retraumatized, disbelieved, and more often than not, punished.

We kept hearing stories of women dying—and the pandemic only made domestic violence worse. The *Poughkeepsie Journal* rarely reported the homicides. I learned that when a man kills a woman, it's barely newsworthy. When a woman kills a man, it's a scandal.

The Dutchess County Sheriff's Office painted a patrol car purple for domestic violence awareness.

I was exhausted.

But the system didn't account for our fortitude. We were Sistered, weatherproofed from the eroding winds of uncertainty, even in the midst of a global pandemic. The system hadn't counted on our resilience, on our hardwired ability to endure the unbearable.

We kept fighting and—thanks to the committee, our "purple" supporters, and Garrard leading the way—we kept growing in numbers, publicly urging the appellate department to do the right thing.

Then finally, in July 2021, a year after the appeal was filed, the decision came down suddenly and without warning. One minute I was writing an email to Garrard about our committee's growing concern about Nikki having a fair second trial in Dutchess County, and the next I was getting a barrage of texts and a link to the New York State Unified Court System. They had posted the DECISION & ORDER. In just one moment, I was given a brand-new future:

The judges decided that Nikki should indeed have been sentenced under the Domestic Violence Survivors Justice Act, and reduced her sentence themselves. Her new sentence was 7.5 years (including time served) plus 5 years supervision. "Life" was off the table.

It was unusual for appellate judges to resentence themselves, we were told, and even more unusual for them to admonish the trial judge in their written response. They didn't comment on the prosecution's misconduct or any other point of the appeal—which was frustrating—but they had a lot to say about the DVSJA, and Judge McLoughlin in particular. They wrote that the county court's decision was based on an "arcane belief/suggestion that the defendant could have avoided the murder by withdrawing from her apartment, which are antiquated impressions of how domestic violence survivors should behave." The court also disagreed with McLoughlin's determination that the abuse was "undetermined."

"Instead," the decision read, "the defendant established, throughout her lengthy testimony, photographs, and other evidence that Grover repeatedly abused her physically and sexually.

"The County Court's finding that there was insufficient proof that the abuse was a significant contributing factor in the defendant's acts is unfounded."

They believed her. They listened to all the arguments, saw all the trial records, and decided that Judge McLoughlin was wrong, *antiquated*, and she absolutely qualified for the DVSJA—therefore strengthening the law for other survivors. It's all Nikki (and all of us) really wanted. The idea that her decision to go to trial was making women feel more scared and trapped, and it weakened a law that took a decade to get passed—that was almost as painful as the verdict itself. But now, with the appellate court's ruling, Nikki was finally heard; she was found.

Along with a pervasive relief that the litigation was over—no looming second trial, with more fundraising and attorney strategy—I also felt a constricting anger. Why 7.5 years? Why not the minimum of 5? Why was she serving one single additional minute of jail time? Why were the prosecutors and judge never going to be held accountable?

Elizabeth and I debriefed on the phone: "I feel like I've been running on a hamster wheel and it all just abruptly stopped," I told her. "Is that it? Is the fight over? Is 7.5 years the very best that can happen?"

Yes, it was a monumental victory—a life sentence taken down to just three more years behind bars. And at the same time, it was *three more years behind bars.* Hundreds of visits to a correctional facility during a raging pandemic. More packages and commissary. More missed milestones. Ben and Faye would be eleven and nine, and Noah would be in high school, when Nikki was finally released.

But Nikki didn't seem to share my anger.

"They believed me," she whispered into the phone, digesting the news that her sentence was now a finite number in single digits—and that she wouldn't need to endure a second trial for the appeal, or to beg a parole board and wait for an answer.

I continued to feel conflicted. I had to accept that my sister would never truly see justice.

We didn't take long to tell the kids.

Luckily we were in a stretch of the pandemic where visits to the prison were open. And so a few days after the appellate court's decision, I brought them to Bedford Hills Correctional Facility.

It was generally an hour-long process, starting in a waiting area that had a colorful poster hanging on the wall with early '90s sports graphics: WEL-COME, FAMILIES! EVERYONE WINS ON OUR TEAM!

Ben had noticed the sign on our very first visit, more than a year before. "What's that mean?" He practically scoffed. "Who wins here?"

I chuckled at his astute observation. "I actually have no idea, Ben. I agree with you."

It was always a hard line to walk—validating that the prison's degradation was wrong, while also making sure they were polite and followed the rules, because at the end of the day, Nikki could face retaliation if we gave the guards a hard time. Luckily Ben and Faye were cute and lovable, and the majority of the guards were kind to them—giving fist bumps, remembering their names, asking questions about their lives. Even so, the kids dreaded the visits, just as much as they *needed* the visits; they always, every single time, left happy and eager to go back again, despite the drudgery.

After an endless span of waiting in the first visiting area, we were called to another room, where we all took off our shoes, emptied our pockets, and walked through a metal detector. The kids instinctively stood with their legs wide and their arms out, a stance they'd taken a hundred times by now. It was their normal.

Then it was a short walk through cold steel doors and along a barbed-wire-lined path, up to the separate visiting area, which resembled a high school cafeteria. Six-foot tables were positioned around the room, keeping everyone at a safe distance. The walls were painted a light lilac purple.

"Oh no, the Trunchbull is here," Ben groaned when we saw one particular female guard sitting at the desk behind plexiglass, whom he'd nicknamed after the villain in *Matilda*. Again, he wasn't wrong. She had a nasty attitude and generally made our visits worse—but he had to be polite.

"I know how hard it is to be nice to people who are mean to you," Nikki had said in the past, when "the Trunchbull" triggered Ben to clench his fists and express an anger much deeper than anything going on in the moment. "But especially since being here, I've learned that it's just not worth losing your temper. Because you know what? The people who put others down and act mean—those are the people who are hurting the most. Something must have happened in her life to make her treat people like that."

We'd already started our coparenting; at this point, we felt like the kids were both of ours. And just as she always did, Nikki made me a better, more empathetic mother.

I reminded Ben and Faye that we had to make sure to follow the rules that day—stay in our seat, on our tushes, no running around. We picked out our snacks at the vending machine, and bought Nikki her favorites: salt-and-pepper potato chips and a Hershey bar with almonds. Some days they had things like salad or microwavable grilled cheese, but typically I let them have whatever junky sweets they wanted. Each bottle of Snapple cost $1.75, a bag of chips was $1.25, a Good Humor ice cream bar was $4.00. Salads, when they had them, were $6 and usually wilted. Typically at least one of the machines was broken or the debit reader was "offline"; a few times I'd put in cash and got returned nickels instead of quarters.

I constantly wondered who, exactly, was profiting from the outrageous costs. I became resigned to these micro-injustices, and that there was no overseeing accountability—not for the jail's robbery in jacked-up prices, not for the prosecution's deceit, and not for the judge who was still sitting on the bench, deciding futures. I'd pocket the nickels and shrug it off as just another absurdity.

Today I also bought a bag of Skittles, and put it in front of where Nikki would sit.

"I wonder what dog she's going to bring," Faye said excitedly, eyes fixed on the door at the back of the room where her mom was sure to walk through. Nikki had recently started working with a special program in the prison that trains service dogs to work with law enforcement and veterans. She had to apply and get accepted, and the program took only those with exemplary behavioral records and the kind of character and temperament to raise therapeutic animals. And so now, to pass the time, she did more than sit in her cell and rip paper for collages; she lived in a special area with the dogs and trainers, and took classes on how to raise them. Many of the other women in her unit were survivors, like her. "We find each other," Nikki had told me.

A major perk, for us, was that Nikki could often bring a dog to the visit—which helped the dog acclimate to kids, and helped the kids reap the therapeutic benefits of the dogs.

Finally the door opened, and Nikki walked in the room wearing a bright pink shirt and her State-issued green pants, a big smile on her face. The kids locked eyes with her and grinned—"She's here! She's here!" Her long dark hair was streaked with gray. A sweet black Lab named Coach was wagging its tail by her side.

They hugged and took in each other's faces over their masks, before settling Coach into a *down* position, laying her on a small towel with a bone to munch. Nikki saw the Skittles bag and flashed me a mischievous grin. We had a plan.

"So," Nikki said, laying out a brown paper napkin in front of her. "I have some news."

Ben and Faye sat in rapt attention.

She opened the corner on the Skittles bag, poured some into her hand, and started lining them up on the napkin.

"Ben, how many Skittles are here?" she asked. Ben leaned his body across the table and counted with an outreached finger. "One, two, three... nineteen."

"Yes, that's right, nineteen. This is how many years the original judge said I had to stay here, and maybe even longer. He said that I might have to stay here for the rest of my life."

Ben's face fell. Faye raised her eyebrows. We had never told them her original sentence. Ben instantly recognized that in nineteen years he would be a grown man.

"But we had new judges, who decided that the original judge was wrong. They said that Mommy can come home in this many years—" And she swiped sixteen Skittles off the table. Ben's face lit up. There were three Skittles left on the table. Purple Skittles.

"Did you make them purple on purpose?" Ben asked. He knew that purple was the color of support and love for Nikki. Our community had hosted family-friendly fundraising events, including one outdoor fall fest called Purple Day.

"I sure did," Nikki said.

The kids smiled even bigger.

Soon the conversation shifted to address the reality that, even though it's so great that Mommy *is* definitely coming home—something we could never say before with true confidence—she was not coming home right then and there. And three years was a long time to wait when that constituted a significant chunk of your short life. Three more birthdays. Three more Christmases.

1,095 days.

1.6 million minutes.

148 more prison visits to endure.

We'd all do that time together.

"It's okay to feel happy that I'm coming home, and sad that there's more time to wait. It's okay to feel two things at once," Nikki reassured them. Faye wilted in her chair.

"Ben, do you remember when you asked me who was more powerful—the people who want me to stay here, or the people who want me to come home?" He nodded. Nikki smiled at him and said, "We are."

Hearing her say that lifted my heart; it was all I'd ever wanted to be able to tell him.

His big brown eyes looked back at her—wise and knowing, because he'd seen too much already. "It's not over until we help all the other mommies who defended themselves get free," he said.

That night, there was a full moon, and like always, the kids and Nikki picked a time to stand outside and look up. "And you'll know I'm looking at the same moon at the same time," Nikki promised.

I watched the kids lay out a blanket in the grass, the same spot where Nikki and Ben had once lain before she surrendered back to jail. I saw them huddle together, arms around each other's bodies, looking up. I imagined Nikki doing the same, standing outside in a prison yard surrounded by barbed wire, with a dog at her feet.

The moon would always be a constant, a symbol of their connection, proof that they're still living under the same sky, on the same planet, even when they feel worlds apart.

I saw them look up, knowing they were making the same familiar wish.

Soon, I whispered.

Knowing it wouldn't be soon enough.

epilogue

Nikki continued to write me. But instead of opening her stories of pain and isolation on loose-leaf paper, I clicked them open on my phone's JPay app. She still typed in all lowercase letters, as if she didn't have inner power to muster a capital. There was no real therapy in prison to process all she'd been through, but they gave her anti-anxiety medication, and a blood pressure pill that prevented her from waking up the entire unit with blood-curdling screams. Every email was monitored; sometimes they'd be denied with no explanation or refund.

dear sister,

a few hours after i received my appellate decision, i was walking up the hill to meds at 6pm. a big, bright yellow butterfly landed next to me and i stopped walking—even when the officer yelled, "addimando, what's the hold up?" i just pointed. it was so beautiful. two more inmates and the officer stopped next to me, looking down at the butterfly whose wing was half missing—not a small tear, a whole chunk, gone. we watched her lift off, fly in circles, and delicately land again.

   "ooh look, she's broken," one of them said.

   i shook my head. "she's not broken," i said. "look, she's still flying."

acknowledgments

If I had to write this book all on my own, I'd still be writing (and rewriting) it. The fact that this book exists is because many, many people helped me to the finish line—proving, once again, that we need one another to achieve absolutely anything.

To Sarah Bryden-Brown, who came to me with a seed of an idea—a recognition that I could and should alchemize my experience into a memoir—and connected me to the people who helped transform it into a book proposal: Adam Burgoon, who believed in this story from the beginning, and Eve MacSweeney, the greatest agent in the world, who championed and helped shape this project from start to finish. Without you three, I never would have carved space to write this book. Thank you.

Karyn Marcus, my brilliant, compassionate, endlessly patient editor—thank you for your unfailing belief in my story and writing, and for bringing this project with you from Simon & Schuster to Grand Central Publishing so that we could see it through to the end. Your enthusiasm and faith that I could do this—even when I doubted that I could—kept me pushing forward. And Becky Cole: Bringing you into the project was the best decision I made, and these finished pages are the end result of your careful, dedicated shepherding and laser-sharp insight. Eve, Karyn, and Becky: I'm a better writer because of you three, and I consider this book to be just as much ours as mine. Thank you, thank you, thank you.

To Nikki: If it weren't for your enthusiastic consent and constant cheerleading, I would not have written this book. Your belief in me made me brave. Your commitment to speaking out and telling the truth—despite the risks—helped lead the way. And your practical on-the-page help in writing this book—through your letters, emails, and our read-aloud phone editing sessions from prison—made this book immeasurably better. You're the best person I know, and I learn from you every day. I love you.

Linsey Gatto, my behind-the-scenes partner in all aspects of this book, along with Rebecca McWilliams and Heather Dell'Amore: Thank you for helping to workshop my writing, and for being my sounding board during the long revision process. And a big thank-you to Elizabeth Clifton, Sarah Caprioli, David Crenshaw, Caitlin Sanford, Kate Cruz, Rhiya Trivedi, Fiona McKenna, and Gemma Hartley for reading early drafts and offering valuable clarifications, corrections, and suggestions. This is a truer, more accurate book because of your input. And thank you to Elizabeth Lesser, Rachel Louise Snyder, Scott Turow, Sheila Kohler, and Tara Brach for reading an early manuscript and generously offering a blurb.

My deepest gratitude to everyone else at Grand Central Publishing for your help, especially: Ben Sevier, Colin Dickerman, Matthew Ballast, Beth deGuzman, Martha Bucci, Janine Perez, Staci Burt, Albert Tang, Shreya Gupta, Taylor Navis, Ian Dorset, Joan Matthews, Bob Castillo, and Elisa M. Rivlin. A huge thank-you also to Sally Marvin at Gallery. This was a real team effort—and you all played a vital role.

To the rest of my committee sisters, if you weren't named already, thank you for holding me up as I slogged my way through (this book *and* this life), and for your supportive and helpful early reading: Carla Goldstein, Katie Johnston, Kellyann Kostyal-Larrier, Larissa Vreeland, Laura Mocodeanu, Melanie Bailey, Nicole Bonelli-Dubinski, Rachel Hawkes, and Wendy Freedman. Thank you to Richard Douglass and Tiffany Teamer for helping me process and better understand myself through [gestures wildly] *all of this*. Thank you to every single "purple person" who has loved and supported us—your contributions, big and small, made it possible for me to take on this project.

Perhaps the biggest recognition should go to Noah, Ben, and Faye, who had to live with me as I wrote this book through a global pandemic. Thank you for sacrificing time while I stared at a screen, understanding when I'd emerge grumpy and dysregulated, and celebrating my accomplishments along the way. You three are the real heroes. I hope—one day when you're old enough to read this book—I've made you proud. You each have stories of your own to tell.

Thank you to my beloved polydactyl cat, Mittens, for spending so many writing sessions curled on my lap, emotionally supporting me through this process.

And thank you to my parents for always believing I'd write a book one day—even if *this* wasn't the book we imagined. I never would have had the courage to pursue this writing path if it weren't for your steadfast encouragement since second grade. I love you.

notes

Author's Note

1 https://survivedandpunished.org/analysis/
2 https://doccs.ny.gov/system/files/documents/2019/09/Female_Homicide
   _Commitments_1986_vs_2005.pdf
3 https://www.aclu.org/other/words-prison-did-you-know
4 https://www.vera.org/publications/price-of-prisons-2015-state-spending
   -trends/price-of-prisons-2015-state-spending-trends/price-of-prisons
   -2015-state-spending-trends-prison-spending

Part I. Truth

1 https://traffickinghub.com/
2 https://bjs.ojp.gov/content/pub/pdf/dccc.pdf
3 https://bjs.ojp.gov/content/pub/pdf/dccc.pdf
4 https://vpc.org/studies/wmmw2020.pdf
5 https://www.nhs.uk/mental-health/conditions/selective-mutism
6 https://www.ncbi.nlm.nih.gov/pmc/articles/PMC7878014/
7 https://www.ojp.gov/ncjrs/virtual-library/abstracts/evidence-based
   -prosecution-prosecuting-domestic-violence-cases
8 https://www.ojp.gov/pdffiles1/jr000250e.pdf
9 https://www.hsph.harvard.edu/news/hsph-in-the-news/homicide
   -leading-cause-of-death-for-pregnant-women-in-u-s/
10 I'm leaving him unnamed, because unlike others in the book, he did not
   consent to having his name in the public trial record.

11 https://www.cdc.gov/violenceprevention/childabuseandneglect/fastfact
    .html

12 https://pubmed.ncbi.nlm.nih.gov/28086178/

13 https://www.childwelfare.gov/pubs/parental-incarceration/

14 https://justicewomen.com/tips_bewarechildprotectiveservices.html

Part II. Reality

1   https://www.cdc.gov/violenceprevention/childabuseandneglect/fastfact
    .html

2   https://survivedandpunished.org/

Part IV. Courage

1   https://vpc.org/studies/amroul2020.pdf

2   https://bja.ojp.gov/sites/g/files/xyckuh186/files/media/document/Plea
    BargainingResearchSummary.pdf

3   "An extensive body of research has concluded that one of the wide-reaching
    negative effects of early childhood sexual trauma is the risk of being sex-
    ually victimized again [https://pubmed.ncbi.nlm.nih.gov/24325940/;
    https://pubmed.ncbi.nlm.nih.gov/15753196/]. Approximately 66% of
    victims are revictimized. Other researchers estimated that the odds of
    being sexually assaulted after age sixteen nearly doubled if one had been
    sexually abused as a child, and these odds increased with each additional
    trauma. Revictimization is also correlated with increased psychological
    distress as a new rape or sexual assault can compound and magnify the
    effects of an earlier trauma. Revictimization has been associated with
    PTSD, depression, anxiety disorders, addiction, interpersonal difficulties,
    problems with affect regulation, coping difficulties, and feelings of shame,
    blame, and powerlessness [https://pubmed.ncbi.nlm.nih.gov/20724297/;
    https://pubmed.ncbi.nlm.nih.gov/15753196/]."

4   https://sanctuaryforfamilies.org/our-approach/client-services/igvsi/

resources

Here is a small sample of supplemental reading to better understand the cultural context for many of the themes in this book—including domestic violence, trauma, patriarchy and misogyny, pornography addiction, abolition feminism, mass incarceration, and the long history of fighting for each other's freedom.

Understanding domestic violence and how it intersects with the criminal legal system:

- *No Visible Bruises: What We Don't Know About Domestic Violence Can Kill Us,* by Rachel Louise Snyder
- *Imperfect Victims: Criminalized Survivors and the Promise of Abolition Feminism,* by Leigh Goodmark
- *Coercive Control,* by Evan Stark

Understanding trauma:

- *Trauma and Recovery: The Aftermath of Violence—From Domestic Abuse to Political Terror,* by Judith Lewis Herman
- *The Body Keeps the Score,* by Bessel van der Kolk, MD
- *The Myth of Normal: Trauma, Illness, and Healing in a Toxic Culture,* by Gabor Mate, MD, and Daniel Mate

Understanding patriarchy, misogyny, and rape culture:

- *Down Girl: The Logic of Misogyny,* by Kate Manne
- *Pornland: How Porn Has Hijacked Our Sexuality,* by Gail Dines
- *Cassandra Speaks: When Women Are the Storytellers, the Human Story Changes,* by Elizabeth Lesser
- *Not That Bad: Dispatches from Rape Culture,* by Roxanne Gay
- *Macho Paradox: Why Some Men Hurt Women and How All Men Can Help,* by Jackson Katz

Understanding the history of abolition feminism:

- *All Our Trials,* by Emily L. Thuma
- *We Do This 'Til We Free Us,* by Mariame Kaba
- *"Prison Makes Us Safer": And 20 Other Myths about Mass Incarceration,* by Victoria Law

For those looking to form a defense committee or support a criminalized survivor, start with the resources at survivedandpunished.org.

And to learn more about Nikki's case, go to westandwithnikki.com, and search for Lemonada Media's "Believe Her" podcast wherever you listen to podcasts.

about the author

Michelle Horton is a writer and advocate living in the Hudson Valley of New York with her son, nephew, and niece. Through the Nicole Addimando Community Defense Committee, she continues to speak out for the countless other domestic violence victims criminalized for their acts of survival.